THE
HOLLOW
CROWN

THE HOLLOW CROWN

ENGLAND CRICKET
CAPTAINS
FROM 1945 TO THE PRESENT

MARK PEEL

First published by Pitch Publishing, 2020

Pitch Publishing
A2 Yeoman Gate
Yeoman Way
Worthing
Sussex
BN13 3QZ
www.pitchpublishing.co.uk
info@pitchpublishing.co.uk

ISBN 978 1 78531 663 0

Typesetting and origination by Pitch Publishing
Printed and bound in the UK by TJ International Ltd.

Contents

Acknowledgements

In this study of England cricket captains since 1945, I don't include the captains or the fortunes of the one-day side, which is a separate story in itself.

I would like to thank the following for their help with my research: Johnny Barclay, Simon Barnes, Mike Brearley, Matthew Engel, David Frith, Vic Marks, Peter Parfitt, Pat Pocock, Ivo Tennant and John Woodcock.

I'd also like to thank the staff of the National Library of Edinburgh for all their efficiency on many an occasion; to Neil Robinson, the Curator of Collections at Lord's, for all his help over many visits and for permission to quote from the MCC Archives; and to Robert Curphey, the Archive and Library Manager at Lord's, for his unfailing efforts on my behalf.

I am most indebted to my agent Andrew Lownie; to Andrea Dunn and Michelle Grainger for their editing and proofreading; and to Jane Camillin, Alex Daley and Derek Hammond of Pitch Publishing, along with Duncan Olner and Graham Hales for all their work in bringing the project to fruition.

Mark Peel

Introduction

WHEN LEN HUTTON stood before the cheering crowds on the balcony at the Oval on 19 August 1953 to celebrate the return of the Ashes after 19 long years, it was his proudest moment as England captain and very probably the most fulfilling of his whole career.

Fifty-two years later, another Yorkshireman, Michael Vaughan, attracted similar scenes of jubilation at the Oval when he too reclaimed the sacred urn after England had lost eight consecutive series against Australia. Compared to the austerity of the 1950s, the celebrations proved rather more excessive, so that after a night of non-stop carousing Vaughan's bleary-eyed team paraded on an open-top bus through London before attending a reception at Number 10 Downing Street, hosted by the prime minister Tony Blair.

Given the mystique that the English have always attached to leadership, their cricket captain enjoys greater prestige than any other position outside royalty, apart from the prime minister and the England football manager. 'When people ask me what my favourite moment in cricket is, I always say it was when I was asked to captain my country for the first time,' recalled Graham Gooch, captain in 1988 and again between 1989 and 1993. [1] When he became England captain, people told Nasser Hussain he was taking on a poisoned chalice, but they turned out to be the greatest years of his life. He absolutely loved the job and considered leading the England side one of his greatest-ever thrills. 'There is no bigger honour,' declared Mike Gatting, captain between 1986 and 1988. 'It's a wonderful feeling.

And, yes, when it's taken away, it's a big part of your life. It's almost like giving up a family.' [2]

Yet whatever the honour attached to the job, it is almost the most demanding and thankless in sport because of the dependence on one person's decision-making. 'The best cricketers the country can produce, and the best cricket captains, have only to take on the mantle of the England captaincy to tumble headlong into self-parody,' wrote *The Times*'s chief sports writer Simon Barnes. 'The job reduces every cricketer that takes it on.' [3] The only way a captain could avoid ridicule, he averred, was to win Tests, be a good ambassador and play magnificently. This level of expectation heaped upon the England captaincy was a legacy of imperial days when the country expected to beat all comers. 'I was 25 years old, blissfully naïve and totally unaware of the roller-coaster ride to come,' recalled Michael Atherton, on taking over the captaincy in 1993. [4] 'You need to be an English graduate to choose your words carefully,' wrote David Gower, captain between 1984 and 1986 and again in 1989. 'You need to be a psychologist to deal with the people around you. And, eventually, you need to be a cricket captain.' [5] 'He must combine tactical finesse, man-management, sound political sense and a sense of moral cohesion while playing at the very top of his game,' concurred Barnes. [6]

England's self-proclaimed mission to forge harmony within the British Empire and promote the spirit of cricket placed a premium on the captain's ambassadorial role. At the farewell dinner at Lord's for the MCC team heading to Australia in 1946/47, the prime minister Clement Attlee reminded them that they were embarking on more than a cricket tour: it was a goodwill mission. It was a message reiterated by other bigwigs before the beginning of subsequent tours. Yet those ethical principles sometimes clashed with the visceral desire to win. In 1953/54 MCC toured the West Indies at a time when the movement for national independence in the islands was gathering pace, giving an added frisson to the cricket. The situation called for tact and sensitivity, but under the uncompromising leadership of Hutton these qualities were often lacking. Numerous incidents of condescension towards their hosts off the field were matched with displays of petulance on it, especially towards the umpires. Whether the unpopularity of the tourists contributed towards the riot in the third Test at Georgetown is a moot point, but, determined to press home his side's advantage at that stage in the game, Hutton displayed commendable composure by not overreacting and England went on to win the match. More controversial umpiring followed in the fourth Test at Port of Spain and in the final Test at Kingston, Hutton himself became embroiled in a major kerfuffle. Returning to the pavilion exhausted at teatime on the third day, having batted for the previous two days, he failed to note the presence of Jamaica's chief minister Alexander Bustamante and to hear his words of congratulations. When Hutton was made aware of his oversight, he immediately apologised to Bustamante, who was fully understanding of his explanation, but the local press treated it as a major insult, only adding to the tension of an already turbulent tour. Hutton's batting went a long way towards establishing England's revival coming back from 2-0 down to level the series, but the burden of captaincy had weighed heavily upon him and he was never the same player again.

Touring the Caribbean remained something of a minefield, and both Peter May and Colin Cowdrey, respective captains on MCC's next two tours there, had to tread carefully, not least when England's on-the-field supremacy precipitated further riots – in the Trinidad Test of 1959/60 and in the Kingston Test of 1967/68. Noting the raw antagonism of the crowds on that latter tour, Cowdrey saw it as his self-proclaimed task to try and keep his cool when everyone else was losing theirs.

The following winter Cowdrey had to negotiate a full-blown political crisis in Pakistan, where opposition to the repressive regime of president Ayub Khan had reached fever pitch. After student disturbances had marred the first Test at Lahore, Cowdrey and manager Les Ames, much against the wishes of their team, felt obliged to travel to Dacca for the second Test, despite the sense of lawlessness that had gripped the city. Their fate was placed in the hands of the all-powerful students who provided the security for the match, and in the circumstances they did it pretty effectively, more than could be said for the final Test at Karachi. Two days of constant disruption gave way to a full-scale pitch invasion on the third day, forcing the abandonment of the match and a rapid escape from Pakistan by the tourists that evening.

Political instability in the developing world continued to call for British self-restraint. Ian Botham, leading England in the West Indies in 1980/81, was confronted with a diplomatic crisis in Guyana caused by the decision of its left-wing government to expel fast bowler Robin Jackman because of his association with South Africa, a situation that led to the cancellation of the Test there. At the beginning of England's tour to India in 1984/85, David Gower faced not only the assassination of their prime minister Indira Gandhi, which threw the country into turmoil, but also the subsequent assassination of the British deputy high commissioner of Western India, Sir Percy Norris, after he'd entertained the team the previous evening. While the tour was placed in some jeopardy, Gower helped persuade his team to remain in India and he motivated them enough to go on and win the series. Twenty-four years later, it was left to another England captain in India, Kevin Pietersen, to follow in Gower's footsteps when a terrorist attack in Mumbai killed 174 people. Following their departure from the country, Pietersen spent many hours persuading reluctant team-mates to return and once back he showed considerable sensitivity towards his hosts and the tragedy they'd suffered.

Compared to the poise of these captains under duress, Keith Fletcher lacked the diplomatic touch when leading England in India in 1981/82, especially his show of dissent when given out in the second Test at Bangalore. More seriously, Mike Gatting also fell short in Pakistan in 1987/88 when sorely provoked by the chicanery of the authorities there. Having publicly excoriated the partisanship of the umpiring after England's heavy defeat in the first Test, he went head to head with umpire Shakoor Rana in the second Test in an unedifying altercation which contained plenty of ripe language. Concerned that British influence with an Allied country in a strategically sensitive region would be compromised unless bygones were bygones, the Foreign Office advised Lord's that Gatting should apologise, a request that both he and his team found abhorrent. When the request became an order, Gatting eventually complied but its very terseness rendered the apology almost meaningless, a blot on his escutcheon that helped cost him the captaincy.

Perhaps most serious of all were the shenanigans associated with England's refusal to play in Zimbabwe in the 2003 World Cup, primarily on grounds of conscience against the Mugabe government. With the England and Wales Cricket Board (ECB) and the International Cricket Council (ICC) washing their hands of the matter, it was left to captain Nasser Hussain, after interminable meetings, to make the decision, a stand that cost England vital points and an early exit from the World Cup. 'Being locked in a room in Cape Town, questioning myself and the players, feeling trapped, having to make a major political and moral decision – this non-cricket side was the most tiring part of the captaincy and one which has left me, still, mentally exhausted,' Hussain declared months later at the time of his resignation. [7]

Bad form can add immeasurably to a captain's burden. Walter Hammond's failure with the bat in Australia in 1946/47, especially in comparison with his great rival Don Bradman, only added to his general moroseness and detachment that proved so detrimental to his team; Nigel Howard's lack of class in India in 1951/52 was such that he was forced to resist pressure to stand down; and Mike Smith, an esteemed captain, was dropped against the West Indies in 1966 after a run of low scores. Mike Denness felt obliged to omit himself from the critical fourth Test against Australia in 1974/75 because of poor form, and Mike Brearley, one of England's finest captains, was constantly dogged by his lack of runs throughout his tenure. Botham found the burden of captaincy doused his creative spark; Hussain endured an horrendous year with the bat in his second year in charge, which brought him to the brink of resignation; and Vaughan was never the same batsman once he became captain.

By the 1980s press intrusion had become ever more intense now that the tabloids were engaged in a fierce circulation war with their rivals and non-cricketing journalists were employed to investigate the players' private lives. When Botham, one of England's most colourful and controversial cricketers, became captain, they seized their opportunity to cause trouble. It so happened that, prior to departure to the West Indies in January 1981, Botham, a part-time footballer with Scunthorpe United, had become embroiled in a scrap with a fellow reveller in a local nightclub and he, along with one of his team-mates, was charged with assault (later to be found not guilty). The story was clearly in the public interest, but the tabloids thereafter never stopped hounding Botham on both professional and personal matters, with some of the attacks on his family being highly intrusive. An impulsive cricketer at the best of times, Botham gave his detractors further ammunition by declaring midway through the first Test at Port of Spain that heads would roll if England lost the match on such an easy-paced wicket. That they did owed much to Botham's reckless dismissal on the final day when he tried to hit the gentle off spin of Viv Richards out of the ground. In a series in which Botham's captaincy and playing ability fell below expectation, the critics rounded on him to excess. The cricket writer and broadcaster Henry Blofeld even wrote in the *Sunday Express* that he captained the side like a great baby, a barb that so riled Botham that he manhandled Blofeld at Bermuda airport on the way home, an incident that was hushed up at the time.

Botham's spat with the media continued until he was relieved of the captaincy several months later, but he remained the prize catch for any tabloid journalist fishing in a murky pool, and his off-the-field antics – real or imaginary – remained an unwelcome distraction for subsequent captains to overcome. It remains something of an irony that one of England's most genial captains should endure such a torrid relationship with the media, but this fate befell Gower, partly because he was in control during some of England's most ignominious defeats. While no side came close to competing with the West Indies in the mid-1980s, Gower twice suffered a 5-0 whitewash against them. Although the first in 1984 elicited a certain sympathy, the same couldn't be said of the disastrous tour to the Caribbean in 1985/86.

After victory against India the previous winter and a convincing 3-1 win against Australia at home, the team headed to the West

Indies confident of giving their hosts a run for their money. Afflicted by the death of his mother days before the tour began, Gower arrived in the Caribbean exhausted and missed the first match against the Windward Islands. That decision was perfectly understandable were it not for a photograph of him and Botham relaxing on a pleasure cruiser while the team slumped to an embarrassing defeat against unfancied opposition. From then on, as England veered from one crisis to another, Gower's relaxed style of leadership became fair game for every critic, especially his willingness to make net practice optional the day after England had lost the Barbados Test in little over three days. Even the veteran cricket correspondent of *The Times*, John Woodcock, felt moved to write at the end of the tour: 'No one who has been in the West Indies with England's cricketers can be in the slightest doubt that there has been a depressing lack of leadership.' [8] Weeks later, following defeat by India in the first Test at Lord's, Gower was ditched unceremoniously by chairman of selectors Peter May.

The critics continued to pursue Gower when he unexpectedly returned as captain against Australia in 1989. Although the omens seemed quite promising, everything he touched thereafter turned to dust from the moment he inserted his opponents in the first Test at Headingley, and they went on to score a match-winning 601/7 declared. As defeat loomed yet again in the second Test at Lord's, Gower became so rattled by the hostile questioning at the Saturday evening press conference that he left abruptly in the middle of it to go to the theatre. What seemed to upset the critics as much as England's abject performance – they lost the series 4-0 and would probably have lost 6-0 had rain not intervened – was Gower's apparent insouciance which was really a veneer for his lack of confidence.

His successor Gatting was berated for oversleeping in Melbourne in December 1986 and missing the opening overs of the match against Victoria. Later he was brought down by tabloid allegations that he'd had sex with a barmaid at the team hotel during the first Test against the West Indies in June 1988. Although he wasn't helped by his graceless demeanour in Pakistan the previous winter, he became a victim of the selectors' muddled thinking: thus, while they accepted his claim that no impropriety had taken place, they still deemed his action of inviting a maid to his room irresponsible enough to lose the captaincy. It was comical stuff were it not so serious. According to former England captain Brearley, any indiscretion on Gatting's part was dwarfed by the failure of the authorities to stand up to the prying notions of the mass media. 'For which is the greater evil: a possible sexual laxity in an England cricket captain or a sneaking, vicious, malicious and possibly libellous account in the popular press? To my mind the Test and County Cricket Board (TCCB) has got hold of the stick at the wrong end.' [9]

With England remaining a soft touch throughout the 1990s, Michael Atherton's four-and-a-half-year stint in charge between 1993 and 1998 was no sinecure. Aged 25 and naturally prickly with the media, he found himself all at sea in July 1994 when caught by the television cameras rubbing dirt on the ball during South Africa's second innings in the first Test at Lord's and for giving a misleading account of the incident to the match referee, behaviour that earned him a £2,000 fine from the chairman of selectors Ray Illingworth. Left to fend for himself at a chaotic press conference at the end of the match in which England had been overwhelmed, Atherton was given a right old grilling. According to his biographer David Norrie, 'Few sporting personalities have ever been so publicly humiliated on and off the field in a single day.' [10] Jonathan Agnew, the BBC's cricket correspondent, declared that he should lose the captaincy, as did an editorial in *The Times,* on the grounds that, like Caesar's wife, the England cricket captain should be beyond reproach. 'I was to learn that the England cricket captain was expected to act with greater moral probity than the highest officers in the land, and it was to push me to the brink of resignation of a job I had held for only a year,' Atherton was later to write. 'Only a small percentage of people in this country will know what it feels like to have the full force of the press pack bearing down.' [11]

After a week being pursued all over the country as he contemplated his future, Atherton chose to stay and he displayed his resilience by scoring 99 in the second Test against South Africa. Unfortunately, he then blotted his copybook by saying that a hundred would have been the best answer to the gutter press. It proved an unfortunate jibe that came back to haunt him as England continued to underperform under his watch. While their failure to qualify for the 1996 World Cup bred some unflattering headlines, it was nothing compared to England's tour to Zimbabwe and New Zealand the following year. Their failure to win in Zimbabwe, coupled with Atherton's deteriorating form with the bat and his general surliness with the media, brought relations to a new low. *The Sun* depicted him as a sheep and the *Daily Mirror* as Mickey Mouse, and only a timely return to form in New Zealand gave him breathing space. The respite was only temporary, however, and after further defeats by Australia at home and on tour in the West Indies he was happy enough to fall on his sword. The criticism aside, he found that the weight of maintaining his own performance, at the same time as carrying the responsibility of the team, was becoming too onerous. 'Eventually, the losses, the periods of poor form and the constant decision-making take their toll. There comes a time when you want the headlines to be about someone else.

'Captaincy is a lonely road and decision-making is a lonely responsibility. Eventually most come to feel that they'd like a bit more company along the way.

'I couldn't switch off. I didn't realise that at the time because my mind was obsessed with cricket and the captaincy. I was becoming completely self-absorbed, to the detriment of those around me. I needed sleeping tablets at night; it was time to get my life back.' [12]

While England's record since 2000 has given subsequent captains an easier ride from the media, partly due to the decline of the tabloid press, the truce only goes so far. After scoring his maiden one-day century against India at Lord's in 2002, Hussain gesticulated angrily to the media centre and showed them the number three on his back in reaction to those critics who thought he should bat lower down; later that summer Vaughan found Hussain in tears at the Oval because a couple of the Channel 4 pundits had indicated that he should stand down as Test captain. It was a sign of his waning influence after three years in charge.

Five years later, it was the same with Vaughan himself. No longer quite the leader of old, and certainly a lesser batsman after his ankle injury in 2006, his relationship with the media began to deteriorate. With the pressure mounting, he grabbed the *Daily Mirror*'s Dean Wilson for taking pictures of the England team at a karaoke night in Sri Lanka in 2007/08. Within months he had resigned, worn out by the all-consuming nature of the job. 'You're always involved in meetings and chat, and never take your mind off the game. You're on the phone a lot and you have to have an instinctive feel for who needs a talking to so your mind never stops.

'What breaks you is losing and when you know you've made mistakes. That hurts you.' [13]

Alastair Cook was treated more leniently before his stock fell appreciably during the whitewash in Australia in 2013/14. The esteemed cricket writer Scyld Berry wrote, 'During that series of 2013/14, watching the England captain being eaten away was the most distressing – or nearest to distressing – experience I have had in journalism. The fresh face of a young Cook became a middle-aged mass of worry lines. He was torn in all directions, by each succeeding crisis, and had no time left for himself.' [14] The pressure continued when England lost to Sri Lanka for the first time at home, with Cook once again contributing little with the bat, pressure that drove him to the point of resignation. He eventually went after the 4-0 thrashing in India in 2016/17, handing over to his successor, Joe Root. Root celebrated his first match in control with a win against South Africa at Lord's, but his honeymoon didn't last. England capitulated at Trent Bridge and prompted universal derision. Vaughan declared in the *Daily Telegraph* that they had failed to respect Test cricket, comments that upset Root, especially since Vaughan, a Sheffield Collegiate club man like himself, had been one of his friends and mentors.

While all holders of high office carry great responsibility, the England cricket captain bears a heavier burden than most. This perhaps explains why they have proved less durable than their Australian counterparts, with 43 of them leading their country since 1945 compared to only 26 in Australia. 'Whether it is poor form, poor results, physical or mental exhaustion or some pungent cocktail of all four, the end comes to them all in the end,' wrote the sports writer Jonathan Liew. [15] Yet even Atherton, a perennial victim of press vitriol, admitted that leaving the England captaincy was a kind of bereavement: 'something we've held dear and cherished', suggesting that this position, with all its pleasure and pain, will continue to attract and repel future captains for years to come.

The Twilight of the Amateur: 1945–52

I N July 1945 the British people took a giant step forward by voting in the first majority Labour government committed to greater equality and social reform. Yet, alongside this mandate for change, there was a yearning for familiarity reflected in the MCC, the private gentlemen's club that had governed the game of cricket since the late 18th century and was renowned for its feudal outlook. Fully embracing the amateur ideal, there appeared little willingness to move with the times, even though the number of amateurs, impoverished by higher inflation and punitive taxation, was diminishing fast. Consequently, MCC were forced into making a number of bizarre short-term appointments that seriously disrupted any sense of continuity in the team.

The first post-war captain was the incumbent Walter Hammond, a professional-turned-amateur when he assumed the captaincy in 1938. Although still able to hold his own against India in 1946, his age, health and temperament told against him when leading MCC in Australia in 1946/47. Beaten 3-0 by superior opposition under his old rival Don Bradman, the 43-year-old Hammond, afflicted by fibrositis, looked well past his pomp and his lack of runs contributed to his dark moods, which did little to boost team spirit. At the end of a gruelling tour he retired, to be succeeded by his vice-captain Norman Yardley.

Yardley was one of the most affable men to ever captain England and he possessed a good cricketing brain, but he lacked the personality to impose himself on the team. Having beaten South Africa in the golden summer of 1947, when Bill Edrich and Denis Compton ran amok, he was unfortunate to come up against two great sides: Don Bradman's 1948 Australians and John Goddard's 1950 West Indians, both of whom proved far too strong for England.

With Yardley unavailable for overseas tours after 1947 because of business commitments, England were subsequently led by five different captains – seven if one counts two stand-ins – on their next five trips. In 1947/48 MCC took the extraordinary step of asking the 45-year-old Gubby Allen to lead in the West Indies, which made him the eldest England captain since W.G. Grace in 1899. Having played no Test cricket for over a decade and barely any first-class cricket the previous summer, it was hardly surprising that Allen pulled a calf muscle while exercising on the boat, causing him to miss the first three first-class matches, including the first Test, and at no stage was he fully fit. The side he led was an experimental one and they paid the penalty for underestimating their hosts by losing the series 2-0 and failing to win a first-class game throughout the tour.

With MCC due in South Africa the following winter, the selectors now plumped for George Mann, the captain of Middlesex and the son of Frank Mann who'd led MCC in South Africa in 1922/23. Without Test experience, Mann's appointment raised a few eyebrows, but his limitations as a top-flight cricketer were more than compensated for by his sterling character, reflected in his outstanding war record. A man described by the eminent broadcaster Brian Johnston as having all the virtues and none of the vices of an old Etonian, he proved a marvellous diplomat, motivator and tactician of a side that won the rubber 2-0 and went through the five-month tour undefeated.

Because of his commitment to the family brewing business, Mann was only to captain England in two more games – the first two Tests against New Zealand in 1949 – before handing over to the 38-year-old Freddie Brown, whose career had experienced a remarkable revival on becoming captain of Northamptonshire that year. After two games in charge against New Zealand and the final Test against the West Indies the following summer, Brown won plaudits for his inspirational captaincy of England in Australia in 1950/51 when his own personal exploits and wholehearted defiance made the series much closer than it might have been. A firm favourite with the home crowds, thousands assembled in front of the pavilion at the end of the final Test at Melbourne to cheer him on and to greet England's elusive victory.

He returned to captain England to victory over South Africa in 1951 before retiring – although he did reappear in one Test against Australia in 1953 – his departure marking a changing of the guard at Lord's.

Walter Hammond

WALTER HAMMOND was born in Dover on 19 June 1903, the only child of a corporal (later a major) in the Royal Garrison Artillery. His early years were spent on service stations in Malta and Hong Kong with parents with whom he wasn't very intimate. Returning home on the outbreak of war in 1914, they settled in Portsmouth and Hammond was educated at the local grammar school before his mother sent him to Cirencester Grammar School in 1918, where he was a boarder. It was there that he learned of the death of his father, killed in action near Amiens. His loss in no way brought him closer to his mother, since he spent most of the holidays on a friend's farm in the Cotswolds.

Although no academic, Hammond's sport, and cricket in particular, really blossomed at school and, on the recommendation of his headmaster, he joined Gloucestershire in 1920. Forced to miss most of the next two seasons after his qualification to play for the county was challenged by Kent, he scored his maiden century in 1923, and in 1925/26 he toured the West Indies with MCC. He excelled with the bat in the representative matches but contracted a serious illness which, in a pre-antibiotic age, nearly cost him his life. While Hammond claimed it was blood poisoning, his biographer David Foot later argued that it was syphilis or a related sexually-transmitted disease, which helped account for his contrasting moods thereafter.

Returning to full fitness in 1927, he scored 1,000 runs in May and made a promising Test debut in South Africa that winter, before scaling the highest peaks in Australia a year later with 905 runs in the series at an average of 113.12.

He enjoyed another profitable tour of Australia under Douglas Jardine's leadership in 1932/33, followed by scores of 227 and 336* in two Tests in New Zealand.

For the rest of the decade, Hammond and Bradman towered over their contemporaries in a class of their own, the former, according to Hutton, the best batsman he ever saw on all types of wickets. Handsome, muscular and immaculately attired, his technique was such that he was all grace and timing, his peerless off-drive unparalleled in Bradman's estimation. 'Hammond in his heyday offered all the glory and the colour of medieval chivalry,' wrote the Yorkshire cricket writer Jim Kilburn. 'He graced a cricket field by stepping on it.' [16]

Yet for all his success and the adulation it brought him, not least with female company, his private life remained troubled, his insecurities heightened by his humble origins, his innate shyness and his failure to form close relationships. His marriage to Dorothy Lister, the daughter of a Bradford textile merchant, in 1929 turned out to be something of a sham and he continued to see other women. While he could be good company, he was moody and uncommunicative with his team-mates, rarely having anything positive to say to them.

Some of this rift was down to his snobbery. Keen to better himself socially, he refined his accent, dressed stylishly, drove a Rolls and consorted with polite society. In order to fulfil his ambition to captain his country, he turned amateur in 1938 and he led them against Bradman's Australians, the rubber ending 1-1 after Len Hutton's 364 at the Oval. He won qualified praise for leading England to victory in South Africa that winter and beating the West Indies at home in 1939, his tactical shrewdness offset by his undue caution and singular personality. 'Wally had spent 14 years of his life as an army sergeant's [sic] son,' declared his Gloucestershire and England team-mate Charlie Barnett. 'It was a difficult upbringing. He had to do as he was told. So when he became a cricketer he expected people to carry out his orders without question.' [17]

After war service in the RAF, the return of peace gave Hammond a new lease of life. He captained England against the Australian Services XI in the Victory Tests of 1945 with rare abandon and led them to victory against India in 1946, but while heading the national averages for the eighth successive year, serious fibrositis limited his number of appearances. With MCC bowing to Australia's request to send a team there in 1946/47, the emphasis would inevitably be on tried-and-tested players. Because of his cachet as one of England's greatest cricketers and his continued prowess with the bat, he remained the logical choice as captain, age notwithstanding. Friends advised him not to go – he was 43 and struggling with his fitness – but the lure of leading MCC in Australia overrode all other considerations. Although the batting, led by himself, Hutton and Denis Compton, looked formidable, the bowling lacked penetration, and with only three players under the age of 30, their prospects against a revitalised Australian side looked bleak.

On arrival in Australia, Hammond was feted, not only for his stature as one of the giants of the game, but also as the captain of MCC out to re-establish historic links between the two countries. Crowds rose to him as he came in to bat, the Mayor of Adelaide called him 'one of the greatest sportsmen of all time' and, when visiting the Melbourne Tivoli to watch the British comedian Tommy Trinder, he entered the theatre to a standing ovation. His double century in the opening first-class match against Western Australia further enhanced his reputation, but little of this goodwill brought him out of his shell. The *Daily Telegraph*'s E.W. Swanton found him rather suspicious of the press and anything but an easy mixer. It was the same with his team. As captain, he normally travelled around Australia in his Jaguar with the manager Rupert Howard while the rest went by train.

Conscious of his side's limitations, Hammond opted for a policy of containment from the very start. Edrich recalls that he told them on board ship that the state matches should be used primarily as practice for the batsmen and consequently they lost the habit of winning. In the game against Queensland prior to the first Test, Hammond's captaincy was subjected to a withering assessment by

Brian Sellers, the abrasive captain of Yorkshire who was covering the tour for the *Yorkshire Evening Post*. If he gave another display like that, Sellers opined, England stood little chance in the Tests. Not only should he show greater consistency in his field placings, he needed to smile more and offer greater encouragement to his players. While Sellers's comments were in bad taste given his position as an England selector, they pointed to a fundamental truth manifest throughout the rubber.

Although Hammond had publicly expressed his hope that his old adversary Bradman, the Australian captain, would be fit enough to play against England, such generous sentiments, even if valid, soon dissipated on the opening morning of the first Test at Brisbane. Entering at 9-1, Bradman proceeded tentatively to 28, whereupon he attempted to drive opening bowler Bill Voce and the ball flew high to Jack Ikin at second slip. The catch seemed clear-cut, but Bradman stayed at the crease and was given not out, the umpire declaring it was a bump ball. The reprieve incensed Hammond, who approached Bradman at the end of the over and muttered, 'That's a bloody fine way to start a series.' He knew the importance of getting the Australian captain early and now, with fortune eluding him, he saw the Bradman of old laying waste to his bowlers as they toiled in the heat. 'Hammond never forgave Bradman for not walking,' wrote the Australian cricket writer R.S. Whitington. 'Indeed, his bitterness over that incident affected his judgement and attitude for the rest of the series.' [18]

His bitterness was exacerbated by Bradman scoring 187 out of his team's 645 before letting loose Ray Lindwall and Keith Miller, Australia's most intimidating pair of opening bowlers since Jack Gregory and Ted McDonald in 1921. Caught twice on a drying wicket after two ferocious thunderstorms on consecutive nights, England had no chance in near unplayable conditions and, valiantly though they fought, they lost by an innings.

From Brisbane, the team went their separate ways. While the majority departed to Gympie to play Queensland Country XI, a brooding Hammond drove Hutton and Cyril Washbrook through the night to Sydney, barely saying a word the whole journey, before depositing them at their hotel and disappearing for the next four days. 'Amazing fellow – Wally was a difficult man to live with,' recalled Washbrook. 'He never asked anybody their opinion.' [19]

Aside from the turmoil in his personal life – his divorce from his wife Dorothy had been splashed across the Australian press and his new love, Sybil Ness-Harvey, a South African beauty queen, was struggling to adapt to life in Britain – events at Brisbane had rekindled his rivalry with Bradman. While their relationship remained correct in public, the England captain was the first and only person known to have spurned an invitation to his home, and he dissuaded his team from socialising with him.

As his troubles mounted, Hammond became ever more aloof. He rarely spent time with his players off the field, and seldom praised and encouraged them. 'He tended to be individualist and uncommunicative,' recollected Compton, 'worse still, he didn't seem to be part of the side. There was an absence of that sense of community and all being in it together which is an important element in keeping up the spirit of a side, and to which, of course the captain has the most vital contribution to make.' [20] 'Hammond in Australia in the first post-war series was a shadow of his former self,' wrote Edrich. 'The rapport we had developed had diminished and his judgement became impaired by the burden of leading a side shorn by war of penetrating bowlers. He became edgy, retiring and irritable, especially when he complained about us fraternising with the Australian Test players.' [21]

His captaincy lacked imagination and enterprise. His instructions that his batsmen should occupy the crease on a perfect wicket at Sydney mystified Compton, as England's timidity against the Australian spinners cost them dear. All out for 255, they were forced to watch Sid Barnes and Bradman score double hundreds in Australia's 659/8 declared, and although they adopted a more positive approach in their second innings they were still badly beaten.

The third Test at Melbourne proved a more even contest and, but for some bad luck and bad judgement, England might well have won. Despite injuries to two of their bowlers, Voce and Edrich, they reduced Australia to 192/6 in their first innings, only for leg-spinner

Colin McCool to rescue them with an undefeated century. In reply to 365, England, with Edrich in fine fettle, finished the second day at 147/1. The next morning, he was soon out, lbw to Lindwall off an inside edge, and when Compton also departed in contentious circumstances, Hammond looked a picture of fury as he made his way to the wicket. He was soon out to a rash stroke.

A century partnership by Ikin and Norman Yardley took England to within 14 of Australia's total, and when they captured their seventh wicket at 341 they still retained an outside chance of winning, until an eighth-wicket stand of 154 between Don Tallon and Lindwall put the match beyond their reach. Throughout this onslaught, Hammond attracted serious criticism by persevering with the same bowlers and adhering to the same field while boundaries were being scored in all directions. 'There was, too, a melancholy note about Hammond's captaincy which was lacking in drive and, sometimes it seemed, in thought,' noted the former Australian batsman turned journalist Jack Fingleton. 'Wright and Bedser often went from the bowling crease to the boundary between overs, while Hammond sailed like a schooner from slip to slip anchorage with hardly ever a consultation with his bowlers and fielders.' [22]

Two centuries by Compton at Adelaide enabled England to once again compete on even terms. During their second innings, it was Bradman's tactics that came under scrutiny as he lined the boundary with fielders, inviting Compton to take a single so they could attack his partner Godfrey Evans, a ploy that brought the Australian captain into conflict with Compton. His century permitted Hammond to declare but, bizarrely, he delayed it until one ball after lunch on the final day, supposedly as revenge for Bradman's delay in informing him that Australia would bat on at Sydney. Bradman called it the most inexplicable decision he'd ever known. Feeling that his rival's poor form was reflected in his negative captaincy, Bradman later wrote that 'Hammond showed little imagination on the tour and did not display the leadership and tact required of an overseas diplomat.' [23]

Although Hammond's absence was entirely due to his fibrositis, which had afflicted him throughout the tour, neither his batting –

168 runs in eight completed innings – nor his captaincy would be missed. The team responded to Yardley's intelligent captaincy by playing with spirit, and although they lost by five wickets the result was closer than the scores suggest.

The brief trip to New Zealand, which followed the Australian leg, at least permitted Hammond to bow out of Test cricket in some style. Cheered all the way to the wicket by the large crowd at Christchurch and given three cheers by his opponents, he rolled back the years with some vintage shots in his 79. It proved some consolation for a traumatic six months in which, ill-fortune aside, he'd been outsmarted by his old rival. Although England were always destined to come second given their inferior bowling and fielding, Hammond, nevertheless, could have run them closer had he shown real leadership. 'It was heart-breaking to see morale, which had started so high when we sailed, sink into a general state of disillusionment,' wrote Swanton. [24] Alec Bedser, a great admirer of Hammond in his youth, had cause to revise his opinion. 'I found him to be below my ideal as captain. I was still inexperienced and would have appreciated some words of advice and encouragement from the great man on the first big occasion of my cricketing life.' [25] Wicketkeeper Paul Gibb, who'd flourished under Hammond in South Africa in 1938/39 but had been discarded after Brisbane, felt liberated at the end of the tour. 'Free perhaps from an ever-present awareness of my erstwhile skipper's presence, free from his quite unpredictable and rather untrustworthy moods.' [26] What particularly shocked him was his failure, and that of manager Rupert Howard, to inquire after the health of spinner Peter Smith and himself on returning to the tour after minor operations.

Hammond's first act on returning home was to marry Sybil, but the gilded life he promised her failed to materialise, and, lured by fanciful talk of starting a joint business in South Africa, he and his young family emigrated there in 1951, only to see their dream fade fast. An alternative job as a general manager of a Durban car firm provided little satisfaction, and after he was made redundant in 1959 he was invited to become the first sports administrator at Natal University. Glad to be back in the open air, the job brought him some respite in his final years, which otherwise were blighted by a near-fatal car accident in 1960. Five years later, in July 1965, Hammond died prematurely of a heart attack in semi-obscurity, a sad end to a singular life in which a man blessed with such talent could never find ultimate fulfilment.

Norman Yardley

NORMAN YARDLEY was born in Royston, near Barnsley, on 19 March 1915, and was raised in some style owing to the fortune accumulated by his grandfather in his retail business and property ventures.

A sporting prodigy at St Peter's School, York, Yardley captained the rugby, the cricket and the squash and was North of England squash champion six times. At Cambridge he won blues in hockey, squash, rugby fives as well as cricket, and after hitting a century against Oxford in 1937, he captained the Blues the following year.

In 1936 Yardley made his debut for Yorkshire and was chosen as Hammond's vice-captain for the MCC tour to South Africa in 1938/39, primarily because of his amateur status. His form in the early games won him a place in the first Test, but he scored only seven and didn't feature again in the series.

On the outbreak of war, Yardley served in the 1st Battalion of the Green Howards, along with his Yorkshire team-mate Hedley Verity, and took part in the Sicily landings in which the latter was killed. Later he was wounded in the Western Desert.

Appointed vice-captain to Hammond on MCC's ill-fated tour to Australia in 1946/47, he emerged as one of the few successes, scoring useful runs, dismissing Bradman three times in succession with his under-rated medium pacers and standing in for Hammond capably in the final Test at Sydney. 'He certainly has the knack of keeping his men equable and happy,' wrote Swanton. 'If there was a little more punch or bite in his make-up one could regard Yardley as a thoroughly satisfactory England captain of the near future.' [27]

In the wake of Hammond's retirement, Yardley was his logical successor to captain against South Africa in 1947. His appointment was broadly welcomed by all those who admired his tactical nous, the result of his baptism in the Yorkshire dressing room of the 1930s, his benevolent personality and cheerful outlook. In contrast to his captain at Yorkshire, Brian Sellers, Yardley adopted a much more consensual style, calling the professionals by their Christian names, listening to all shades of opinion and praising whenever he could. Never a rigid disciplinarian, he preferred to deal with breaches of protocol with a quiet word of advice rather than a public dressing down, a style of leadership more conducive to the England dressing room than the rough-and-tumble atmosphere of the Yorkshire one.

The touring South Africans, led by Alan Melville, looked stronger in batting than bowling, although it was the latter who took them to the brink of victory in the first Test at Trent Bridge. Forced to follow on 325 behind, England were toiling at 170/4 when Yardley joined Compton. They added 108 that evening and Yardley, with a match to save, called for an hour of concentrated net practice for the remaining batsmen the next morning. His words had a galvanising effect as they fought with their backs to the wall. Compton with 163 and Yardley with 99, his highest Test score, led the way with a fifth-wicket stand of 237, Evans hit a breezy 74 and the last-wicket pair of Eric Hollies and Jack Martin put on 51. Set 228 to win in 138 minutes, South Africa finished on 166/1.

The second Test brought a turn of the tide as Edrich and Compton captivated their home crowd with their imperious stroke-play in a stand of 370 for the third wicket. England made 554/8 declared and, forcing their opponents to follow on, they went on to win by ten wickets.

Another epic stand between Edrich and Compton in the third Test at Old Trafford formed the backdrop to England's seven-wicket victory, and, with Hutton returning to form at Headingley, England clinched the rubber 3-0.

A high-scoring draw at the Oval brought Yardley his second fifty of the series in which he'd been commendably consistent. 'In captaincy he is of sanguine temperament and modest assurance,' *Wisden* wrote of him. 'He has ideas without being opinionated, and he is as prepared to receive advice as to give it. He is himself in all circumstances and consequently enjoys the respect and confidence of his fellow-players.' [28]

Because the family finances had been hit by the punitive rates of war-taxation, and with a young family now to care for, Yardley's business commitments ruled him out of MCC's tour to the West Indies that winter.

In 1948 he succeeded the redoubtable Sellers as captain of Yorkshire, but an early-season attack of lumbago and a shortage of runs persuaded the selectors to invite Walter Robins, a former captain of England, to lead his country against Bradman's Australians. Under his dynamic leadership, Middlesex had won the championship in 1947, but having seen how advancing years had played havoc with Gubby Allen in the West Indies, the 42-year-old Robins refused to tempt fate. Yardley, meanwhile, saved face by scoring 90 for Yorkshire against Middlesex on the eve of the first Test, and once he'd assured the selectors of his fitness, they gave him a vote of confidence.

Now that Yardley was back in the saddle, he resolved to frustrate Australia's free-scoring batsmen by getting his bowlers to bowl a leg-stump line at them to a packed on-side field. His plan dominated the second day of the first Test as England, dismissed for a paltry 165 in their first innings, attempted to get back into the game. They certainly curbed the Australian run rate and visibly irritated Bradman, who ground out the slowest of his 29 Test centuries but failed to stop his team from amassing a total of 509, the foundation of their eight-wicket victory.

England were again outplayed at Lord's, chiefly because of the failure of their batsmen to withstand the pace of Lindwall. Hutton in particular looked distinctly uncomfortable in the second innings, but the decision to omit him for the next Test for Gloucestershire's George Emmett caused consternation. As one of England's selectors,

Yardley couldn't escape responsibility for this blinding error, and his failure to explain the rationale behind it to his Yorkshire team-mate reeked of insensitivity. 'I heard the news that I had been left out over the radio,' Hutton wrote many years later. 'The selectors never offered me a reason or explained what was behind the decision. Had they done so it might have softened the blow.' [29]

Despite Emmett's failure in his sole Test, England came out on top in the rain-affected draw and, with Hutton back for Headingley, they assembled there in good spirits. In a high-scoring contest, England led by 38 on first innings and scored 365/8 declared in their second innings, batting on for two overs on the final morning to get a second use of the heavy roller in the hope that it would break up the pitch. Requiring 404 for victory, history was very much against Australia, especially since no Test side had ever scored more than 350 to win in the fourth innings, but England's omission of spinner Jack Young now came back to haunt them. Two-nil down in the rubber and needing to attack, Yardley placed his faith in Compton's occasional left-arm spin. Compton soon dismissed Lindsay Hassett but Evans missed stumping Arthur Morris and Jack Crapp dropped Bradman at slip. Grateful for their reprieves, both batsmen went to town against Hutton's occasional leg spin, enabling Australia to lunch more easily at 121/1. A post-prandial assault by Morris on Compton forced him out of the attack, and with England continuing to flounder in the field – seven chances were missed altogether – their morale quickly sagged. Both Morris and Bradman went remorselessly on, adding 301 in just over three hours, and thanks to their magnificent batting Australia won by seven wickets with 15 minutes to spare. In the wake of their crushing defeat, Yardley came in for much criticism, but while his captaincy hadn't been flawless – four overs of Hutton and the under-bowling of both himself and medium pacer Ken Cranston – he was ill-served by his team's shoddy display. According to the former Australian leg-spinner turned critic Bill O'Reilly, he did 'a remarkably good job as captain' and even his use of Hutton was a 'gamble worth taking'.

Despite four changes for the final Test at the Oval, England remained a demoralised outfit and Australia barely had to break a sweat to win by an innings. Yardley's double failure completed a miserable series with the bat (although he topped the bowling averages), calling into question his continued presence in the team. Business commitments once again prevented him from touring South Africa that winter and his services weren't required against New Zealand in 1949, but with George Mann, his successor, no longer available for England, and with doubts about Freddie Brown's age, Yardley was recalled for the first Test against the West Indies in 1950.

Confronted with a turning wicket at Old Trafford, he left out his best bowler, Alec Bedser, in order to play three spinners. Winning the toss, England slumped to 85/5 before a swashbuckling maiden Test century by Evans gave them the early initiative, which they never surrendered as the West Indies succumbed to spinners Eric Hollies and Bob Berry to lose by 202 runs. *The Times* praised Yardley for his excellent captaincy, but at Lord's it was a different story as the West Indies came of age. Led by the batting exploits of Frank Worrell, Everton Weekes and Clyde Walcott and the mesmeric spin duo of Sonny Ramadhin and Alf Valentine, they ran out clear winners by 326 runs.

Before the third Test, Yardley declared his unavailability for the forthcoming tour to Australia, a decision regretted by many, since he was still regarded as the obvious man to captain. In what appeared to be a misjudgement, Yardley, on winning the toss at Trent Bridge, elected to bat first on a seaming wicket. England were bowled out for 223 and, with Frank Worrell leading the way with a majestic 261, the West Indies amassed a first-innings lead of 335.

England batted with greater resolution in their second innings but still lost by ten wickets, a sombre end to Yardley's England captaincy. It was his misfortune that nine of his 14 Tests in charge should be against Bradman's Australians and Goddard's West Indians. Yet despite his indifferent record of won four and lost seven, there were plenty of his team-mates willing to sing his praises. 'I played under Yardley for Yorkshire and England and a kinder and a more considerate captain never walked on to a field,' opined Hutton. [30] Edrich considered Yardley the best captain he played under, his willingness to get to know his team particularly admirable, and Compton was of a similar view. 'But I have always thought that Yardley was too charming and too tactful ever to make a really good captain of a Test side or even of a Yorkshire side,' wrote Evans. [31] That was certainly the view of Illingworth regarding his captaincy of Yorkshire, in particular his failure to bring divisive characters such as Johnny Wardle and Bob Appleyard to heel.

Yardley continued to captain Yorkshire till 1955 – without ever winning the championship outright – and after his playing career he worked as a wine merchant, a cricket journalist and a summariser on BBC Radio's *Test Match Special*, in addition to serving on the Yorkshire committee. Sadly, his time as the county's president was overshadowed by a fractious internal dispute regarding the future of their premier batsman, the controversial Geoff Boycott. When the committee voted not to offer him another contract, a group of his supporters passed a vote of no confidence in the committee in January 1984, at which point Yardley resigned as president. He died in 1989, aged 74.

Gubby Allen

GUBBY ALLEN was born in Sydney on 31 July 1902, a fourth-generation Australian whose uncle Reginald played for Australia in the 1880s. Moving to England in 1908, the Allens settled in Datchet, near Eton, where they became close friends of Sir Pelham Warner, the former captain of England, a significant connection given the crucial influence that the latter was to have on Gubby's career.

After three years in the Eton eleven, Allen won consecutive blues at Cambridge as an accomplished all-rounder with match figures of 9-78 in their win against Oxford in the 1922 Varsity match. Leaving Cambridge without completing his degree, he gravitated to the City, where he became a successful stockbroker. Never playing more than half a season with Middlesex as an amateur, he rarely failed to cut a dash when he turned out for them. In 1929, arriving late for their game against Lancashire at Lord's because of work, he took 10-40, eight of his victims clean bowled.

Making his debut for England against Australia in 1930, he scored his maiden Test century against New Zealand in 1931 and was selected for the MCC tour to Australia in 1932/33. Although refusing to bowl bodyline, much to captain Douglas Jardine's chagrin, he proved an invaluable foil to the opening pair of Harold Larwood and Bill Voce with his 21 wickets in the series.

His disapproval of bodyline and Warner's patronage as chairman of selectors helped gain him the captaincy of the MCC side to

Australia in 1936/37. Although something of a martinet, he cared deeply about his men and won their respect with his leadership on the field. His bowling greatly contributed to England winning the first two Tests before they ran into the genius of Bradman. Despite the disappointment of losing the series 3-2, the tour achieved its prime objective of repairing the breach in Anglo-Australian relations caused by bodyline and much of this was down to Allen's deft diplomacy.

Work and injuries severely restricted his appearances in the years prior to the war and, afterwards, he only played twice for Middlesex in 1946/47. It was thus a considerable surprise that Allen should be asked to captain/manage the MCC team to the West Indies in 1947/48. The tour had been arranged at short notice as a goodwill gesture to the West Indies Board of Control, since there had been no major tour there for 13 years, and MCC, fatally underestimating the challenge they posed, picked an unproven side containing only three players, Jack Ikin, Godfrey Evans and Joe Hardstaff, from the tour to Australia the previous year.

On 23 December 1947, the side left Liverpool in an empty banana boat with accommodation for fewer than 20. The journey across the storm-lashed Atlantic was turbulent enough to cause a mass outbreak of sea sickness. Not surprisingly, Allen didn't find much enthusiasm from the older players when he tried to keep them up to the mark with his keep-fit classes. Ironic then, that he pulled a calf muscle while skipping on the boat, forcing him to miss the first three matches. As he watched two promising Barbadians, Everton Weekes and Clyde Walcott, punish MCC's bowling, Allen was found by assistant manager/wicketkeeper Billy Griffith with his head in his hands. He'd seen enough already to realise that his team weren't strong enough to compete effectively with their opponents.

While knowing few of his men at the outset of the trip, Allen made every effort to get to know them and concern himself with their welfare. In post-dinner conversations he talked to them about the game and its personalities and advised them about their technique. Although a touch autocratic at times – he arranged a personal catching practice for the young Yorkshire batsman Gerald Smithson after he dropped a skier in the first Test – he leaned on Griffith to help him bridge the generational gap. While the young players such as Jim Laker admired Allen for his courage and leadership, he did cross swords with his vice-captain, Cranston, and the senior professional, Hardstaff, both of whom were bon viveurs who resented his attempts to place a curfew on their carousing.

After missing the Barbados leg of the tour, including the first Test, Allen returned to combat in Trinidad, only to find a growing casualty list. In the return game against the colony, MCC fielded four substitutes at one time, and in these trying circumstances he sent an SOS to Lord's, requiring a replacement. Given the sensitivities of their hosts about his under-strength side and the need to raise British prestige, he stressed the need for a player of class, and was rewarded with Hutton, although he arrived too late for the second Test at Port of Spain. In the absence of both openers, Dennis Brookes and Winston Place, and with no other obvious alternative to partner Middlesex's Jack Robertson, Allen solved the problem by getting Ikin, Laker and Griffith, a useful lower-order batsman, to face him in the nets. He chose the latter, and eschewing any compliments, he simply told him, 'Just bloody well stay in.' Curbing his natural impulse, Griffith, playing in his first Test, followed instructions to the letter by scoring 140, his maiden first-class century, an innings that helped England salvage a draw.

They entered the third Test at Georgetown bolstered by the presence of Hutton and the return from injury of Hardstaff, but the curse returned when Allen broke down in the third over and was unable to bowl again in the match. England lost by seven wickets, and the fourth Test by ten wickets, finishing the tour without a victory. The gulf between the two sides underlined the folly of sending such an experimental side and asking Allen to captain at his age, although, when he was fit, Swanton thought he looked a class above the rest.

Wedded to cricket, Allen wielded great influence at Lord's for the rest of his life, not least as chairman of selectors between 1955 and 1961, and MCC treasurer between 1964 and 1973. He was knighted for his services to cricket in 1986 and died in 1989, aged 87.

Kenneth Cranston

KENNETH CRANSTON was born in Liverpool on 20 October 1917, the son of a dentist, and, like his brother Ronald, who died young, he showed outstanding sporting ability at Liverpool College. He also played for Neston in the Liverpool and District Competition and the Lancashire second eleven before the war, impressing the county coach Harry Makepeace so much that he considered him the greatest natural talent he'd ever taught.

After graduating from dental school, he served as a dental surgeon in the war, playing cricket for the Royal Navy and the Combined Services, and witnessed the Japanese surrender to Lord Mountbatten at Singapore.

Appointed captain of Lancashire in 1947 as an amateur without having played a first-class match, Cranston tended to listen to the committee rather more than the professionals, which somewhat impeded team spirit.

With his telegenic looks and his robust stroke-play, he became an immediate favourite with the large crowds who flocked to Old Trafford post-war. His brisk fast-medium earned him a call-up for England in the third Test against South Africa that summer, and in the fourth Test at Headingley he took four wickets in an over without conceding a run to end the tourists' second innings.

Appointed vice-captain to Allen on MCC's tour to the West Indies in 1947/48, he found himself in charge for the first three matches, including the first Test at Bridgetown because of the captain's torn calf muscle. In the absence of Allen and his opening partner, Harold Butler, Cranston opened the bowling himself, along with Somerset's Maurice Tremlett. The home side ended the first day in a commanding position at 244/3 but, helped by overnight rain, Cranston immediately turned to off-spinner Laker to exploit the conditions and he responded with 6-25 as the last seven wickets fell for 52. England made 253 and needed 395 to win but they were on the ropes at 86/4 when bad weather ended play prematurely. 'Cranston the England captain set a fine example in the field,' reported *Wisden*, 'and little fault could be found with his handling of his limited bowling resources.' [32]

Although Cranston managed only limited success in the three remaining Tests, it didn't detract from his enjoyment of life in the Caribbean. His hedonism brought him into conflict with Allen who was rather more puritanical in his outlook. 'I remember once having to divert Gubby when we were on our way to the ground for early morning practice and I bumped into Ken Cranston returning to the hotel in his dinner jacket,' recalled Griffith. [33]

Left out of the England side against Australia the following summer, Cranston was recalled for the fourth Test at Headingley but failed with both bat and ball. He did, however, help Bradman who sought his professional advice about his bad teeth. At the end of the season, he resigned the captaincy of Lancashire to concentrate on his dental practice – much to general regret. He maintained strong links with Lancashire and was their president in 1993/94. When he died in 2007, aged 89, he was then England's oldest Test cricketer.

George Mann

GEORGE MANN was born in Byfleet, Surrey, on 6 September 1917, the elder of two sons to Frank Mann, who led Middlesex and England in the 1920s. A lusty middle-order hitter and a brilliant fielder, Mann played in the same Eton eleven as his brother John, captaining it in 1936, and won blues at Cambridge in 1938 and 1939.

During the war, Mann served with distinction in the Scots Guards and was judged the best regimental officer in the British Army. He won the MC in 1943 and the DSO in 1945, his citation speaking of his consistent courage and outstanding leadership in the Allied advance from Rome to Florence.

He missed the 1946 season while recuperating from war wounds but returned in 1947 and contributed to Middlesex's winning of the championship by captaining the side in Walter Robins's absence. He captained the next two years, leading them to third place in 1948 and to a share of the title with Yorkshire in 1949.

Owing to Yardley's unavailability for MCC's tour to South Africa in 1948/49, the selectors plumped for Mann. Because he'd never played for England, his appointment raised some eyebrows, but his limitations as a top-flight cricketer were more than compensated for by his personal qualities. A man of charm, intelligence, firmness and unselfishness, he proved an inspired choice, and together with the manager, Brigadier Mike Green, the secretary of Worcestershire, he ran a very successful tour.

Unlike the two previous tours to Australia and the West Indies, the selectors picked a better-balanced side, with the batting revolving around Hutton, Washbrook and Compton and the bowling depending on Bedser and Doug Wright.

Because there had been no tour to the Union since Hammond's ten years earlier, and with the Second World War forging special links between Britain and the English-speaking white South Africans, the tour aroused much interest wherever the team went.

On becoming captain, Mann was given two bits of advice by his father, who'd captained MCC in South Africa in 1922/23: stay well clear of the press and never accept a private dinner on tour. He ignored the first bit but adhered religiously to the second, ensuring that he was always available to his players.

His authority was enhanced by a forceful century in the opening game against Western Province, winning a warm endorsement from Len Hutton. A superb fielder himself who chased everything to the boundary, Mann placed a great emphasis on this part of the game, and in time his enthusiasm brought about a vast improvement as they became the best MCC fielding side that Swanton ever saw.

After six wins and two draws in their first-class matches, England entered the first Test at Durban in good heart against opponents whose traditional depth in batting had been strengthened by the inclusion of 19-year-old fast bowler Cuan McCarthy. Set 128 to win in 125 minutes and soon reduced to two hours because of a sharp shower, they went for glory. After an encouraging start, they collapsed against McCarthy, whose suspect action occasioned much comment but no complaint. His 6-25 kept South Africa in the game, and 11 were still needed when the number ten, Cliff Gladwin, strode jauntily to the crease in appalling light. At the beginning of the final (eight-ball) over-bowled by Lindsay Tuckett, South Africa's opening bowler, the target had been reduced to eight, and, amid unbearable tension, that had been narrowed down to one needed off the final ball. Gladwin swung heartily to leg and missed, but as the ball rebounded off his thigh and fell close to Tufty Mann (no relation) at square leg his partner Bedser charged down the wicket and made his ground to record an epic win.

The England batting, led by an opening stand of 359 by Hutton and Washbrook, dominated the drawn second Test and comfortably saved the third Test after being behind on first innings. For the fourth Test, Mann showed his mettle by demoting his first-choice wicketkeeper Evans. Having thrown a glass of beer over the manager in a fit of pique after the third Test, Evans then further blotted his copybook in the return match against Rhodesia by prolonging an appeal long after the umpire had ruled the batsman not out. Mann, a great stickler for the proprieties of the game, told him that it was the most unsporting appeal he'd ever heard, and, convinced that Evans needed to be brought to heel, he subsequently wrote him a note to say he'd been dropped for disciplinary reasons. He was replaced by reserve wicketkeeper Griffith.

On another easy-paced wicket at Johannesburg, England gained a first-innings lead of 122, but, mindful of their narrow lead in the series, Mann's declaration setting South Africa 376 to win in four and a half hours wasn't overgenerous. Another draw resulted, meaning that all came down to the final Test at Port Elizabeth. With South Africa one down in the series, the onus was on them to increase the tempo once they had won the toss, but on another docile wicket they failed to do so. Nevertheless, their total of 379 looked quite imposing when England lost their fourth wicket at 149, whereupon Mann played the innings of his life. Mixing sound defence with powerful drives, he defied his opponents for over four hours to finish undefeated with 136.

With time against them, South Africa's failure once again to accelerate defied reason. Finally, in an act of some desperation, their captain Dudley Nourse declared, setting England 172 to win in 95 minutes. They could easily have played out time but, in keeping with his positive approach, Mann accepted the challenge and promoted himself in the order. Hutton and Washbrook gave them a solid start and a quick-fire 42 by Compton saw them pass 100 in 53 minutes, only then for the roof to start caving in. Seven wickets were down for 153 before Gloucestershire's Jack Crapp stopped the rot, hitting ten off the penultimate over to give his side victory by three wickets.

With MCC easily disposing of the Combined Universities in their final match, they emerged from a tour of 23 matches unbeaten, emulating Hammond's achievement ten years earlier. Results aside, the games had been played in a great spirit and, with Mann the perfect ambassador, MCC made friends wherever they went. Writing years later, Swanton rated the side the most popular he'd experienced and the only side between 1938 and 1955 that reached their full potential both on and off the field. Mike Green, in his end-of-tour management report, attributed much of the credit to Mann. 'There is no doubt as to his leadership and his example on the field, however hot or late in the day, could not be faulted. In addition, as the tour progressed, he gained confidence and experience and so the use of his field and the use of his bowlers was first class.' [34] Green also commented on Mann's ability to enthuse his players and achieve unity so that even those not selected for the Tests remained upbeat.

Mann continued to captain England in two Tests against New Zealand, both drawn, scoring 49* in 25 minutes in the first Test at Headingley, before he stood down because of his growing business commitments, barely playing first-class cricket again after the end of that season.

For the next 30 years he helped to manage the family brewing concern, Mann, Crossman and Paulin, and distinguished himself in cricket administration, most notably as chairman of the TCCB from 1978 to 1983, chairman of Middlesex from 1980 to 1983 and its president from 1983 to 1990. He died in 2001, aged 83.

Freddie Brown

FREDDIE BROWN was born in Lima, Peru, on 16 December 1910, his father being engaged in an import and export agency business there. After education at St Peter's School in Chile, he went to St Piran's Prep School in Maidenhead, where he was taught googly bowling by the South African all-rounder and notable coach Aubrey Faulkner. At The Leys School, Cambridge, he enjoyed four years of unbroken success, with more than 2,000 runs and nearly 200 wickets, establishing himself as a formidable striker of the ball. On the advice of Faulkner, he switched to leg breaks at Cambridge and topped the bowling averages in 1931 with 66 wickets.

That summer Brown made his debut for England against New Zealand and, having completed the double for Surrey in 1932, he toured Australia with Jardine's side , although he didn't play in a Test.

Because of his work with Lloyd's Insurance Brokers, his appearances for Surrey were intermittent for the rest of the decade.

Commissioned into the Royal Army Service Corps, he helped evacuate the British Army from Crete in 1941, for which he was awarded the MBE for gallantry. He played cricket against Australia's future captain Lindsay Hassett for their respective Services XI in a game in Cairo before he was captured at Tobruk with the Yorkshire fast bowler Bill Bowes, and together they spent the rest of the war in prisoner-of-war camps in Italy and Germany.

Brown played little cricket post-war until a new job with British Timken in 1949 permitted him to captain Northamptonshire, an unfashionable county that had been rooted to the bottom of the table for the previous two years. His arrival injected a fresh sense of purpose. He ordered his new charges back for three weeks' training before the season began, and from his first match he made it clear to the committee that he was in charge. A rumbustious, Falstaffian personality with sandy hair and a rubicund face, he barked out his orders and brooked no dissent. He addressed the professionals by their surnames and insisted they not only called the amateurs 'Mr', but also gave them prior use of the showers.

Yet for all his class-based attitudes, he won his players' grudging respect because he never demanded anything of them that he wouldn't do himself. Although aged 38, he revelled in his new responsibilities and repeated his 1932 achievement with Surrey of completing the double. Following an eight-wicket match haul for the Gentlemen against the Players at Lord's in July, and his success in reviving Northamptonshire – they finished sixth in the championship that year – he replaced Mann as England captain. He led the side with gusto in the final two matches against New Zealand, but a combination of three-day Tests and flat wickets consigned the matches to draws.

Brown's mediocre form at the beginning of the 1950 season meant that Norman Yardley captained England against the West Indies, but Yardley's unavailability, and that of Mann, to tour Australia that winter created a void which Brown was able to fill. Any doubts about his age were swept aside by his stupendous innings of 122 out of 131 in 110 minutes to rescue the Gentlemen against the Players. Before the match had ended, he'd accepted an invitation to lead England in Australia; then, days later, he presided over the final Test against the West Indies, a match which England lost by as convincing a margin as they had in the previous two Tests.

That summer had exposed weaknesses in the England middle order, a weakness compounded by the flawed selection of the team to Australia. The undue emphasis on youth, including three Cambridge graduates, David Sheppard, John Dewes and John Warr, was partly down to Brown's disregard of Edrich and Laker.

Brown used the voyage out to successfully weld his team together and, unlike Hammond, spent time in their company as they travelled around Australia. 'The fact that we were such a happy and contented band throughout the trip was largely due to the leadership of Freddie Brown,' wrote Trevor Bailey, one of the six amateurs who were given preferential treatment. 'To those of us who were young and amateurs, he [Brown] was friendly and fatherly,' wrote Dewes. 'For others, I suspect, he adopted a different manner.' [35] 'Our amateurs were a little on the soft side,' recalled Brian Close. 'The amateurs wanted to enjoy the cricket, they did not want to be bothered by a young lad like me who had come out of the Army. They played to the best of their ability, but then after that they wanted to enjoy the hospitality. The point was the standard of leadership in those days was poor. They failed to understand players and their talents.' [36]

Hampered by unusually bad weather, MCC's form prior to the first Test was unimpressive. Brown was slated for his team's casual approach to practice, and when injury forced him to miss the games against Victoria and New South Wales, Compton, his vice-captain, showed little grip as captain. With Australia, under Hassett, unbeaten in any Test post-war, England were all but written off, but Brown had no time for such defeatism. He roused his team with a pre-Agincourt speech on the eve of the first Test and then led them out the next day with resolution written all over his face. Whether encouraging or cajoling in the field, Brown, attired in his trademark white knotted handkerchief tied around his substantial neck, conveyed his determination to his team and they responded admirably by dismissing Australia on a plumb wicket for 228. 'It was captaincy supreme,' wrote the sports journalist Vivian Jenkins in *Wisden*, 'and I like to think that here was one instance, at least, where professionals managed to put off the lure of averages, and press report and transient personal glory. They were playing for England, and their skipper Freddie Brown, and nothing else.' [37] A monsoon that evening washed out the next day's play and further rain on Sunday delayed the start until half an hour before lunch on Monday. On a true Brisbane 'sticky', England struggled to 68/7 – Hutton 8* – before Brown declared to give Australia a taste of their own medicine. They made 32/7 and also declared to get their opponents in again that evening. With several batsmen guilty of throwing their wickets away, England limped to stumps at 30/6. The next morning, in better conditions, the carnage wasn't quite so great, but England could only manage 122, leaving Hutton, batting at number eight, undefeated on a brilliant 62. In such a low-scoring match, it seemed the height of folly to bat him so low in the order. Although there was some validity in holding back some of the leading batsmen until the wicket had improved, the chances were that Hutton, the leading exponent of uncovered wickets, would have stiffened the resolve in both innings, a point of view that Brown later accepted.

He continued with the error of batting Hutton down the order at Melbourne. On a seaming wicket, England gained an early advantage by bowling out Australia for 194, only to then collapse to 54/5. They were rescued by Brown who, by taking the attack to the Australians, entranced the 60,000-crowd with his exhilarating 62 and earned himself a thunderous ovation on his dismissal. Thanks to him and Evans, England led by three on first innings and Brown now played his part with the ball by breaking the back of the Australian batting with his medium-paced cutters. Requiring only 179 to win, the England batting once again failed to pass muster and they lost by 28 runs, much to the disappointment of many in the crowd who were willing them on to victory. As the two captains left the ground, it was Brown who was surrounded and cheered by well-wishers, much to the bemusement of Hassett, who waited for his rival to free himself.

Brown's spirited batting again came to the fore at Sydney. Entering at 187/5, he won over the Hill, the hardest cricket crowd in the world to satisfy, as much by his gargantuan personality as the audacity of his hitting. After he was bowled by Lindwall for 79, the cricket writer Neville Cardus remarked that the crowd almost groaned with sorrow. 'His reception, as he walked back to the pavilion's cool shade, was so royal that it might all have been a procession with the red carpet down and the decorations up.' [38]

All out for 290 on a good wicket, England's plight was exacerbated by the loss of two of their bowlers, Bailey and Wright, due to injury while batting, leaving Bedser, Warr and Brown to bear the burden of the attack. In stifling heat, they bowled 123 (eight-ball) overs between them, Brown's rubicund face becoming redder and redder as he soldiered on, but, for all their heroics, Australia gained a first-innings lead of 136. With their mystery spinner Jack Iverson near unplayable on a wearing pitch, England collapsed to 123 all out, ensuring that the Ashes remained down under.

Hutton aside, England were outplayed at Adelaide, but at Melbourne in the final Test they finally came good. Still recovering from a damaged shoulder sustained in a minor car accident in Adelaide, Brown was reluctant to bowl, but with Bailey injuring his ankle early on, he soon returned to the fray to inflict serious damage by removing Arthur Morris, Keith Miller and Neil Harvey without conceding a run. He later dismissed Hassett for 92 to finish with 5-49, his best Test figures.

Dismissing Australia for 217, England, helped by 156* from Reg Simpson, gained a first-innings lead of 103 and once again bowled out their opponents cheaply. Needing only 95 to win, a painstaking 60* from Hutton saw them through to victory by eight wickets. Their success delighted many in the crowd and thousands assembled in front of the pavilion calling for Brown. Twenty minutes later he appeared on the balcony to great acclamation, the most tumultuous reception ever accorded an England captain, opined the renowned Australian cricket writer Ray Robinson. Brown congratulated Australia on their victory in the rubber and in turn received a glowing compliment from Hassett. Later that evening, at the team hotel, the England players gathered around Brown and drank his health in champagne, ending with 'For he's a jolly good fellow'. According to Australian off-spinner Ian Johnson, he did a magnificent job with his indomitable spirit. 'Brown made severe demands upon his team but asked for nothing that he was not prepared to give himself.' [39]

After Australia, Brown won the two-match series against New Zealand and then led England to a 3-1 victory against South Africa the following summer, his enterprising approach contrasting with his opposite number, Dudley Nourse. In the first Test at Trent Bridge, Brown declared 64 runs behind on first innings to get South Africa back in again on a rain-affected pitch, but, despite Bedser's 6-37, the task of scoring 186 in over five hours proved too taxing for his batsmen.

At Lord's, another rain-affected pitch played to England's advantage this time and with spinner Roy Tattersall taking 12 wickets they won by an innings.

They won again at Old Trafford and, after a draw at Headingley, England wrapped up the series at the Oval by beating South Africa by four wickets, with Brown contributing an aggressive 40.

His retirement from the England captaincy brought him many plaudits. 'Frederick Richard Brown will be remembered in days to come as a great England cricket captain,' wrote Jenkins in *Wisden*. 'It will not be so much for what he and his team accomplished on the 1950/51 tour to Australia – they lost the series, four games to one – but because of what he personally all but inspired them to accomplish.' [40]

Evans, enthused by his buoyancy and aggression, thought he captained the side wonderfully, but not everyone was so admiring. Edrich wrote that he didn't get enough out of his players because his understanding of them was limited, while Compton thought he was too stubborn to be a great captain.

Brown wasn't quite finished yet. Becoming chairman of selectors in 1953, he responded to his captain Hutton's request that he play against Australia at Lord's. In a Test immortalised by the Watson-Bailey stand on the final day that saved England from defeat, Brown didn't disgrace himself with either bat or ball. He retired from county cricket at the end of that season but remained active as manager of the MCC tours to South Africa in 1956/57 and Australia in 1958/59 – an unpopular appointment with most of the players – chairman of the Cricket Council from 1974 to 1979 and president of the National Cricket Association. He died in 1991, aged 80.

Nigel Howard

NIGEL HOWARD was born in Hyde, Cheshire, on 18 May 1925. His father, Rupert Howard, had played briefly for Lancashire before becoming its secretary between 1933 and 1949, during which time he twice managed MCC tours to Australia; and Nigel's younger brother, Barry, also played for Lancashire.

At Rossall School, Howard excelled at golf and hockey as well as at cricket. He made his debut for Lancashire in 1946 and within two years he'd established himself as a stylish batsman and fine fielder. In 1949, helped by his amateur status and his father's connections, he was appointed the county's youngest captain, aged 23. The job proved a demanding one. He faced constant interference from the committee, which undermined his authority with supporters, critics and team-mates alike, nearly all of whom thought Washbrook, the senior professional, should be captain.

Yet, politics aside, Howard proved an enterprising captain, willing to accept any reasonable declaration in pursuit of victory, and encouraging the younger players like Tattersall and Brian Statham. In 1950, his best year with the bat when he averaged nearly 40, he led Lancashire to a share of the championship, a feat not again repeated until 2011, and they continued to flourish thereafter, finishing third for the next three seasons.

In 1951 he captained the Gentlemen against the Players, the prelude to his appointment as captain of MCC to India, Pakistan and Ceylon that winter. Without a win in their first 20 Tests, India lacked the cachet of Australia and South Africa, and six months on the subcontinent held out little appeal to England's senior players. Consequently, it was a scratch side comprising old sweats and young bucks that came together under Howard and his vice-captain Donald Carr, the former captain of Oxford, neither of whom had had Test experience.

On arrival at Bombay, the team received a rapturous welcome, but while often the recipients of sumptuous hospitality they also came face to face with the realities of everyday India: the tiring rail journeys, the oppressive heat, the sleepless nights, the primitive sanitation and the constant stomach ailments. 'Poor Nigel is so scared of illness,' the manager Geoffrey Howard (no relation) wrote to his wife. 'The flies are a nuisance up here but he is really stupid about them. Now I have upset him by warning about the dangers of dog-bites and hydrophobia.' [41] 'He was very young and his upbringing had been so materialistic,' the manager later reflected. 'In a way he'd had things too easy in his life. He'd got where he had because of his father.' [42]

After beginning the tour with four draws out of five, England, without their best batsman Tom Graveney because of illness, entered the first Test as underdogs against an opposition who were no pushover on their own wickets. Exposed to this exacting environment, Howard leant greatly on senior professional Allan Watkins, constantly seeking his advice, over-bowling him and, when batting with him, accepting his offer to shield him from the leg-spinner. With his side heading for defeat, it was Watkins with an undefeated century, along with Carr, who managed to salvage a draw.

With Graveney back for the second Test, the question was: who should make way for him? Watkins, a member of the selection committee, thought Howard, who was averaging 16 on tour so far, should stand down. 'Poor Nigel can't get going. I'm afraid he is just not good enough for Test cricket,' wasn't only the opinion of the manager. [43] It was commonly held throughout the team, but Howard, primed about such a possibility by Lord's prior to the tour, refused to demote himself, and Carr, who had helped save the previous Test, was dropped instead.

Led by Graveney's 175, England gave a much-improved performance in the second Test and went close to pulling off a surprise victory. The third Test was a drab draw, but in the fourth Test at Kanpur the tourists played above themselves to win by eight wickets. On a turning wicket the Lancashire spinners, Malcolm Hilton and Tattersall, well supported by Howard's attacking captaincy, twice dismissed India cheaply.

Kanpur proved to be Howard's finale for the tour. For a man who'd never really taken to India and who'd worried constantly about his health, all his phobias now came to pass as he developed pleurisy. Although out of his depth as a batsman with a top Test score of 23, he led the side capably, apart from his mistrust of opening bowler Derek Shackleton, who only played in one Test, and by playing in the right spirit he helped cement good relations with India in the post-independence era.

He continued to lead Lancashire for another two years before devoting himself to the family textile firm. He retired to the Isle of Man in 1976 and died there from a heart attack three years later, aged only 54.

Donald Carr

DONALD CARR was born in Wiesbaden, Germany, on 28 December 1926, the youngest of three sons of an officer of the Royal Berkshire Regiment, and a keen sportsman who played football for Oxford University, hockey for the Army and cricket for Berkshire.

At Repton School, where his father had taken the post of bursar on leaving the Army, Donald developed into one of the leading schoolboy cricketers in the country, captaining the Public Schools against a Lord's XI in 1944.

In 1945, still aged 18, he played in the third Victory Test against Australia, and after a short service commission in his father's old regiment, he went up to Oxford in 1948, winning blues in both football and cricket. He captained the latter in 1950 and in 1951 he helped Oxford beat Cambridge at Lord's, the same year in which he headed the Derbyshire batting averages.

On the basis of his form and his amateur status, he was appointed vice-captain of MCC's experimental side to India, Pakistan and Ceylon that winter. Unlike his captain, Howard, the gregarious Carr felt very much at home on the subcontinent and proved an ideal ambassador, a quality he later displayed as manager of three MCC tours.

Chosen for the first Test at Delhi, he emerged as one of England's heroes for his dogged resistance in the second innings. Entering at 116/3, with his side still 99 in arrears, he and Watkins defied the Indian spinners for over five hours, putting on 158, and after

Carr left for 76 Watkins persevered to the end, his undefeated 138 securing his team an honourable draw.

Carr celebrated their escape by riding a bicycle around a restaurant that evening, but neither his efforts nor his position as vice-captain guaranteed him a place in the second Test. With Graveney, their leading batsman, now recovered from illness, and Howard unwilling to drop himself despite his wretched form, it was Carr who was thrown to the wolves. 'I was a bit disappointed, as you can imagine, but he [Howard] certainly wasn't going to stand down,' he later recalled. 'I suppose it was inevitable, really, and I've sometimes wondered what I would have done in similar circumstances.' [44]

He returned to the front line as captain in the fifth Test at Madras because Howard was indisposed with pleurisy. One up in the series after their convincing win in the fourth Test, England approached the game full of confidence, but their batting succumbed to the wiles of spinner Vinoo Mankad, who returned match figures of 12/108. Carr made a determined 40 in the first innings but England's total of 266 presented few terrors to the Indian batsmen. They replied with 457/9 before their spinners went to work again, dismissing England for 183, their first Test victory.

Carr captained the side for the remaining games in Ceylon, but he never played for England again. He did lead an MCC A team to Pakistan in 1955/56 and captained Derbyshire with panache between 1955 and 1962, becoming one of their finest-ever players. After his playing days, he immersed himself in the complexities of cricket administration, distinguishing himself as a conscientious assistant secretary of MCC between 1962 and 1974 and secretary of the TCCB between 1973 and 1986. He also proved his worth as manager on three MCC tours to South Africa in 1964/65, India and Pakistan in 1972/73 and to the West Indies in 1973/74. He died in 2016, aged 89.

The Victorious Fifties:
Hutton and May
in Charge

ALTHOUGH MCC had remained true to Lord Hawke's philosophy of never appointing a professional to captain England, they were swimming against the tide of history. Some counties began appointing professionals as captains, most notably Warwickshire who won the championship under Tom Dollery in 1951. When Nigel Howard, the young amateur captain of Lancashire, led a second-string England side to India in 1951/52 and barely scored a run, MCC finally entered the modern world by appointing Len Hutton as England's first professional captain.

Reared in the austere Yorkshire dressing room of the 1930s when winning was everything, Hutton brought a more competitive edge to England's cricket at a time when political independence movements in the developing world placed a greater premium on winning Test matches. Never the most accomplished of diplomats and man-managers, Hutton struggled to lay down the law in the West Indies in 1953/54 when his team's gamesmanship and breach of protocol came under fierce scrutiny. The resulting bad publicity unnerved the selectors enough to contemplate replacing Hutton with the amateur David Sheppard for the forthcoming tour to Australia, but in the end public support for Hutton and natural justice decreed that the latter remained in charge. One of the world's greatest batsmen and a master strategist, he employed his formidable opening attack of Frank Tyson and Brian Statham to maximum effect in Australia by slowing down the over rate and constantly changing the field. The winner of the Ashes twice and unbeaten in six series, his success came at a cost because the physical and emotional strain of leading England, not least on tour, brought about his premature retirement in 1956. His legacy lived on in the form of his vice-captain Peter May, whose privileged background and old-fashioned courtesies concealed a ruthless determination to win, and in pursuit of his goal he played risk-averse cricket.

Immediately establishing himself with his magisterial batting, May led an all-conquering England side for nearly four years, and even after their ignominious defeat in Australia in 1958/59 his captaincy remained unassailable, his position buttressed by his close relationship with chairman of selectors Gubby Allen. Had illness and a certain disillusion not intervened, May might well have captained England for several more years, but after their loss to Australia in 1961 he retired having captained his country a record 41 times. His departure marked the end of a golden era when the post-war captaincy reached its zenith. Thereafter, in a less deferential age, England cricket captains, along with other establishment figures, were forced to undergo much greater scrutiny.

Len Hutton

LEN HUTTON was born in Fulneck, Yorkshire, on 23 June 1916. His father was a builder of Scottish origin and his mother was a descendant of the Moravians, a central European Protestant sect that settled in Fulneck in 1744 and adhered to the values of hard work, respectability and self-sufficiency.

The Huttons were a keen cricket family. Len's father and all three of his brothers played for Pudsey St Lawrence, the local club of Herbert Sutcliffe, the legendary Yorkshire and England opener, and he made his first appearance for the second eleven aged 11. Two years later, he played for the first eleven and, coached by his mentor Sutcliffe, he developed an immaculate technique.

In 1934 Hutton first played for Yorkshire, striking up a prolific opening partnership with Sutcliffe, and in 1937 he made his England debut against New Zealand at Lord's. He began with nought and one, but in the next game at Old Trafford he hit a century, and in the following year he achieved lasting renown by scoring a record-breaking 364 against Australia at the Oval.

A wartime accident in a gym during commando training injured Hutton's arm so badly that three bone grafts were needed to repair the fracture. He spent eight months in hospital in constant pain and full of anxiety as to whether he would be able to play cricket again, before he was finally discharged, but with his left arm shorter and weaker.

Although the accident injected a touch more caution in his batting, Hutton remained a cricketing colossus whose Test record stands comparison with any of his contemporaries, Bradman aside.

Because of changing times post-war, the tradition of amateur captains was becoming ever more obsolete, but even so the decision to appoint Hutton as England's first professional captain in 1952 was by no means universally popular. E.W. Swanton, while acknowledging the merit of his appointment, warned that his attitude to the broad tactics of the game, commonly said to be characteristic of the Yorkshireman, seemed to his fellow players to cloud his judgement.

Hutton displayed plenty of Yorkshire canniness and grit when it came to cricket. The puritan values of his upbringing that shaped his personality and batting certainly applied to his captaincy. 'You don't play cricket for fun, Peter, you know,' he once said to May. Commensurate with this mentality, he valued containment above adventure, shunning generous declarations, preferring pace over spin and disdaining anyone in his team who appeared casual. Armed with an encyclopaedic knowledge of the game, his planning was meticulous. Every change in the bowling or fielding was made with the expressed hope of pressuring the batsman. He rarely let a game drift.

Yet, while undoubtedly a superb tactician, he wasn't a natural leader of men. 'The captaincy of the English cricket team was the most important office in all sport,' reflected Geoffrey Howard, the manager of MCC in Australia in 1954/55. 'It meant a lot to Len, but he'd never been captain of Yorkshire. He was very confident of his own ability as a player but, until the later stages of his career, I don't think he ever saw himself as a leader.' [45] Part of this was down to his parvenu status. Hutton later wrote: 'As I considered myself a stopgap, I was at a disadvantage among selectors with amateur backgrounds and distinguished playing records. I rather felt like a head boy called to a meeting of housemasters.' [46] It was notable that when the former England captain Freddie Brown, now chairman of selectors, played under his captaincy against Australia at Lord's in 1953, Hutton continued to refer to him as 'skipper'.

Hutton's shy, reclusive personality made him an inscrutable figure who rarely displayed his emotions. Although he would listen to senior team-mates such as Evans or Bailey, he rarely discussed tactics, held team meetings or said anything while batting. 'He was a chap who didn't communicate to anyone at all, all the time I knew him,' recalled Bedser, who played alongside Hutton for all of his Test career. [47] Much of his talk was oblique. Ray Illingworth, recalling his early years at Yorkshire in the 1950s, wrote that Hutton never gave useful advice and that any comments of his would normally be of a sardonic nature. Yet those who could penetrate his outward reserve, such as David Sheppard and Colin Cowdrey, found him to be kind and helpful. 'When he liked you, he could pass on tips about batting that you might not learn in a season at the crease,' recalled Cowdrey. 'But you had to accept that he was going to help you in his own individual way.' [48]

Pitted against an Indian team vulnerable to the pace of Fred Trueman, Hutton faced few challenges in his initial series as captain, England winning the four-Test series 3-0. He cemented his authority with two centuries and won the compliments of the editor of *Wisden* by insisting on the highest standards of fielding. Alluding to Hutton's innate caution, the editor hoped that if a spirit of enterprise was required in the forthcoming series against Australia, he would rise to the challenge regardless of the consequences.

Such enterprise was foreign to Hutton's concept of leadership. A common criticism in the first two Tests against Australia, both drawn, was his failure to press home his attacking advantages. On the second day of the second Test at Lord's, he and Graveney, in reply to Australia's first innings of 346, had given their side the perfect start with a second-wicket stand of 168, but, with the opposition in retreat, Hutton instructed his partner to call off the assault in the last hour. Accordingly, they added a mere 34 in that time and Graveney was out in the first over the next morning. Thereafter, despite Hutton's 145, England surrendered their early advantage and, losing three quick wickets at the start of their second innings, they only survived due to a four-hour partnership of 163 between Willie Watson and Trevor Bailey on the final day.

The Old Trafford Test was a rain-ruined draw and in a truncated game at Headingley, owing to more bad weather, England fought doggedly to avoid defeat. With Australia requiring 177 to win in two hours, Hutton, thinking that the wicket would be receptive to spin, erred badly by opening with Tony Lock to attacking fields. The Australians raced to 100 in the first hour, and with 66 needed in 45 minutes Bailey urged Hutton to slow down the over rate by using him. He proceeded to bowl six overs of leg theory, which cost a mere nine runs, and Australia finished 30 runs short. While they seethed in private, feeling they'd been cheated of victory by time-wasting, a view shared by a number of the England team, Hutton was unrepentant, saying that he'd merely played the Australians at their own game.

With everything resting on the decider at the Oval, England recalled Trueman and Laker and the former took 4-86 in Australia's first innings of 275. England gained a narrow lead of 31 and then, on a wearing pitch, Laker and Lock dismissed their opponents for 162. Needing 132 for victory, they won by eight wickets and regained the Ashes after 19 years. 'When I saw the crowds, happy and cheering, massed in front of the pavilion at the Oval,' recollected Hutton, 'I knew the struggle had been worthwhile.' [49]

His success against Australia guaranteed him the captaincy of the MCC tour to the West Indies that winter. The press billed it as the unofficial world championship, which added tension to the cricket, as did the fragile political backdrop in the Caribbean, where demands for independence from the mother country grew ever greater. With so much at stake, much would depend on Hutton's leadership both on and off the field. His status as MCC's first professional captain won few adherents among the snooty colonial elite in the Caribbean, and, given his self-contained personality, the choice of manager would be critical. Hutton wanted the outgoing Billy Griffith, an able assistant manager on the previous tour to the West Indies, but, because of his new position as assistant MCC secretary, he wasn't available. Consequently, MCC plumped for Charles Palmer, the Leicestershire captain who had presided over a major resurgence of their fortunes. Yet, for all his personal qualities, the 34-year-old Palmer, three years younger than Hutton, lacked the stature, experience and force of personality to cope with the potential pitfalls of such a trip. Although he established good relations with Hutton, especially in the latter stages of the tour, he could do little to wean him away from his deep-seated insularity. Recalling the frequent socialising in the West Indies on the previous tour, which he found most wearisome after a day's play, and never one for small talk, Hutton asked for fewer official functions. More heinous was his tendency to make deeply unflattering remarks about his hosts and dissuade his players from fraternising with them, much to their bewilderment.

Hutton's defensive frame of mind badly backfired in the first two Tests. On a placid wicket at Kingston, his policy of fielding four pace bowlers at the expense of his spinners, Laker and Wardle, proved flawed as his opponents accumulated 417. England could only muster 170 against Ramadhin and Valentine, and although they made a better stab of it at their second attempt they still lost by 140 runs.

For the Bridgetown Test, England brought in Laker for Alan Moss and, more controversially, Palmer for Trueman, since the former wasn't Test ability and his one first-class match on the tour had been three weeks earlier. Batting first on another unblemished surface, the West Indies made 383 before Ramadhin and Valentine again reduced England to near paralysis. On a soporific third day, they managed a mere 128 runs in 114 overs as Hutton opted for occupation of the crease. Concerned that the adventurous Graveney was using his feet to the spinners, he told him to grind it out. Responding to orders, Graveney took over two hours to score 15 before meekly hitting a full toss back to Ramadhin. It was a baffling approach and one that called for reappraisal when England batted again. Set 495 to win, Hutton loosened the noose on his batsmen, and they looked all the better for playing their natural game. Four batsmen, including Hutton, scored half-centuries, and although they lost by 181 runs they broke the stranglehold that Valentine had previously imposed on them. Never again did he pose them a serious threat.

With the team under fire for their gracelessness in adversity and morale at a low ebb, there was a pressing need for real leadership. Vice-captain Bailey arranged a dinner for the senior players, at which he, Compton and Edrich pledged to rally support behind Hutton, while the captain agreed to adopt a more positive approach.

In the third Test at Georgetown, the captain duly led from the front with a chanceless 169 in England's first innings of 435. A wonderful opening spell by Statham ripped the heart out of the West Indian upper order and they were in deep trouble till a plucky eighth-wicket stand between J.K. Holt and Clifford McWatt raised hopes they might avoid the follow-on. The stand had added 98 when McWatt was run out going for a risky second run. The decision was a mere formality, but, given the toxic political climate in British Guiana, and with many a bet riding on the 100 partnership, it proved highly unpopular with the crowd. As Ramadhin replaced McWatt in the middle, scuffles broke out and bottles were hurled at the umpire. In the face of such mayhem and the requests from the local officials that Hutton remove his team from the field, the England captain stood his ground. He wanted more wickets that evening, and when the game resumed ten minutes later Laker bowled Ramadhin.

The next day, the West Indies duly followed on and were dismissed for 256, England winning by nine wickets. The match was an all-round triumph for Hutton, with press and players at one in their praise of his tactical nous and composure under fire. According to Compton, 'Len never had a greater moment. He was cool, nerveless, courageous, quite unconcerned about the demonstrating crowds which surrounded him in angry thousands.' [50]

With the fourth Test ending in stalemate at Port of Spain, everything hinged on the final game at Kingston. Hutton's dismay at losing the toss on the most docile of wickets was soon tempered by Bailey's devastating spell with the new ball. His 7-34 was primarily responsible for dismissing the West Indies for 139, whereupon Hutton took over, and in hour after hour of unwavering concentration his monumental double century edged his side ever closer to victory. Although the home side provided stiffer resistance in their second innings, England won comprehensively by nine wickets to square the series. From his bunker mentality in the first two Tests, Hutton emerged into the sunlight, displaying greater authority thereafter, much of it built around his phenomenal batting. His efforts in the heat had left him physically and mentally drained, as had the various controversies that confronted him throughout the tour.

The trouble began in the first match against the Combined Parishes in Jamaica when Trueman peppered George Headley, the ageing idol of West Indian cricket, and struck him a painful blow on the arm. A young, gauche Yorkshireman from a mining background, Trueman's more outlandish behaviour habitually offended his hosts. Playing against British Guiana, he expressed dissent when several decisions went against him, although it later transpired that it was Wardle rather than him who had sworn at the umpire.

Trueman was again at fault in the match against Trinidad when he felled the popular leg-spinner Wilf Ferguson with a bouncer after the two of them had exchanged words. His refusal to apologise only added to the indignation, and when England twice displayed dissent towards the umpires in the fourth Test the Yorkshire-born journalist J.S. Barker, now living in Trinidad, wrote an open letter to Hutton regretting the loss of England's reputation for good sportsmanship. 'Trueman gave me much concern,' Hutton wrote in his captain's report, 'and until a general improvement is made in his general conduct and cricket manners, I do not think he is suitable for MCC tours, particularly a tour such as the one to the West Indies.' [51] His assessment of Trueman was supported by Compton, although both he and Evans thought that he had been too lenient with him.

Off the field, it was a similar story. According to Swanton, the manners in the West Indies were shocking as the team too often alienated their hosts with their condescending behaviour. On the Saturday evening of the Bridgetown Test, Trueman and Lock were accused of jostling two elderly ladies in a lift and being drunk, when the real offenders were Compton and Evans. That same day, Graveney stepped out of line at a cocktail party when confronted with some disparaging remarks about his team-mates' drinking by an expatriate, and he was reported to the governor. Amid rumours that he was about to be sent home, it needed a meeting between the governor and Palmer and Hutton to pour oil on troubled waters.

In the final Test, Hutton himself inadvertently caused a stir by failing to acknowledge the compliments of the Jamaican chief minister, Alexander Bustamante, for his double century as he walked off the field at tea deep in concentration. The truth was that he'd failed to recognise the chief minister amid the mass of applauding spectators, and although Bustamante was more than happy with Hutton's explanation when they met up after play the local press wasn't quite so willing to let the matter drop. It was but the final altercation of a trouble-ridden trip. *The Times* called it the second most controversial tour in history after bodyline, *Wisden* remarked that it had failed to further good relations between the two countries and Swanton described the tour as a diplomatic and sporting disaster of the first magnitude. He attributed much of the blame to Hutton and his philosophy of disparaging the opposition, while Compton blamed his captain's aloofness for the team's charmless demeanour.

Given these reservations about MCC in the West Indies, the doubts about Hutton's leadership had by no means disappeared. With the forthcoming tour of Australia in mind, several selectors, led by Walter Robins, began to cast their gaze on the amateur David Sheppard, whose inspirational captaincy had taken Sussex from 13th to second in the championship the previous year. In the absence of Hutton because of illness, Sheppard deputised in the second and third Tests against Pakistan, winning one and having the better of the draw in the other, but, ultimately, public opinion dictated that Hutton stayed at the helm. He played his part in picking a team for Australia which omitted Trueman and Laker but included Frank Tyson and Colin Cowdrey, two promising youngsters who fully vindicated the trust placed in them.

Before departure, Hutton assured Cowdrey's father that he would look after the 21-year-old Colin and he was as good as his word, getting to know him and apprising him of the challenges he would face in Australia. 'Losing is foreign to their nature,' he used to say. 'Australians have made me fight for every run I have ever made. It's a hard game against them. The grounds are hard, the men are hard: you need to be harder than they are to beat them.' [52]

When Cowdrey learned of his father's death on arrival at Perth, Hutton was deeply affected and, while never mentioning his father again, he took him under his wing, showing a more sensitive side rarely apparent to others. 'He is an enigma', manager Geoffrey Howard wrote to his wife. 'He just cannot let you in on himself. He is full of sterling worth and a very good fellow: such a pity he won't really let you get to know him.' [53] Speechmaking, press conferences and socialising proved a great ordeal and off duty he kept himself from his players, especially some of the younger ones. Pace bowler Peter Loader complained that he barely spoke to him all tour, while Simpson and Graveney felt frozen out after early failures, until the latter made a triumphant comeback in the final Test. More bizarrely, Hutton didn't visit Bedser once when laid low by shingles in Perth and caused him much hurt by his failure to inform him personally of his omission from the second and third Tests.

Although the batting proved inconsistent in the lead-up to the first Test at Brisbane, MCC remained unbeaten. Placing his faith in an all-out pace attack on what he assumed would be a seaming wicket like the one in the Queensland game, Hutton gambled by fielding first on winning the toss, much to the astonishment of his opposite number, Ian Johnson. It proved to be a monumental misjudgement as Australia scored 601/8 declared on the most placid of surfaces to beat England by an innings. Hutton's error with the toss depressed him greatly, and on the rest day he shut himself away in his room. He did, however, become more upbeat at the end of the match, convinced that he had the wherewithal to beat Australia.

His optimism was boosted by Tyson's 6-68 against Victoria, his bowling all the better for his new shorter run, and with Bailey a reliable third seamer, Hutton now took the hardest decision of his career to omit Bedser, a great bowler now past his pomp. In a taut, low-scoring match, the second Test at Sydney turned out to be a classic, with victory ultimately going to England on the back of Tyson's 6-85 in the second innings, wonderfully supported by Statham. The mood in their camp was transformed overnight, but the strain of captaincy was getting to Hutton, especially since he was short of runs and again faced the prospect of omitting Bedser at Melbourne. On the night before that Test, he was having coffee with fellow Yorkshireman Bob Appleyard in the team hotel when Compton, Edrich and Evans appeared all dressed up for a night on the town. 'Look at those three. They'll say they need to relax,' he said to Appleyard, 'but this is the time to be thinking about the match.'

Such was his agitated state that Howard arranged for a doctor to examine him in the morning. The doctor pronounced him fit, much to his consternation. In a hoarse, quavering voice, he announced his intention of standing down and handing over the captaincy to May. It was then that Edrich, summoned to Hutton's room by Howard, took charge. Knowing that Hutton's talismanic presence was vital to England's morale, they pleaded with him to think again. Eventually he agreed, and they accompanied him to the ground.

A brilliant century by Cowdrey rescued England from a disastrous start against Miller, but 191 still represented a disappointing score. In stifling conditions on the second day, Hutton used his bowlers in short spells as they made frequent inroads into the Australian batting, but their failure to bowl no more than 54 (eight-ball) overs in five hours raised the ire of both their opponents and the large crowd. When questioned about this tactical ploy, Hutton's defence that he was merely helping his younger bowlers with field placings lacked conviction. He wasn't only trying to preserve the energy of his fast bowlers in the heat, but also to frustrate Australia's batsmen, particularly Harvey, by restricting their scoring opportunities.

Forty runs behind on first innings, England, thanks to a masterly 91 by May, made 279 in their second innings, at which point Tyson, with 7-27, sent Australia tumbling to defeat.

Two-one down in the series, Australia won a good toss at Adelaide, but Hutton used his bowlers in short spells and they did well to restrict Australia to 323. England gained a narrow lead of 18 and Hutton then introduced Appleyard early into the attack. It proved a shrewd move since his fellow Yorkshireman picked up the first three Australian wickets very cheaply before the close. With the wicket beginning to break up, it seemed that Appleyard would be the match-winner, but Hutton surprised everyone by opening with Tyson and Statham the next morning. They bowled unchanged for 90 minutes, dismissing six Australians for 24 runs, and England, needing 94 for victory, survived early shocks to win by five wickets. The Ashes had been retained and Hutton, despite a disappointing series with the bat, had accomplished one of his great ambitions, primarily on the back of Tyson and Statham. He later wrote: 'There were no better moments in my career than when I saw my long-term strategy to use fast bowlers as the spearhead of my thrust produce my hoped-for results.' [54]

On inheriting the captaincy, he hadn't reckoned with the full glare of the spotlight, and this was particularly the case on tour in Australia. So intense had been his mental exertions in the Sydney Test that a case full of letters congratulating him on his victory remained unanswered. His reluctance to play at Melbourne has already been noted, and after his second-innings dismissal there he walked in wearily and slumped motionless on the dressing-room bench, his head in his hands, without even bothering to take his pads off for an hour.

On the final day of the Adelaide Test, as the match reached its climax, he paced the dressing room unable to settle or sit. He asked Compton to open in the second innings and then went in himself without informing him about his change of mind. 'It looked to me as if Len had almost had enough, as if the mental strain of the whole thing was becoming almost unbearable,' Compton later recollected. [55]

Although he briefly joined the team celebrations that evening, the campaign had left him exhausted. Statham found him the next morning sitting on a bench outside the team hotel at Glenelg smoking a cigarette and staring out to sea. They sat together barely exchanging a word.

After completing the tour on a triumphant note by dismissing New Zealand for 26 at Auckland, Hutton, on return, was appointed captain for the Test series against South Africa. On leading MCC against the tourists at Lord's, he was applauded all the way to the wicket when going out to bat on the Saturday evening, but over the weekend he was struck down with lumbago which forced him to quit the captaincy with immediate effect. He never played for England again and retired from first-class cricket the following January. Knighted for his services to cricket that year, he went on to be a journalist, broadcaster and, briefly, a selector, as well as working for J.H. Fenner engineering firm. He died in 1990, aged 74.

Raised in an austere age when encouragement wasn't much in vogue, Hutton was never a great man-manager, but his supreme batsmanship, his encyclopaedic knowledge of the game and his fervent desire to win amply compensated. Appointed as England's first professional captain, he led them in the Yorkshire tradition which valued grit and attrition over adventure and flair. It wasn't pretty to watch, but his record of six unbeaten series and two Ashes triumphs speaks for itself. Not only was he one of England's finest captains, he was also one of its most influential ones, since his defensive approach was carried on by his successors, May and Cowdrey, right through to Illingworth and beyond. The amateur era was well and truly over in spirit, if not entirely in form.

David Sheppard

DAVID SHEPPARD was born in Reigate on 6 March 1929, the son of a solicitor. A late developer at Sherborne School, his cricket came on apace in his last two years through sheer application and tenacity.

In 1947 he made his debut for Sussex, and after National Service he went up to Cambridge in 1949. There, in the last golden era of university cricket, he scored a record 3,545 runs in his three seasons. In one of his early games, he made 227 against the West Indians at Fenner's, sharing an opening stand of 343 with John Dewes, and he was picked for England before the season was out.

He toured Australia with MCC in 1950/51 and he hit his maiden Test century against India in 1952. That summer he captained Cambridge, his hard-nosed approach not appreciated by everyone, and the following year he steered Sussex from 13th to second in the county championship, a position not repeated again until 1981. According to Jim Parks, the Sussex and England wicketkeeper-batsman, he was the best captain he played under in his 25 years of first-class cricket, his firmness and will to win tempered by his encouragement and concern for his players.

Sheppard's final year in full-time cricket was in 1953, after he started his studies for Holy Orders, yet when Hutton was unavailable to captain England against Pakistan in 1954 it was Sheppard who replaced him. As an amateur, the cut of his jib appealed to the selectors. He enhanced his reputation by leading England to an innings victory at Lord's and having much the better of a draw at Old Trafford, and after the shenanigans of the MCC tour to the West Indies the previous winter, there was talk of him leading in Australia in 1954/55. With the blessing of the Archbishop of Canterbury, he indicated his willingness to place his studies on hold if he were offered the captaincy, but in the end the selectors stood by Hutton. The editor of *Wisden* averred that 'if charm and personality were the only qualities required for Australia, Sheppard would have filled the position adequately. Unfortunately Sheppard was one of the batting disappointments of F.R. Brown's team in 1950/51 and he did not inspire confidence by his performances in the representative matches of 1954.' [56]

Despite a modicum of first-class cricket, Sheppard was recalled against Australia in 1956 and against the West Indies in 1957, becoming the first ordained priest to play for England and performing admirably against both countries.

In 1962 he once again played for England, enticed back by Robins, the chairman of selectors, who thought his flair and enterprise would make him the ideal captain of MCC in Australia–New Zealand that winter. Ultimately, the vote went to the incumbent Ted Dexter, partly because of concerns that Sheppard, a leading opponent of apartheid in South Africa, might question the White Australia policy, but he played in all eight Tests and preached to large crowds in all the major cities.

As he climbed the ecclesiastical ladder, his association with cricket became increasingly spasmodic, but he did lead the resistance to MCC's handling of the D'Oliveira Affair in 1968 and he successfully opposed South Africa's tour to England in 1970.

After serving as Bishop of Woolwich between 1968 and 1975, Sheppard became a respected, if controversial, Bishop of Liverpool, clashing with the Thatcher government over its perceived neglect of the inner cities. He retired in 1997, was elevated to the House of Lords in 1998 and died in 2005, aged 75.

Peter May

PETER MAY was born in Reading on 31 December 1929. His father was the director of the family electrical engineering business; his mother was a talented tennis player who encouraged his interest in ball games.

At Charterhouse School, May flourished under the coaching of George Geary, the former Leicestershire and England all-rounder, who rated him the best young bat he'd ever seen. He headed the batting averages, aged 14, scoring a century against Harrow in less than two hours, and in his last year, when captain, he made 146 for the Public Schools against the Combined Services, the next top score being 18. After two years as a writer in the Royal Navy and playing for the Combined Services, May went to Cambridge, captaining the football eleven, winning an Eton fives half-blue and scoring nine hundreds for the cricket team.

Making his debut for Surrey in 1950, his progress was so rapid that he was picked for England in the fourth Test against South Africa at Headingley the next year, marking the occasion with a century.

Dropped after the first Test against Australia in 1953, he returned for the decider at the Oval and helped regain the Ashes after 19 years. Appointed vice-captain to Hutton in Australia in 1954/55, he formed a close relationship with the captain, and when illness forced Hutton to quit prior to the series against South Africa in 1955 he took over at short notice. Any doubts about his relative youth and inexperience of leadership – he never captained Cambridge and had yet to captain Surrey – were laid to rest by his personal example, not least his sheer volume of runs.

Tall, handsome and self-effacing, May was the personification of a cricketing knight, a modern-day crusader. With his conscientious and unselfish lead, he lived according to his high ethical standards, always accepting the umpire's decision and acting with dignity in both victory and defeat. Although a shy person, he would mingle with his men and spoke up for them at every opportunity. Shunning favourites, he treated them all fairly and brought out the best in difficult players such as Wardle, Trueman and Illingworth, not least by his encouragement and praise. Yet beneath the boyish diffidence there lurked a steely desire to win and an expectation that his players would give their all, a trait accentuated by his tutelage at Surrey under Stuart Surridge and with England under Hutton. Those who fell short were admonished by a facial expression or a quiet aside. 'The politeness was deceptive,' wrote Bailey, 'there was a hard and unforgiving streak; and a bright mind combined with an inner steel. Peter at his best combined some of the drive of Surridge with the tactical tightness of Hutton. His considerable personal charm tended to camouflage his toughness on the field.' [57]

Although willing to accept advice, May knew what he wanted and once set on a particular course he was rarely deflected from it. Like Hutton, he valued attrition above adventure, so that the trend towards slower over rates, defensive field placings and cautious batting continued.

Against Jack Cheetham's South Africans, a fast-improving side, he began with 89 in the first Test at Trent Bridge, the start of a most prolific series in which he carried the England batting with an average of 72.75. Having won easily at Trent Bridge, England had to fight much harder at Lord's. One hundred and seventy-one behind on first innings, they were primarily indebted to May's 112 to keep them in contention. Needing 183 to win, South Africa had no answer to Statham, who bowled unchanged to take 7-39, leaving England victors by 71 runs.

May continued to score heavily but the South African batsmen, led by opener Jackie McGlew, began to find some form and they won the next two Tests. With the rubber all square, everything came down to the final Test at the Oval. In a low-scoring game, it was the batting of May that made all the difference. Buttressed by a narrow lead of 39 on first innings, May's 89* in the second innings helped England to a total of 204, before Laker and Lock took over. Taking nine wickets between them, they bowled South Africa out for 151, giving them victory by 92 runs.

May was even more imperious the following year when, in a summer of bad weather and poor pitches, England beat Australia 2-1 to retain the Ashes. After a draw in the first Test, they lost badly at Lord's, with only May making runs against Miller, who enjoyed a match haul of ten wickets. At Headingley, England had the worst possible start at 17/3 but Washbrook, recalled at the age of 41, rather against May's better judgement, proved just the man for a crisis. He helped him add 187 in England's total of 325, and, with Laker and Lock capturing 18 wickets between them, they won by an innings.

It was a similar story at Old Trafford, except that this time Laker and Lock took all 20 wickets, 19 of them going to the former in one of the most remarkable feats in cricket history.

Having remained productive all series, May scored 83* and 37* in the final Test, ensuring England a draw in a rain-affected match, although a slightly bolder declaration might well have gained them another victory, since Australia finished 27/5.

In a series dominated by the ball, May's average of 90 once again marked him out as the world's premier batsman, which helped consolidate his authority as captain. According to the sports journalist Norman Cutler, one of the most satisfying features of England's triumph was May's shrewd and aggressive captaincy. 'Every weakness shown by the Australian batsmen was ruthlessly exploited, his tactics were thoughtful and cunning and always with an eye for victory. He was never frightened to change his shrewdly placed and aggressive field if it helped the bowlers; he had the courage to pitch a key bowler even at the most vital stage of the game and was adept at the use of cricket psychology.' [58]

His opposite number, Johnson, certainly rated him, believing he could become one of England's great captains. 'He possesses that slightly ruthless streak that is so essential in captaining a Test match side on the field, yet he has with it an innate charm which allows him to mix freely and pleasantly when the day's play is over.' [59]

So far May's prolific batting, combined with his powerful attack, had seen off South Africa and Australia at home, but on tour to South Africa in 1956/57 the first chinks in his leadership appeared. At first everything went according to plan. By making himself available to all, he helped foster an excellent spirit in the team, a spirit enhanced by their conclusive victories in the first two Tests. Another victory seemed likely in the third Test when South Africa, needing 190 for victory, had slumped to 49/4 against Wardle, England's leading bowler on tour, at which point a brief onslaught by Ken Funston on Wardle persuaded May to take him off and settle for a draw. His decision cost England dear, since the home team, inspired by off-spinner Hugh Tayfield, came back to win the final two Tests.

May's own form, so prolific in the provincial matches, completely deserted him in the Tests, which could well have added to his general caution.

He returned to predominance the following summer, beating the West Indies 3-0, as well as leading Surrey to the top of the championship, an achievement then without parallel. His greatest impact came in the first Test at Edgbaston when his 285* and fourth-wicket stand of 411 with Cowdrey rescued England from likely defeat and took them to the brink of victory. In the process they saw off Ramadhin, England's tormentor in the first innings with 7-49, who was never the same threat again.

Having beaten New Zealand all too easily the following summer, England sailed for Australia in 1958 on a tide of optimism, only to be engulfed in storms that sunk them without trace. Even before their departure, Wardle had had his invitation withdrawn because of his dismissal by Yorkshire, and Laker had locked horns with May over his alleged lack of effort in a couple of county matches. It set the tone for a tour that was marred by rancour and division. A touring side that contained such a clash of personalities and conflicting interests had no chance of building up any esprit de corps. 'We were not a team,' remarked opener Peter Richardson. 'We'd been together for too long and quite frankly we'd all got fed up with each other.' [60] 'The actual atmosphere surrounding the team could be described as half way between uneasy and poisonous,' noted Edrich in his capacity as a journalist. [61]

In the opinion of Tyson, May, more than any other captain he knew, lacked the common touch. 'Each man is entitled to be aloof and pursue his own way, but this policy in a cricket captain, particularly off the field, can be disastrous.' [62] The arrival of his fiancée, Virginia Gilligan, before the first Test placed added distance between captain and team. 'It was one of the weaknesses of the party that neither the captain nor vice-captain was socially minded,' wrote Graveney. 'There is much to be said for both May and Cowdrey but charm isn't enough to hold a touring party together. Something more tangible is needed.' [63]

Unlike Hutton, May relied little on his senior professionals, Evans and Bailey. He ignored their pleas for Cowdrey and him to bat higher in the order after the first Test – in the second Test they went in even lower at five and six – and brushed aside their suggestions regarding bowling and fielding changes. 'Peter seemed to have no humour in him,' wrote Evans, 'and humour is often a very saving grace on the field when the players are tired or bored or a bit downhearted. There's no fun when you're playing under Peter.' [64]

What particularly upset them was May's reaction to the Australian throwers. When MCC played Victoria, their attention was drawn to their opening bowler, Ian Meckiff, whose lack of rhythm, sudden jerk and his great inaccuracy convinced them that he threw. Evans approached manager Freddie Brown and proposed that they make an official complaint about his action. Brown agreed to discuss it with May, but they decided to let sleeping dogs lie, partly because they didn't want to be undiplomatic and partly because they didn't rate him as a bowler. It was, said Evans, the crime of the century.

Winning the toss at Brisbane, May, mindful of Hutton's blunder four years earlier, elected to bat first on a greenish wicket and paid the penalty as England were bundled out for 134. Their bowlers, notably Bailey and Loader, fought back well to restrict Australia's lead to 52, but, following the early loss of Richardson, May promoted

Bailey to number three. He responded with a 458-minute vigil for 68, which encapsulated all too clearly England's sterile approach. On a stultifying fourth day, they managed only 106 runs and were ultimately all out for 198, whereupon Australian debutant Norman O'Neill lifted the match to a different level to guide his side home to an eight-wicket victory.

At Melbourne, England endured the worst possible start at 7/3 before a classic century from May afforded them some respectability. All out for 259, they kept Australia's first-innings lead down to 40 thanks to Statham's 7-57, but all the hard work was undone in two hours of mayhem. Up against Meckiff, cheered on by his home crowd, they collapsed to 87 all out and lost by eight wickets. While the England press corps raged against Meckiff's suspect action, morale among the tourists plummeted, a mood May was unable to change. For the first time he became the object of press vitriol, not least for allegedly spending excessive time with his fiancée at the expense of his team, an onslaught from which he never quite recovered. 'Having been peerless as both batsman and captain,' recalled Cowdrey, 'Peter was quite taken aback by the hostility of the criticism, and badly hurt.' [65]

After a tedious draw at Sydney, all hinged on the crucial fourth Test at Adelaide. Much would depend on whether Laker, England's most successful bowler at Sydney with seven wickets, would be fit. His withdrawal minutes before the start upset his team-mates, who thought he should have risked all in such an important match. 'I'm sorry Jim was so tired and couldn't play today,' May told them as they travelled back to the hotel at the end of a gruelling first day. 'We'd played our hearts out,' recalled Richardson. 'Peter was angry – he'd been let down as we all had – but his remark was as nasty as he would ever get. It is not easy to be forgiving in such circumstances.' [66]

May's comment reflected his frustration at the day's events. His gamble to insert Australia on winning the toss had badly backfired as the pitch offered little to the pacemen, and the Australian openers Colin McDonald and Jim Burke put on 171 for the first wicket. Their final total of 476 proved too formidable for the England batting and they lost by an innings. By the time they lost by nine wickets in the final Test, their humiliation was complete. For all the original optimism about May's team, they had not only lost 4-0, they'd been outplayed in every department. Not one player returned with his reputation enhanced.

While no captain could be held responsible for these individual shortcomings, the fact that such a talented side fell apart so quickly reflected badly on May. 'Whether or not his policies were decided by others,' remarked Harry Gee in *Wisden*, 'the fact remained that May never seemed to communicate to his team the driving force which Benaud gave to Australia.' [67] It was Edrich's opinion that neither May nor Brown understood the players: Brown because his brusque manner didn't recognise the various shades and nuances in other people's characters, and May because he buried himself behind an impenetrable shell. His captain's report, which stated that 'the side was a very happy one', running contrary to everyone else's recollections, seemed to suggest this.

May was used to having match-winning bowlers for both Surrey and England, and his tactical ingenuity had rarely been tested, but, up against superior opposition in Australia, his lack of ideas and imagination was all too glaring. Aside from his defensive field placings, which drew censure from Bradman, England's dilatory over rate was worse than on the previous tour.

After the drubbing in Australia, the selectors discarded many a leading player from the 1950s, and, although there was no question of them dropping the pilot, May was instructed to adopt a more positive approach against India. In a one-sided series, England beat them 5-0, May leading them in the first three games before being incapacitated with an abscess and missing the rest of the season. He was available for the winter tour to the West Indies and led a side that contained a number of new prospects, such as Ken Barrington, Ted Dexter and Mike Smith. Given May's experience and cachet as England's premier batsman, his writ ran large through the team, but he did have to fend off the strictures of manager Walter Robins, an amateur of the old school, appointed to restore order in the ranks. No sooner had they left home by boat, he started laying down the law as to how they should play. 'Robins continued to harry us day after day, throughout the voyage,' wrote Cowdrey, 'and with typical courtesy but no lack of firmness, Peter May would not be drawn.' [68] He vetoed Keith Andrew, Robins's choice of wicketkeeper, preferring Roy Swetman, insisted on playing off-spinner David Allen in all five Tests as opposed to Tommy Greenhough, a leg-spinner like Robins, and played a more defensive form of cricket than his manager would have liked.

After a high-scoring draw in the first Test at Bridgetown, England overcame a proliferation of bumpers by the West Indian quicks and an ugly riot at Port of Spain to win by 256 runs. One up in the series, May's men increasingly played attritional cricket to preserve their slender lead. 'I know Peter May originally intended his team to play open and attacking cricket,' Robins wrote in his manager's report, 'but it takes two to make a game and the bowling tactics of the West Indies in the first Test put our captain's and team's backs up, and from then on every Test was a battle, with our fellows honestly believing that they were fighting for their country.' [69]

With Cowdrey in vintage form and Trueman bowling magnificently, England fought off a spirited West Indian comeback at Kingston to earn a draw. The game was marred, however, by the contentious refusal of May to grant West Indian batsman and potential match-winner Rohan Kanhai a runner when he developed cramp during the closing stages. His refusal was contrary to the Laws of Cricket (Law 2), which stated that Kanhai didn't need to seek consent if injured during the game, and when this was pointed out to him afterwards May apologised to Kanhai and his captain Gerry Alexander.

May's misjudgement may well have been related to his fragile condition, unknown to all at the time. The internal wound stemming from his operation the previous summer had reopened in Trinidad, causing him considerable discomfort, and he paid regular visits to the doctor thereafter to have the wound dressed. His condition deteriorated when he arrived in British Guiana and on medical advice he stopped playing immediately. He flew home to have another operation and missed the whole of the following summer. Cowdrey once again deputised and, employing similar tactics to May, he managed to draw the final two Tests in the West Indies and win the rubber, a result few anticipated several months earlier.

May returned to first-class cricket in 1961, but a groin strain kept him out of the first Test against Australia, and when he returned for the second Test he asked not to be captain. After England's disappointing five-wicket defeat at Lord's, he resumed control at Headingley and won convincingly to level the series. At Old Trafford, they had the opportunity to go 2-1 up, but a plethora of botched opportunities cost them dear. Most critical of all was May's decision to remove David Allen from the attack after Australian all-rounder Alan Davidson had hit him for 20 in an over. On a wearing pitch, Allen had just taken three wickets without conceding a run, leaving Australia 157 in front with one wicket left, but, with the new ball making little impact, Davidson and last man Graham McKenzie added 98. Needing 256 to win in three hours and 50 minutes, a glorious innings by Dexter gave England renewed hope as they reached 150/1, before Australia's captain Richie Benaud, bowling his leg spin around the wicket, dismissed Dexter and May, bowled behind his legs, in one over. It was the game's defining moment. England lost their last nine wickets for 51 and with them went the Ashes.

The fifth Test at the Oval – a draw in Australia's favour – marked the end of May's international career. Although still only 31, his enthusiasm for the game had begun to wear thin, the pressures of captaincy and his illness contributing, and with a young family to support his gaze began to turn towards the City. He worked as an insurance broker and underwriter for Lloyd's but continued his links with cricket as an England selector, subsequently becoming chairman between 1982 and 1989, an unhappy time when he struggled to establish a rapport with a new generation of players. He died in 1994, aged 64.

For the vast majority of his captaincy, May bestrode the cricketing universe, his success as captain matched by his aura as the world's finest batsman. Fortunate to have such a powerful attack at his disposal, he experienced nearly four years of unbroken success, and even after his reverse in Australia in 1958/59 he remained untouchable, helped by his close relationship with the chairman of selectors, Gubby Allen. Too defensive and unimaginative to be considered among the great captains, May's record of 20 wins and ten losses, nonetheless, stands comparison with most, and his retirement marked not only the end of a golden era of English cricket, but also the apogee of the autocratic captaincy.

The Age of Attrition: 1961–80

T HE 1960s was a turbulent age for cricket, with controversy stalking it both on and off the field. While the game became embroiled in political disputes, most notably the ethics of playing cricket against apartheid South Africa, it was failing as a spectacle now that the accent was on attrition. In an iconoclastic decade when those in authority lost much of their traditional deference, England cricket captains were held increasingly accountable for the performance of their team at a time when they no longer dominated the cricketing universe.

As a top-flight amateur groomed for high office like May, it was always assumed that Colin Cowdrey, so long his deputy, would follow in his footsteps once he retired, but his sublime talent couldn't obscure a diffident personality prone to indecision. Consequently, it was his fellow amateur, Ted Dexter, who captained England for the next three years without suggesting that he, too, was true leadership material. While lacking nothing in confidence, his aloof temperament and quixotic theories failed to inspire his team. After losing consecutive rubbers to the West Indies in 1963 and to Australia in 1964, he resigned the captaincy. He was succeeded by the unflappable Mike Smith, whose deep concern for his players made him one of England's most popular captains. Cautious by nature, he drew 0-0 in India in 1963/64 and won 1-0 in South Africa the following year, but his shortage of runs, especially in the drawn Ashes rubber of 1965/66, made his position vulnerable. Following a double failure in England's comprehensive defeat by the West Indies in the first Test at Old Trafford, Smith was summarily discarded in favour of Cowdrey. It was the beginning of a much more precarious era for the captaincy, since Mike Brearley was the only England captain to escape the axe between 1966 and 1989.

For Cowdrey, his return to the captaincy was to be brutally short. After drawing against the West Indies at Lord's, he felt the full force of national disillusionment in the wake of successive defeats at Trent Bridge and Headingley and he was replaced by Brian Close for the final Test, the first time that England had employed three captains in one series.

Close had proven his leadership credentials as captain of Yorkshire since 1963 and he immediately made his mark by beating the West Indies by an innings at the Oval. The following summer he easily disposed of India and Pakistan, but his abrasive temperament alienated many within the Lord's establishment. A bout of brazen time-wasting in Yorkshire's championship match against Warwickshire at Edgbaston in August 1967 led to his downfall as the MCC committee vetoed his appointment to captain in the West Indies that winter. Amid bitter allegations of class bias, the selectors once again fell back on Cowdrey and this time he didn't falter. Batting imperiously and leading with greater authority than previously, he pulled off an unlikely series win in the West Indies, and after leading England against Australia at home and Pakistan away he looked set fair until laid low by a snapped Achilles tendon in May 1969. His replacement, Ray Illingworth, the newly appointed captain of Leicestershire, was viewed merely as a stand-in, but so effortlessly did he take to his new role that it was he and not Cowdrey who captained in Australia in 1970/71.

On tour Illingworth fell out badly with his manager David Clark and the MCC establishment with his brand of dour, uncompromising cricket, but his success in regaining the Ashes after 12 years made him untouchable. He continued to rule the roost till a heavy defeat by the West Indies in 1973 cost him his job. His successor, Mike Denness, never looked secure in the role and, having dropped himself in Australia in 1974/75 because of his lack of runs, he gave way the following summer to the South African Tony Greig. In contrast to Denness, the charismatic Greig looked every inch a leader as he loved performing on the biggest stage. Having led his team to an impressive 3-1 victory in India in 1976/77, he seemed destined for a long spell in charge till fate intervened.

At a time when players were poorly remunerated for representing their country, Greig was only too happy to act as a leading recruitment agent to the Australian media tycoon Kerry Packer and his breakaway World Series Cricket, a breach of trust which brought about his immediate sacking and his replacement by his vice-captain Mike Brearley.

Although never a batsman of Test standard, Brearley's tactical ingenuity and adept man-management won him the overwhelming support of his players, not least the prickly Geoff Boycott and the irrepressible Ian Botham. He immediately won acclaim by uniting the pro and anti-

Packer factions in his team to beat Australia 3-0 to regain the Ashes and thereafter he continued to beat everyone in sight for the best part of three years. He retired after his one reverse in Australia in 1979/80, only to be recalled the following year to lead England to a dramatic series win against Australia, when his poise under fire at both Headingley and Edgbaston was the difference between victory and defeat. He left a rich legacy which few could build on.

Ted Dexter

TED DEXTER was born in Milan on 15 May 1935. His father was a prosperous insurance broker there and he spent much of his school holidays in Italy, cultivating his passion for golf, a sport that saw him become one of Britain's finest amateur players.

At Radley College, he was widely admired for his all-round sporting prowess. Captain of the cricket eleven, he displayed a shrewd cricket brain as well as a haughty mien, which, along with his charismatic presence at the crease, gained him the nickname of 'Lord Edward'.

After two years on National Service in Malaya, he went to Cambridge, captaining both the golf and cricket teams and scoring enough runs in his last year, 1958, to win his first Test cap against New Zealand at Old Trafford.

A notable failure as a replacement on the MCC tour to Australia in 1958/59, he established himself as a batsman of the highest class in the West Indies a year later, able to decimate any attack with his immense power off both front and back foot. Two centuries in the Caribbean were followed by a memorable 180 to save the first Test against Australia at Edgbaston in 1961 and a stunning 76 at Old Trafford to give England a chance of winning a match they ultimately lost.

Appointed captain of Sussex in 1960, Dexter oversaw a major improvement in his first year, but, with his many outside distractions, he found it difficult to maintain his interest in county cricket or in his team. According to his team-mate John Snow, Dexter was a big-time player, one who responded to atmosphere, liked action and enjoyed the chase and gamble, but lost interest when the game was dull.

Mike Brearley offered a similar assessment: 'In all three matches that I played under him in South Africa in 1964/65, there were periods in which he had lost interest and was more concerned with getting his golf swing right at square leg than with who should be bowling or with what field. He was an excellent theorist on the game; but when his theories failed to work, or he had no particular bright ideas, he would drift; and the whole team drifted with him. I would guess that Dexter was, in those days, more interested in ideas than in people.' [70]

Given his privileged background and brilliant batting, Dexter was the obvious man to captain England in India and Pakistan in 1961/62, once May and Cowdrey declared their unavailability. With Trueman and Statham also staying at home, his threadbare pace attack made little impression on the bland wickets of the subcontinent and England were beaten 2-0 by India. The responsibility for defeat could hardly be attributed to Dexter, especially given his success with the bat, but his waning enthusiasm and aloof temperament did little to inspire his team-mates.

Alarmed by the declining tempo of Test cricket, the incoming chairman of selectors, Walter Robins, publicly called for something more enterprising, and he even contacted Sheppard, who'd played little cricket since ordination in 1956, to see whether he would consider captaining MCC on their 1962/63 tour to Australia. Flattered by the thought, Sheppard returned to first-class cricket in 1962, and his consummate century for the Gentlemen against the Players was widely assumed to have won him the greatest prize in cricket. In the end, Sheppard was deemed too much of a risk given his time away from the game and his radical politics, and in a straight fight between Dexter and Cowdrey, the former gained preference because he was seen to have the personality to match his charismatic opposite number, Benaud. MCC did, however, take the unusual step of asking the Duke of Norfolk, the president of Sussex and racing companion of Dexter's, to be manager on the grounds that he could handle him.

With Cowdrey as vice-captain and Sheppard on the selection committee, the tour saw the final rites of the amateur tradition since Dexter's interest in racing, his wife Susan's modelling commitments and Sheppard's preaching attracted as much publicity as the cricket – rather to the detriment of team spirit. Dexter's absence from MCC's fixture against South Australia to go racing drew some critical comment from sections of the travelling press corps, which in turn irked the Duke of Norfolk enough to threaten non-cooperation with them in future.

Having made many a commitment to brighter cricket at the beginning of the tour, Dexter gave himself a hostage to fortune in light of the uncompromising nature of Ashes cricket. Australia held the urn, and although their captain, Benaud, was seen as the fervent champion of brighter cricket, he could resort to something more attritional if he deemed it to be in his side's interest. Australia had slightly the better of the first Test at Brisbane, despite Dexter providing the most memorable moments with two innings of characteristic brio.

He continued in positive vein in the second Test at Melbourne when, in a game of fluctuating fortune, England, playing the more purposeful cricket, won by seven wickets. Victory provided Dexter with his greatest sense of elation in his career, an understandable enough feeling since he had been primarily the author of that triumph. Having scored a superb 93 in the first innings, he handled his bowlers adroitly in Australia's second innings, especially his refusal to overuse his strike bowler Trueman, keeping him fresh for the second new ball. Trueman responded accordingly by mopping up the tail, leaving England 234 to win. They quickly lost opener Geoff Pullar on the fourth evening, but rather than send out a night-watchman, Dexter came in himself. The next day he suggested to his partner Sheppard that they put pressure on the Australians by running them ragged. They did precisely this and by the time Dexter was out for 52, England were well on the way to victory, and with Sheppard scoring 113 they ultimately won by seven wickets.

The upbeat mood post-Melbourne turned out to be all too fleeting as they fell to earth at Sydney. Confronted with a slow-turning pitch, they committed a cardinal error by playing an additional seamer instead of off-spinner David Allen, an omission which led to some expensive overs from Barrington's part-time leg spin. Despite Fred Titmus's 7-79 restricting Australia's first-innings lead to 40, England collapsed to 104 all out in their second innings and they lost by eight wickets.

For the fourth Test, England committed another howler by playing a second off-spinner, Illingworth, rather than a third seamer on an unusually lively Adelaide wicket. That said, Dexter showed enterprise by introducing Illingworth early into the attack. He immediately bowled Lawry leaving Australia 16/2. Had Neil Harvey not been missed off successive balls off Illingworth, and again at 26 off Dexter, England might well have won. He went on to make 154 out of Australia's 393 and, leading England by 62 runs on first innings, the home team made little effort to force a result.

With the Ashes at stake in the final Test, England won the toss and batted first, but, on a dreadfully slow Sydney pitch, they made little effort to seize the initiative, crawling to 195/5 at the end of the first day. By the time Australia were dismissed for 349 at lunch on the fourth day, they led by 28, but with quick runs the priority, Illingworth was unaccountably asked to open instead of Cowdrey and Dexter failed to come in before Barrington, whose 94 took four and a half hours. Consequently, he felt unable to declare till lunch on the final day and Australia, set 241 to win in four hours, played out time, much to the disgruntlement of the crowd, who heckled the players and left the ground in droves.

The general disillusion regarding the series and the general state of Test cricket was widespread, but somehow all the flak fell on Dexter, perhaps because all his repeated promises to play attacking cricket had come to nothing. Although he proved more entertaining than most with his spectacular hitting, his captaincy remained broadly defensive, not least his bowling changes. 'At the beginning of the tour he was tremendous,' wrote Graveney. 'But Ted lacked staying-power. I think his mind wandered after the second Test. Captaining a team for six months was too much for him.' [71] 'He did not always bring his dashing approach into his captaincy and in general his leadership lacked inspiration,' commented Leslie Smith in *Wisden*. [72]

While Dexter wrote critically about Trueman and Illingworth in his end-of-tour report regarding their lack of team spirit, Illingworth in turn regretted the gulf between amateurs and professionals, the lack of organised practice and the failure of Dexter to empathise with his players. Peter Parfitt, a middle-order batsman, was asked to open the batting because Cowdrey no longer wanted to do so and was dropped for the second Test having scored 80 in the first Test; John Murray was axed as first-choice wicketkeeper without any explanation, and off-spinner Allen was cajoled by Dexter to change his line of attack, much against his will, an initiative Dexter later regretted.

In fairness to Dexter, a drawn series against Australia was better than many anticipated and there was little opposition to him continuing as captain against the West Indies under Frank Worrell. Up against a superior side containing names such as Gary Sobers, Wes Hall and Charlie Griffith, it was no disgrace to lose the series 3-1.

He missed the winter tour of India but was back in harness for the visit of Bobby Simpson's Australians. In a rain-affected series which produced little scintillating cricket, Australia won 1-0 by virtue of a seven-wicket victory in the third Test at Headingley. The crucial moment came when Australia, in reply to England's first innings of 268, were 187/7 and floundering against the spinners Titmus and Norman Gifford, at which point Dexter took the new ball. Unfortunately, Trueman and his opening partner Jack Flavell bowled poorly and Peter Burge, in one of his finest innings, hit Trueman all over Headingley. He put on 105 for the eighth wicket with Neil Hawke, and his 160 gave Australia a match-winning lead of 121. England lost by seven wickets and Dexter was castigated for taking the new ball. At the end of another disappointing series, blighted by turgid cricket from both sides, John Woodcock of *The Times* thought that England had failed to pull together. 'On top of this, England were not tactically perceptive. Dexter is a magnificent hitter of the cricket ball. But as a strategist he is too often unaccountable or obtuse.' [73] *Wisden*, too, raised questions about his leadership, and Benaud thought that he'd been outsmarted by Simpson, but his resignation from the captaincy was entirely his own initiative, and, following his defeat by future prime minister Jim Callaghan in Cardiff South East in the general election that October, he toured South Africa with MCC as vice-captain to Smith. Liberated from the ultimate responsibility, he visibly relaxed and was a leading contributor to England's 1-0 victory.

He also scored heavily against New Zealand the following summer until a broken leg caused by a freak accident with his car prompted his retirement from regular first-class cricket, although he did reappear in two Tests against Australia in 1968. Amid his multifarious activities, which included forming his own PR company, Dexter remained in touch with cricket as a columnist and broadcaster, until, in 1989, he became the first salaried chairman of selectors. Although he made an important contribution to the future evolution of the game, his four years in charge were marred by selectorial blunders and an uneasy relationship with the media.

At first reading, Dexter's record of won nine, lost seven and drawn 14 doesn't read too badly, but seven of those victories were against Pakistan and New Zealand. He failed to win any of his four toughest series and lost three of them. At his best he could grasp an initiative and rally his side by his own inspirational example, but these occasions were the exception rather than the rule. 'I liked the man a lot and he could bat beautifully,' remarked Trueman, 'but he was no captain of England. He had more theory than Darwin, but little practical experience to back it up.' [74] 'Ted was one captain I never fully understood,' wrote Statham. 'I don't think anyone in the dressing room did, either. He did things at times that were difficult to understand. He made moves, and bowling changes, which were completely out of keeping with the run of the game and which sometimes resulted in the opposition wriggling off the hook.' [75] Titmus was another bowler who disliked Dexter's reluctance to consult about field placings and his tetchiness if he didn't get full cooperation. This failure to communicate with his team and involve them in tactical discussions was Dexter's fundamental flaw, according to opener John Edrich. They still remained a lot of individuals not a team. According to Bailey, Dexter did have difficulty understanding players whose outlook was different to his own, making him appear aloof and unsympathetic. 'In fact, underneath there dwells an individual who is shy, generous, romantic and remarkably catholic in his tastes, and with a sentimental streak which is very far removed from the somewhat egocentric picture that is often regarded as his true image.' [76]

Bailey summed him up well. Because of his privileged background and immense talents, Dexter always seemed destined to lead when his aloof, enigmatic personality suggested otherwise. Yet those who penetrated his outer defences discovered a well-meaning, generous personality whose overall contribution to English cricket has never been fully appreciated.

Colin Cowdrey

COLIN COWDREY was born in Ootacamund, India, on 24 December 1932, the only child of Ernest Cowdrey, a tea planter and a good enough cricketer to play for a European XI against MCC during their tour to India in 1926/27. Determined that Colin should learn the rudiments of the game from his earliest years, he devised an exacting schedule on the lawn next to their home, which left no detail untouched.

Separated from his parents throughout the war years, Cowdrey was educated at Homefield Prep School, where he came under the imposing authority of headmaster Charles Walford. Walford's harsh, austere regime divested him of much-needed confidence but did wonders for his cricket. By the time he went to Tonbridge School, aged 13, he was a player of exceptional ability, and in his first year he almost beat Clifton single-handedly in the showpiece game at Lord's. Five years in the eleven not only made him the outstanding schoolboy cricketer in the country, it also gave him a thorough grounding in the game's etiquette.

At Oxford, his class was apparent enough to impress Hutton and win him a place on MCC's tour to Australia in 1954/55. He scored a memorable century in the third Test at Melbourne and made a significant contribution to England's retention of the Ashes.

In 1957 he shared a record fourth-wicket partnership of 411 with May against the West Indies at Edgbaston to deprive their opponents of victory, and the following year he was appointed May's vice-captain on the 1958/59 tour to Australia. Defeated 4-0, Cowdrey was one of the few England players to emerge unscathed, and later that summer he captained his country in the final two games against India when May was indisposed.

Two years earlier, Cowdrey had taken over the captaincy of Kent, a county that had fallen on hard times. Very much an amateur in background and style – his father-in-law, Stuart Chiesman, was chairman of Kent – Cowdrey's brilliance as a batsman and his debonair charm gave him a certain aura. Yet for all his deep knowledge of the game and paternal concern for his team, he wasn't a natural leader. Whether it was his solitary childhood or austere schooling, he lacked the self-confidence to make decisions. Loathing confrontation, he'd often get the secretary-manager of Kent, Les Ames, or the chairman of the cricket committee, David Clark, to inform certain players that they'd been dropped.

A follower of the Hutton and May school of captaincy, Cowdrey practised caution over adventure. His pragmatic approach brought him into conflict with Walter Robins, manager of MCC's 1959/60 tour to the West Indies. A staunch apologist for the amateur tradition, Robins had been disconcerted by the sterile cricket played by both sides throughout the series, with England the more culpable party. Having won a decisive victory in the second Test at Port of Spain, they sat back on their lead thereafter, and by slowing down the over rate and setting defensive fields they managed to contain the powerful West Indian batting.

Although the tactics originated with May, Cowdrey continued them when he assumed the captaincy for the final two Tests. England comfortably drew at Georgetown, but a middle-order collapse in their second innings at Port of Spain caused some jitters before a record seventh-wicket stand between Mike Smith and Jim Parks carried them to safety. Having laboured so hard to win a series in the West Indies, an outcome few thought possible at the beginning of the tour, Cowdrey refused to adhere to Robins's Corinthian ethos by making a challenging declaration on the last day. His stance, supported by the rest of his team, enraged Robins and had ramifications for Cowdrey when Robins became chairman of selectors in 1962.

While May missed the whole of the 1960 season to recuperate from an internal operation, Cowdrey continued in charge against South Africa. In a one-sided series, which England won 3-0, he had little opportunity to parade his wares. He continued in office for the first two Tests against Australia in 1961. Fortunate to escape with a draw at Edgbaston, Cowdrey had the chance to stamp his authority at Lord's now that May was back in the side, but little went right for him in England's five-wicket defeat. Not only did he fail twice with the bat, but he also lost control in the field when Australia's last two wickets added 102. He gave way to May, who remained in charge for the rest of the series, before retiring from Test cricket.

Having been the crown prince for several years, Cowdrey seemed May's natural successor, but by declaring himself unavailable to tour India and Pakistan that winter the captaincy was given to Dexter. When Dexter returned, the jury was still out about his credentials, and with an MCC tour to Australia pending the selectors gave Cowdrey another opportunity to stake his claim in the third Test against Pakistan the following summer. He performed creditably enough in England's third successive win and was due to captain the Gentlemen against the Players in an unofficial Test trial, with both Dexter and Sheppard under his command, before kidney trouble forced his withdrawal. Dexter replaced him as captain and, days later, he was chosen to lead England in Australia with Cowdrey as his deputy.

A year later Dexter opted out of another tour to India to pursue his political ambitions and Cowdrey was chosen instead, but once again he was beset by misfortune. A broken arm sustained against Wes Hall in the Lord's Test of 1963 had taken longer to heal than anticipated, forcing his withdrawal from the tour. Smith took over and proved such a popular choice that, when Dexter relinquished the captaincy for good at the end of the 1964 season, he was appointed captain of the tour to South Africa. The decision so upset Cowdrey that he declared himself unavailable for the trip, and by the time he had second thoughts he was too late to warrant inclusion.

Smith led England in the next 20 Tests, until their heavy defeat by the West Indies in the first Test at Old Trafford in 1966 when he paid the penalty for his lack of runs. Cowdrey took over at Lord's and began well. England led by 86 on first innings and reduced the West Indies to 95/5 in their second innings. Only Sobers and his cousin, David Holford, stood between them and victory, but Cowdrey, instead of going for the kill, allowed Sobers to dictate by spreading the field. Both batsmen grew in confidence and guided their team to safety with an unbroken stand of 274.

Although England lost at Trent Bridge, they'd fought hard, but at Headingley they folded all too easily. Bob Barber, returning to the England side after an absence of six months, was struck by the dramatic decline in morale. 'I have always said I don't think Kipper [Cowdrey's nickname] should ever have been captain of any team,' he declared. 'It was such a different atmosphere in the dressing room compared with the tour of Australia. I felt too many players were thinking that they could lose inside three days and they could all go home. It was just dreadful in there.' [77]

Barber's criticism of Cowdrey was sharpened by what he saw as his lack of faith in his leg spin. When finally introduced into the attack at Headingley at 324/4, he troubled both Seymour Nurse and Gary Sobers, the West Indies' two centurions, but by then it was too late. At the end of a depressing game, Cowdrey had little cause to feel satisfied. A double failure with the bat and defeat by an innings led to some cutting criticism. 'For Cowdrey, this was a personal disaster,' wrote Brian Scovell in the *Daily Sketch*. 'His own contribution with the bat – 29 in two innings – was negligible. And he failed to galvanise his men with the necessary spirit and guts to bridge the gap in skill between the sides.' [78]

In this climate of disillusionment – this was England's fifth consecutive series defeat at home by a major cricketing nation – Cowdrey became the prime casualty of a wholesale purge – removed not only from the captaincy but also from the team. His successor, Brian Close, oversaw a remarkable transformation of the team with an innings victory at the Oval, and by continuing his winning sequence at home to India and Pakistan the next year he seemed destined to lead MCC in the West Indies. His abrasive personality, however, wasn't to everyone's taste, and his delaying tactics for Yorkshire against Warwickshire in a vital championship match in August 1967 precipitated his sudden downfall. With Smith unavailable to captain in the West Indies, the selectors found themselves returning cap in hand to Cowdrey. Although the chairman Doug Insole made a public admission that Close had been their preferred choice as captain, Cowdrey soon regained his zest for the job as he looked forward to an exciting new era.

Bolstered by the appointment of Les Ames, the former England wicketkeeper and secretary-manager of Kent as tour manager, Cowdrey brought a greater authority to the England captaincy than hitherto. He struck a positive note by batting at number three and playing at his very best throughout. While the West Indies started the series as favourites, their fearsome opening attack of Wes Hall and Charlie Griffith was well past their best, whereas England possessed a formidable batting line-up and a devastating fast bowler in John Snow. Forced to follow on in the first two Tests, the home side were saved by the clock at Port of Spain and by an unseemly riot at Kingston. The third Test was a dull draw and the fourth Test at Port of Spain seemed to be heading the same way until Sobers's controversial declaration on the final afternoon. Inviting England to score 217 runs in 165 minutes on an unblemished surface, and without the participation of his one fast bowler, Griffith, because of injury, it seemed generous to say the least. Cowdrey's innate caution inclined him to spurn the challenge but, once persuaded to chance his arm by his team-mates at the tea interval, he batted brilliantly. His 71 and Geoff Boycott's undefeated 80 carried England to a memorable seven-wicket victory with minutes to spare.

With the final Test at Georgetown played over six days and Sobers in prime form, it required a defiant sixth-wicket stand between Cowdrey and Alan Knott on the last day to rescue England from the depths of 41/5. Playing with great resolution and skill, they took the game into the final 70 minutes, and when Cowdrey was out Knott continued to hold the fort before last-man Jeff Jones successfully negotiated Lance Gibbs's final over to save the Test and win the series. Although Sobers berated Cowdrey's defensive tactics, the truth was that he'd been outmanoeuvred by him. 'Cowdrey took a tremendous weight on his shoulders on that trip, more than I've seen an England captain accept before,' recalled Graveney. 'He skippered the side brilliantly, batted magnificently and did everything right.' [79] His assessment was endorsed by the *Evening News*'s E.M. Wellings in *Wisden*: 'I am quite certain that no other captain could have led the side so well and performed the numerous duties of captaincy so flawlessly in the exacting circumstances of this tour.' [80]

The tour was the high watermark of Cowdrey's career. His stock was high enough to be appointed for all five Tests against Australia, but it was soon to depreciate in light of an abject performance in the first Test at Old Trafford. Fielding only three full-time bowlers, England allowed an inexperienced Australian side to score 357 and then they batted poorly in both innings to lose by 159 runs.

They picked a better-balanced side for Lord's and an aggressive 83 from Colin Milburn injected a much-needed touch of brio into their play. Having declared at 351/7, they bowled Australia out for 78 and would surely have won had bad weather not intervened.

Rain again curtailed England's chances of winning at Edgbaston, a game notable for Cowdrey's century in his 100th Test. A leg injury kept him out of the draw at Headingley, which enabled Australia to keep the Ashes, but at the Oval he looked every inch a leader. England gained a first-innings lead of 170 and went hell for leather for quick runs on the fourth afternoon. By lunchtime on the final day Australia were staring defeat at 85/5, whereupon a ferocious storm flooded the ground in minutes.

With the Australian dressing room celebrating yet another reprieve, Cowdrey appeared a forlorn figure as he surveyed the waterlogged ground with his trousers pulled high over his boots, but, ever the optimist, he helped supervise a mass mopping-up operation featuring members of the crowd, as well as the ground staff, and with 80 minutes remaining play resumed. On a saturated pitch the Australian sixth-wicket pair of John Inverarity and Barry Jarman proceeded comfortably for the first 40 minutes before Cowdrey threw the ball to Basil D'Oliveira, a renowned partnership-breaker.

He promptly bowled Jarman, at which point Cowdrey immediately restored Derek Underwood to the attack, and with the pitch now beginning to play tricks, he worked his way through the Australian lower order. With six minutes left, he had opener Inverarity lbw and England had pulled off another famous victory to bring some cheer to what had otherwise been a frustrating summer.

Had events taken their natural course then Cowdrey would have captained MCC in South Africa that winter, but the failure to pick D'Oliveira unleashed a major political crisis which forced the tour to be cancelled. An alternative tour to politically unstable Pakistan proved scant compensation, since the cricket ranked a poor second to perennial questions about the team's security. In the end, after two draws, both games marred by crowd trouble, a major riot by politically active students opposed to the autocratic regime of President Ayub Khan put paid to the Karachi Test. Although unknown at the time, it turned out to be Cowdrey's final game as England captain. Several months later, while batting for Kent in a one-day match, he snapped his Achilles tendon, ruling him out of the Tests that summer against the West Indies and New Zealand. Illingworth replaced him as captain and performed so capably that he continued in charge the next year when England played the Rest of the World instead of the proposed tour by South Africa.

Because of his poor start to the season, Cowdrey wasn't considered for the first Test but recovered enough to play in the next two games under Illingworth. With the captaincy for Australia to be decided in the later stages of the third Test, Cowdrey hoped that his greater experience and expertise as a Test cricketer would help realise his lifelong ambition. Instead, the selectors opted for Illingworth and his more assertive personality. 'To my mind, unlucky as it was for Colin,' wrote chairman Alec Bedser, 'it would have been a rank injustice if at that point Illingworth had been asked to move aside as he had done everything the selectors had asked of him.' [81]

Shattered by his rejection, Cowdrey reluctantly accepted the vice-captaincy, a decision he soon regretted as he was constantly at loggerheads with Illingworth. Losing form and confidence, he faded into the background in what proved to be a miserable tour for him personally.

With his England career seemingly over, Cowdrey gave his all to Kent and scored his 100th century at Maidstone in 1973. On the strength of his form the following summer, he readily joined Mike Denness's tour to Australia as a replacement, a brave if unavailing attempt to combat the hostility of the pace bowlers Dennis Lillee and Jeff Thomson. After his retirement in 1975, he worked for Barclays in a PR capacity and maintained a close link with cricket, most notably as president of MCC in its bicentenary year, chairman of the ICC between 1989 and 1993 and chairman of the MCC cricket committee. In this latter capacity he was the driving force behind the Spirit of Cricket, a preamble to the recodification of the Laws of Cricket in 2000, commending the values of fair play and respect for one's opponents.

Colin Cowdrey was knighted in 1992, and in 1997 he became the first British peer ennobled exclusively for his contribution to sport. He died in 2000, aged 67.

While a number of Cowdrey's contemporaries, such as May, Dexter and Illingworth, captained England in more Tests, no one in the post-1945 era has ever captained them over such a long period. The reasons he never made the crown his own relate partly to bad luck and partly to the absence of a natural assertiveness, essential to great leadership. 'He was intelligent, charming and had generosity,' noted Mike Brearley. 'But he was not a good captain because his problem was himself; he lacked decisiveness and was too concerned about how things (and he) looked.' [82]

That said, his record of eight victories and four defeats from 27 games compared most favourably with many of his successors in the 1980s and 90s, and his record of winning twice in the West Indies – in 1959/60 he was only in charge of the final two Tests – speaks for itself.

Mike Smith

MIKE SMITH was born in Westcotes, Leicester, on 30 June 1933, the son of a businessman. Educated at Stamford School, he captained both the cricket and the rugby, a players' captain who didn't pull rank even then.

After two years of National Service, he achieved renown at Oxford by scoring centuries in the Varsity match in three successive years – 1954 to 1956 – the last as captain. He also gained a rugby blue, forming a dynamic partnership at half-back with Onllwyn Brace, and in 1956 he played for England against Wales at Twickenham, England's last double international.

In 1957 he moved from Leicestershire to Warwickshire to become its captain and the following year he made his Test debut, but while remaining prolific in county cricket – in 1959 he scored 3,000 runs – he struggled to establish himself at the highest level. As vice-captain to Dexter on MCC's tour to India and Pakistan in 1961/62, he was omitted for the fourth Test after a run of low scores.

Neglected for the next couple of years, Smith was given another opportunity when several players opted out of the tour to India in 1963/64. Originally named as vice-captain to Cowdrey, he ended up going as captain when Cowdrey was forced to withdraw, because his broken arm, sustained in the Lord's Test of 1963, took longer to heal than anticipated.

It proved to be an apt choice because Smith loved touring and was well versed in the art of leadership.

Aside from being vice-captain to Dexter in India and Pakistan, he had been a long-time captain of Warwickshire. According to all-rounder Tom Cartwright, he was a good man to play for. He appreciated other players' abilities and he let them get on with it. His teams were always happy, a view endorsed by Barber, the former Lancashire captain, who compared the relaxed Warwickshire dressing room very favourably with the one he'd left at Old Trafford.

Although an Oxford-educated former amateur, Smith, with his casual appearance and classless accent, was very much a captain for the professional age. While conscientious in carrying out his formal duties, he was at his happiest relaxing with his team in the bar. 'MJKS would come out to dinner with you in the evening and have a laugh and a joke,' recalled John Murray. 'I can't remember Colin or Dexter doing that.' [83]

Modest, fair-minded and reliable, he was trusted implicitly by his players. Unlike some of his predecessors, he consulted and encouraged, not least those who underperformed. An accomplished batsman, particularly against spin, and a brilliant short leg, he led by personal example. A fine tactician, he knew the game inside out, but while expecting everyone to give their all – he reserved some of his most telling rebukes for non-bowling fielders who left unnecessary work to those who had to bowl – there were no recriminations if they lost. Cricket was a game to be enjoyed.

Unlike the preceding tour to India in 1961/62, the 1963/64 tour was to be much shorter, encompassing five Tests in just under two months, yet despite their extensive preparations the team fell prey to the onset of illness, a frequent hazard on the subcontinent. With several of their players suffering from stomach disorders during the first Test, they did well to earn a draw, but in the run-up to the second Test at Bombay the casualty list lengthened extensively. In addition to Barrington's broken finger, Phil Sharpe, John Edrich and John Mortimore all succumbed to Asian flu, and Micky Stewart, the eleventh man standing, lasted till teatime on the first day before he threw up. Consequently, England were forced to field a most unbalanced side containing two wicketkeepers, two spinners and four quicks.

Having toiled manfully to restrict their opponents to 300 in their first innings, England's makeshift batting order struggled against the Indian spinners. Closing the second day at 116/6, they appeared to be heading for defeat, but a spirited 84* by Titmus and stout resistance from the tail kept the first-innings deficit down to 67 runs.

Once again, India failed to press home their advantage and a belated declaration allowed England to claim the most honourable of draws.

Bolstered by the arrival of Cowdrey and Parfitt as replacements, they more than held their own in the next two Tests, and in the final Test at Kanpur they forced India to follow on. The decision was an error, since a combination of a lifeless wicket and three successive days in oppressive heat took their toll. England bowled badly and India easily saved the match to leave the series all square at nil all.

Although the team had been badly afflicted by illness, it brought them closer together, a great tribute to the leadership of manager David Clark and Smith, the most harmonious manager-captain partnership that the veteran cricket writer John Woodcock ever witnessed. 'Of course, we were lucky with the chaps who were chosen to go,' Clark wrote to the secretary of MCC, Billy Griffith. 'There were really no lame ducks who didn't fit and no prima donnas and everyone settled down into a team very quickly. Mike influenced this to a great extent, his experience and personality were wonderful for such a tour.' [84]

With Dexter back in charge against Australia in 1964, Smith didn't feature throughout the series, but he was the obvious candidate to lead MCC's 1964/65 tour to South Africa following Dexter's resignation. As in India the previous year, Smith proved adept at getting the best out of each player. He made a special effort to reach out to Boycott, whose inauspicious start with the bat had sent him into his shell. Eventually succeeding with 193* against Eastern Province, he wrote fondly about Smith in his autobiography: 'If he lacked anything tactically compared to men like Close and Illingworth, he more than compensated for that in terms of his personality and attitude – very important to a young man like me on his first tour. Mike took everything in his stride, and was always willing to talk about problems rather than apportion blame. When I was struggling for runs before the match in Port Elizabeth he took time out to offer advice and reassurance. I would have done anything for him.' [85]

Without a win in 12 Tests, England began the series as underdogs against Trevor Goddard's South Africa, who had unearthed real talent in Eddie Barlow, Colin Bland and the Pollock brothers. Their Achilles heel was their lack of a decent slow bowler and, with the Durban wicket conducive to spin, England gained an early advantage when Smith won the toss and batted first. A flurry of runs, including centuries from Barrington and Parks, enabled him to declare at 485/5, the perfect platform for the spinners Titmus and Allen to get to work. They ran through the South African batting twice and England won by an innings.

They had the better of the draw in the second Test, but thereafter South Africa offered tougher resistance. The third Test at Cape Town witnessed the one unpleasant incident of Smith's time as captain when Barlow edged Titmus to slip on 41 and was given not out. Taking exception to Barlow's unwillingness to walk, Titmus called him a cheat and his reprieve rankled so much that none of the England players applauded his fifty or his hundred. The South Africans were unimpressed and Smith ordered Titmus to apologise on pain of being sent home.

The rumpus overshadowed the match itself. In response to the home side's 501/6 declared, Smith's painstaking century helped England to a respectable 442, which all but ensured a draw.

Anticipating a touch of green in the pitch at Johannesburg for the fourth Test, Smith omitted Allen for Cartwright and inserted South Africa on winning the toss. It proved a costly error as the openers Goddard and Barlow put on 134 for the first wicket and England thereafter had to battle hard to save the match.

Reeling from a spate of injuries to their pacemen, the tourists were forced to call up Somerset opening bowler Ken Palmer, who was coaching in Johannesburg, for his one and only Test. Not surprisingly, a pace attack of Ian Thomson, Palmer and Boycott posed few problems for the South African batsmen. Brearley, a member of the tour party, recalls being appalled and embarrassed when England only bowled

29 overs in one two-hour session. They then batted 207.5 overs to score 435 in reply to South Africa's 502, a mammoth go-slow which helped them to draw the Test and win the rubber in addition to going through the tour undefeated. While lavish in his praise of Smith's overall leadership, Donald Carr criticised him and his South African counterpart in his manager's report for adopting ultra-defensive tactics in the field, especially regarding the over rates. His comments fully registered with the MCC committee, some of whom had been out in South Africa, and they urged the selectors to do everything in their power to overcome defensive attitudes by some leading players.

Smith retained the captaincy for the home series against New Zealand and South Africa. England easily beat the former 3-0 but lost 1-0 to the latter and Smith himself had a lean summer with the bat averaging 22.57 in six Tests. His popularity, however, remained unimpaired and he was appointed captain of MCC in Australia in 1965/66, although manager Billy Griffith was given unprecedented overall control. His appointment reflected the determination of Lord's to counter public disillusion with the modern game and Smith's defensive captaincy by promoting attacking cricket.

After the disappointment of the previous MCC trip to Australia, Smith's team arrived to relative indifference, but their attacking instincts from the first game against Western Australia made the locals sit up and take note. With Smith working harmoniously with Griffith and the amateur-professional divide of the previous Australian tour consigned to history, this was a popular, contented team, the happiest that the long-serving Sydney dressing room attendant had seen.

While MCC's form prior to the first Test was encouraging, the lack of penetration in their bowling suggested that regaining the Ashes would be beyond them. Australia, without their captain Simpson, had the better of the first Test and England had the better of the second Test. At Sydney, a magnificent 185 from Barber laid the foundations of England's victory as Australia, again without Simpson, lost by an innings. On a wearing pitch, Smith was an inspiration at short leg, and on taking the final Australian wicket the England players held back to allow their captain to lead them off.

One-nil up and two to play, England held most of the cards but their impetuous batting on an excellent Adelaide surface saw them slump to an innings defeat.

Increasingly Smith fell back on containment in the final Test at Melbourne, so that a combination of bad weather and undue caution by both sides eradicated any hope of a positive result. It was a disappointing end to a successful tour in which England had performed creditably to share the rubber. Once again Smith won many a plaudit for his unselfish leadership, but unlike the previous two tours his batting had disappointed, his Test average of 17.83 in stark contrast with his team-mates, seven of whom averaged 40 or more.

With growing doubts about his form, Smith knew that he was very much on trial when appointed for the first Test only against Sobers's West Indians. Losing the toss at Old Trafford, England's sloppy fielding allowed their opponents to score 484 and, on a turning wicket, they subsided all too meekly to Gibbs's off spin. Smith made only 5 and 6 and in light of his team's resounding defeat he was unceremoniously discarded. Many people, including Sobers, thought he should have been given another chance but Smith, ever the philosopher, offered no complaints. Although too defensive to be rated a great captain, he was in every other case a very good one. No England captain, with the possible exception of Brearley, commanded such loyalty from his players and such respect from the opposition, and the three tours he led constituted an era of good feeling between MCC and India, South Africa and Australia.

In the same year that Smith lost the England captaincy, he led Warwickshire to success in the Gillette Cup. Had he not announced his retirement at the end of the 1967 season, he might well have taken MCC to the West Indies. Within two years he was back, and in 1972 he played in the first three Tests against Australia. After his final retirement in 1975, he and his family ran a country club outside Warwick. He was also chairman of Warwickshire between 1991 and 2003, an ICC match referee and he managed England's tours to the West Indies in 1993/94 and to Australia in 1994/95.

Brian Close

BRIAN CLOSE was born into a working-class family in Rawdon, near Leeds, on 24 February 1931. An able student at Aireborough Grammar School, Hedley Verity's alma mater, his headmaster urged him to go to university to read mathematics, but his heart was set on a career in cricket. (He was a good enough footballer to play for Bradford City.) His father and grandfather were both league cricketers and Close considered himself fortunate to have learned the game in the hard school of the Yorkshire leagues. He made his debut for Yorkshire in 1949 and acquitted himself so capably that he was chosen for the third Test against New Zealand, aged 18, still the youngest cricketer to have represented England.

National Service with the Royal Corps of Signals restricted him to only one game with Yorkshire in 1950, but his success for the Combined Services won him selection on MCC's tour to Australia that winter. Stubborn and impetuous, he failed dismally in his sole Test at Melbourne and, insensitively handled by captain Freddie Brown and the senior players, he found the trip a demoralising experience, denting his confidence for some time after. Despite success for Yorkshire, he never commanded a regular place in the England team and when culpable of an injudicious shot against Australia in the Old Trafford Test of 1961, he received a disproportionate share of the blame for England's shock defeat.

In 1963 Close succeeded Vic Wilson as captain of Yorkshire, and by winning four championships and two Gillette Cups over the next seven seasons he became the third most successful leader in the county's history. In contrast to the bitter divisions of the Yorkshire side of the 1950s, he forged a healthy team spirit by treating everyone as equals and involving them in dressing-room discussions. A tough, unselfish player, who flourished in the heat of battle, he was an inspiration to his bowlers by his blind courage at short leg and his extraordinary resistance to pain. As befitted a racing fanatic, Close was a gambler who was prepared to lose a match in order to win it. An implicit believer in his ability to shape the cricketing weather, he was the past master at heaping pressure on the batsmen through his bowling and fielding changes. In tandem with Illingworth, he used to upset Cowdrey's poise by crowding him with fielders in front of the wicket to stop him playing the spinners with his pads, the result being that he rarely made runs for Kent against Yorkshire.

After England slid to an abject defeat against the West Indies at Headingley in 1966, it wasn't just the home crowd that called for Close to become captain. The selectors duly obliged, and in a side containing five changes for the Oval Test he insisted on Illingworth's inclusion.

Back in England colours for the sixth time, Close approached the challenge with his usual ebullience. He told the team to forget Headingley and go out and win. Losing the toss, they took the field with a renewed zest and kept the pressure on the West Indian batsmen with their attacking fields and positive out-cricket.

Before the lunch interval, Close introduced leg-spinner Barber into the attack and Barber responded by taking 3-49 in 15 overs, including the prize wicket of Sobers. Even during a fifth-wicket stand of 122 between Sobers and Kanhai, England remained upbeat, and with the tail contributing little the West Indies were all out for 268 on a good pitch.

England in turn struggled, and at 166/7 they seemed destined to lose yet again, but this time they didn't buckle. Graveney with 165 and Murray with 112 put on 217 for the eighth wicket, and then, incredibly, Ken Higgs and Snow added 128 for the last wicket.

Bolstered by a lead of 259, England took four cheap wickets on Saturday evening. The crucial moment came early on Monday morning. After the night-watchman Holford was run out and Sobers walked to the wicket, Close asked Snow to bowl a shortish delivery first ball, fathoming that the West Indian captain would rise to the bait. Snow bowled to plan and Sobers went for the hook. He caught the bottom edge of the bat and the ball rebounded into Close's hands at short leg.

'As the catch came, nothing could have been easier,' reported Swanton in the *Daily Telegraph*, 'but how many fielders would have been still holding their ground and not taking evasive action at that moment Sobers shaped his stroke?' [86]

England won by an innings and 34 runs and Close took his bow on the Oval balcony in front of the cheering crowds, days before Yorkshire won the championship.

He continued his winning ways against India and Pakistan the following summer. He defended Boycott after his fellow Yorkshireman was dropped for slow scoring in the first Test against India, despite making 246*, and made light of the criticism he attracted for not making the tourists follow on in the third Test by still winning easily.

After disposing of India 3-0, England faced stronger opposition from Pakistan. After drawing the first Test at Lord's, Close played a significant part in their ten-wicket victory at Trent Bridge, putting on 95 with Barrington in tricky conditions and handling his attack shrewdly on the final day. Three times a wicket fell immediately after he'd changed the bowling. Only in the Oval Test during Asif Iqbal's momentous 146 in Pakistan's second innings did he err tactically with an unduly attacking field, but with runs to play with he could afford to be a touch profligate.

One other point should be made. In seven Tests as captain, Close only scored 201 runs at an average of 20.1 – although he took 12 cheap wickets – and had he remained as captain his lack of runs might well have become a matter of some contention.

Although Close had restored self-respect to English cricket, there were still those at Lord's who disliked his combative style and doubted whether he had the right temperament to lead MCC on a highly charged tour to the West Indies. A letter from a former West Indian cricketer, abhorring the professionalism of Len Hutton's

MCC side and advocating a return to the days of appointing university graduates as captain, found an echo with Donald Carr, the assistant secretary of MCC. 'We must keep this letter as it clearly represents my views,' he wrote in the margin. [87] Their reservations were given added substance by Close's tactics on the final day of Yorkshire's vital championship match against Warwickshire at Edgbaston on 18 August. To prevent their opponents from scoring 142 to win in 100 minutes, they deliberately indulged in blatant time-wasting, upsetting spectators and critics alike. John Woodcock was so appalled that he advocated the return of Smith as England captain instead of Close.

Convinced that the whole affair had been overblown by sections of the press hostile to him, Close refused to apologise, an oversight which didn't help his cause when a report of Yorkshire's conduct reached Lord's. Summoned to appear before the County Advisory Executive Committee on the day before the final Test against Pakistan, he was publicly censored for his team's delaying tactics, an unprecedented rebuke for an England captain.

Although buttressed by the support of the chairman of selectors, Doug Insole, and his England team-mates, Close was shattered by the verdict and found himself unable to sleep properly during the next week. Only the cricket field afforded him some relaxation as his future was being decided among the game's hierarchy.

It was during the Oval Test that the *Sunday People* charged him with attacking a Warwickshire supporter in the members' enclosure at Edgbaston. Although there was little truth in the story – Close had merely put his hand on a Warwickshire member and asked him whether he was responsible for insulting him as he entered the pavilion at lunchtime on the second day – the press hounded him throughout the rest day to gauge his reaction to it. Returning to the team hotel that evening, he slipped round to the back where he lay hidden on the floor behind some packing cases till the night porter, hearing of his plight, let him in the back door. 'If this had not been such a serious matter,' Close later wrote, 'the sight of the captain of an England Test team crouched behind some packing cases would have been farcical.' [88]

By then his fate had been sealed. Although he remained the selectors' choice to captain MCC in the West Indies, his nomination was vetoed by the MCC committee who took into account his brush with the spectator, although this hadn't formed part of the Advisory Committee's remit. When Insole informed him of the news at the end of the Test, Close called it the bitterest moment of his life in cricket. His opportunity to test his revitalised side against the world's best had been snatched away from him for an offence that others had committed with impunity, most notably Hutton against Australia at Headingley in 1953 and Worrell against England at Lord's in 1963. 'To condemn the offence is right,' declared an editorial in *The Times*. 'But it is no less important to show a sense of proportion towards the offender. Close has erred, but this one episode should not be enough to deprive him of the England captaincy.' [89] Others detected an establishment coup to restore the urbane Cowdrey to favour, but whatever the truth it brought the curtain down on Close's England captaincy (aside from leading them in three one-day matches against Australia in 1972 as stand-in for the injured Illingworth). Whatever his faults, he had the potential to be one of England's greatest captains, and, in an age of dour mediocrity, his enterprise would have made Test cricket a more worthy spectacle.

His career continued along its controversial path when he was dismissed by Yorkshire in 1970 for expressing his dislike for the one-day game. Yorkshire's loss was Somerset's gain, since he revived an unfashionable county and inspired a younger generation of their players, including Ian Botham, to dream big. He was even recalled to the Test team against Clive Lloyd's West Indians in 1976, aged 45, and won admiration for his unflinching resolution in the face of some brutal fast bowling, most notably on a suspect wicket in the third Test at Old Trafford. After his retirement from Somerset in 1977, he continued his links with the game by coaching Yorkshire's colts, serving on its committee and becoming its president in 2008. He died in 2015, aged 84.

Tom Graveney

TOM GRAVENEY was born in Riding Mill, Northumberland, on 16 June 1927, the son of an engineer who worked for the arms manufacturers Vickers Armstrong in Newcastle upon Tyne. His elder brother Ken later captained Gloucestershire.

After his father died in 1933, his mother remarried and the family moved to Bristol, where Graveney was educated at the grammar school. He excelled at all sports and in 1944 he joined the Army, serving with the Gloucestershire Regiment in the Middle East.

In 1948 he joined Gloucestershire and was awarded his county cap at the end of the season. A wonderfully elegant batsman whose driving drew comparison with his idol, Hammond, Graveney made his debut against South Africa in 1951 and easily topped the averages on MCC's tour to India that winter. He remained a regular in the England side over the next four years but failed to live up to his potential, primarily because he was seen as too casual. Dropped in 1956, he returned in triumph against the West Indies the following summer, only to be discarded once again after the disastrous tour to Australia in 1958/59.

Appointed captain of Gloucestershire in 1959, he proved a sound rather than inspiring leader. The county finished second that year but slipped to eighth the following year, giving the committee the chance to replace Graveney with the amateur Tom Pugh. Disillusioned by his treatment, Graveney left the club and signed for Worcestershire. After a year's qualification, he emerged a harder, more determined player and his prolific run-scoring helped Worcestershire to win the championship in 1964 and 1965. Bizarrely, England continued to ignore him following a disappointing tour of Australia in 1962/63 until his dramatic recall against the West Indies in 1966. Returning in triumph, he scored a sublime 96 at Lord's and finished with 165 at the Oval, giving him an average of 76 for the series.

Graveney continued to score freely for England, and when vice-captain Titmus was forced out of the West Indies tour in March 1968, after losing four toes in a boating accident, he replaced him. He also took over the captaincy in the third Test against Australia that summer when Cowdrey pulled a leg muscle, surprising everyone with his positive approach. Had bad weather not intervened on the final day, England would probably have won. As it was, Australia went to Headingley one up and determined to cling on to the Ashes.

With neither Cowdrey nor his Australian counterpart Bill Lawry fit to play, it was Graveney, handicapped by a deep hand wound, who tossed up with Barry Jarman. Jarman won and, on a slow pitch, Australia batted with extreme caution to make 315. England found the conditions no easier, scoring 302, and on a dour fourth day their bowlers made little headway against batsmen content to occupy the crease. Graveney's reliance on his spinners, Illingworth and Underwood, eventually paid off on the final morning as the last five Australian wickets fell for 39 runs, leaving England to score 326 to win at an average of 66 an hour. It was a tough assignment, and hard though Edrich, Dexter and Graveney tried, they were always behind the clock.

When Graveney was out for 41 at 164 he told the incoming batsman Keith Fletcher to 'play for a draw but make it look good'. Fletcher and Barrington followed instructions, ensuring the Ashes remained with Australia.

Graveney continued as vice-captain on MCC's chaotic tour to Pakistan that winter. Missing out to Illingworth when Cowdrey was forced to stand down as captain against the West Indies in 1969 because of a snapped Achilles tendon, Graveney was then suspended for organising a match for his benefit on the rest day of the first Test. His England career, at the age of 42, was over.

He retired from Worcestershire at the end of 1970, having averaged 62.66 for that season, to become player-coach of Queensland. He returned after two years to run a pub before becoming a BBC cricket commentator. In 2004 he was appointed president of MCC and he died in 2015, aged 88.

Ray Illingworth

RAY ILLINGWORTH was born in Pudsey on 8 June 1932. His father was a versatile craftsman, qualified as an undertaker and cabinet maker, who employed him after he left school. Raised in a close-knit community of terraced houses, he enjoyed a happy childhood playing sport, and by the age of 15 he was playing for Farsley first eleven in the Bradford League. Days before his 17th birthday, he caused a stir by scoring 148 against Pudsey St Lawrence in the Priestley Cup, the knock-out competition of the Bradford League.

Two years of National Service gave him plenty of cricket with the RAF and the Combined Services, and in 1951 he made his debut for Yorkshire. Their side contained many a great player, but it was riven by dissension and the failure of the captain, Yardley, to stand up to the hard men such as Wardle and Appleyard undermined morale. Illingworth later wrote: 'Such was the hard, vicious school in which the young players of the 50s had to make their way. No word of encouragement, no helpful tips, no pat on the back, which would have meant so much from these established Test players – and heaven help you if things went wrong. You either swallowed the insults and gritted your teeth or you went to pieces.' [90]

Critical of Yardley for his failure to show true leadership, Illingworth was later a great admirer of Ronnie Burnet who led Yorkshire to the county championship in 1959. Despite being a very average player, the 39-year-old Burnet lifted morale by eliminating the factions, getting the team to play for each other and reaching out to one and all. 'Ronnie Burnet sowed the seeds of that philosophy in my mind more than any other man,' wrote Illingworth, 'and it is a philosophy I have never forgotten.' [91]

Illingworth's fortunes as a highly accomplished all-rounder (a canny off-spinner and dependable middle-order bat) flourished under Burnet, and in 1958 he won his first cap for England against New Zealand. He played again the next year but was in and out of the side over the course of the next decade, unable to do justice to his ability.

A great tactician, Illingworth was Close's right-hand man during the glory years of the 1960s, and the Yorkshire committee's willingness to let him leave in 1968 following a contractual dispute proved a serious error. He went to Leicestershire as captain, a position that had increasingly appealed to him, and he made an unfashionable county a force in the land. A tough competitor who gave little away – he was very conscious of his bowling average, which explained his reluctance to bowl himself when the batsmen held sway – he put his profound knowledge of the game to excellent use. An astute reader of conditions and pitches, and of a batsman's weaknesses, he knew which bowler to bowl at which end, the type of length they should bowl and the kind of field they needed.

Recalling the Yorkshire unrest of the 1950s, Illingworth saw it as the captain's duty to give a firm lead and to come down hard on troublesome individuals who placed their interests above those of the team. At the same time, he would always listen to his players and fight hard for their welfare. Most importantly, he instilled such faith in them that they believed anything was possible, never more than in a tight corner when his coolness under fire often proved the difference between victory and defeat.

Within weeks of taking over there, he was the selectors' surprise choice as caretaker captain of England following Cowdrey's snapped Achilles tendon. He was fortunate that the West Indies were a shadow of the side they'd been on their previous tour, despite the presence of Sobers, Gibbs and Basil Butcher, and he began with a ten-wicket win against them at Old Trafford. The West Indies rallied at Lord's and it needed maiden Test centuries from debutant John Hampshire and Illingworth himself to steer their side out of trouble.

With Lord's ending in a draw, Illingworth regarded the deciding game at Headingley as his finest hour as England captain because his tactical ingenuity helped turn potential defeat into narrow victory. Set 303 to win, the West Indies were cruising at 219/3, with Butcher batting beautifully, whereupon he was given out controversially to Underwood. With Sobers now at the wicket, Illingworth immediately brought back seamer Barry Knight, who had twice dismissed him in the series, and he promptly did it a third time by bowling him for 0. Illingworth then replaced Underwood with himself, reasoning that he was better equipped to bowl at left-handers, and having dismissed Clive Lloyd he turned back to Underwood, who had his Kent team-mate John Shepherd caught behind for 0, at which point four wickets had fallen for nine runs.

On the morrow, with the West Indies needing another 73 for victory, Illingworth opted to take the new ball and his pacemen cleaned up the tail, giving England victory by 30 runs and the series 2-0. His reward was the captaincy for the three-match series against New Zealand and he lost no time imposing his authority. Irked by the failure of his leading bowler, Snow, to carry out his instructions in the later stages of the Headingley Test, he asked that he be left out of the next game, and he rang Snow himself to explain his thinking, a gesture which Snow respected even though he disagreed with the decision.

In a rain-affected series, Illingworth played an important all-round part in England's 2-0 win. With no tour that winter, his chance to lead MCC in Australia in 1970/71 appeared to rest primarily on Cowdrey's return to fitness. The latter's start to the 1970 season was so inauspicious that he wasn't considered for the first Test against the Rest of the World, a late substitute for the cancelled South African tour. Illingworth, in contrast, batted superbly in the first three Tests, and with his stature enhanced it was no surprise that he landed the prize.

Less satisfying for him was having Cowdrey as vice-captain since they were unable to work constructively with each other.

Although only one England team had won in Australia since Douglas Jardine in 1932/33, Illingworth set out to put this right. Much would depend on his two leading players, Boycott and Snow, both mercurial characters who needed firm but sensitive handling. Illingworth laid down the law from the opening first-class match against South Australia, insisting that the former shouldn't bat ad infinitum to the exclusion of others, and rebuking the latter for his lethargic effort. While promising not to over-bowl him prior to the Tests, he demanded total commitment in return, a pact that Snow was prepared to accept, and from then on they marched fully in step together.

With Illingworth and Lawry, his Australian counterpart, similar in their attritional approach – although the latter was less able to impose pressure – it wasn't surprising that the first two Tests ended in stalemate. England's hopes had been diminished by a serious injury to their fastest bowler Alan Ward, which forced him to return home, but Snow looked a real threat and Bob Willis, Ward's replacement, proved a valuable acquisition. A potential spanner in the works was the attitude of manager David Clark, an old-style amateur whose cricketing philosophy differed from that of his captain. His remarks at the end of the second Test that he would rather see Australia win the series 3-1 than have all the Tests drawn exacerbated relations between him and the players.

That gulf was further exposed at Melbourne when torrential rain caused the third Test to be abandoned after three blank days. With the Australian Board of Control desperate to recoup their losses, Clark and other MCC dignitaries, without consulting the players, agreed to the Melbourne Test being rescheduled. The idea of playing four Tests in six weeks without any additional remuneration brought into the open team grievances about the formal dress code, parsimonious meal allowances and the number of receptions to attend. Illingworth organised a meeting and managed to get some additional remuneration, but it paled in contrast to what the Australians received.

If nothing else, these grievances helped bring the team closer together. Illingworth encouraged them to congregate in the captain's suite where they could share a beer and relax, so that even the reserves were made to feel important, and he imposed no limits on a player's socialising provided he performed the next day. After encountering opposition to D'Oliveira's selection for Australia because of his colourful nightlife in the West Indies three years earlier, Illingworth stood up for him in committee and later told him he was not to let him down, a request with which D'Oliveira was only too happy to comply. On the penultimate night of the final Test, with the match finely balanced, he sought Illingworth's permission to attend a concert by the popular Puerto Rican guitarist Jose Feliciano. Illingworth left the decision up to him but warned him about the potential pitfalls of a late night out before such a crucial day's play. D'Oliveira accepted his advice and opted to stay in and watch television instead.

Illingworth also backed his players to the hilt with the press and public. When Underwood was jeered by the Hill at Sydney for dropping a catch, Illingworth moved him to another position away from his tormentors.

England won the fourth Test at Sydney thanks to some magnificent batting from Boycott and some superb fast bowling from Snow, and they drew at Melbourne. They then had the better of the draw at Adelaide in a game marred by the controversial run out of Boycott in England's first innings. Objecting to what was a marginal decision, Boycott dropped his bat, and stood hands on his hips in disbelief and glared at the umpire. He left to a crescendo of boos and Illingworth felt obliged to apologise to the umpires.

Leading by 235 on first innings, the England captain was pilloried for not enforcing the follow-on, but his logic made sense. His pace bowlers were exhausted, the pitch was getting easier and he fretted about facing Johnny Gleeson, Australia's unorthodox spinner, in the final stages. With runs aplenty from both sides in the second innings, the match finished in a tame draw.

With the series to be decided at Sydney, England went into the Test without Boycott, who'd broken his arm in an inconsequential game. Ian Chappell, making his debut as Australia's captain in place of the ousted Lawry, inserted them on a damp wicket and bowled them out for 184, Illingworth top scorer with 42.

England fought back to have Australia 177/7 before a stubborn eighth-wicket stand between Greg Chappell and Terry Jenner halted their progress. With frustration building, Illingworth took the second new ball and in his second over Snow hit Jenner on the side of the head as he ducked into a ball that barely rose above stump height.

As Jenner was helped from the field, umpire Lou Rowan warned Snow for intimidatory bowling. Aggrieved that he'd been warned for bowling one bouncer, Snow protested vehemently and was supported by Illingworth, who in both word and gesture disputed the umpire's decision. The altercation only fuelled the anger of the 29,000 crowd. Bottles were hurled onto the field and, after Snow was manhandled by a drunk as he took up residence on the boundary at the end of the over, Illingworth, concerned about the safety of his players, led them off the field without consulting the umpires. On reaching the dressing room, he was ordered to return by Clark, but he only relented when the umpires warned him that a failure to return would mean his side forfeiting the match.

After a seven-minute delay, during which the ground was cleared, the team returned to a mixed reception to play out the final overs.

Facing a deficit of 80 on first innings, the England openers Edrich and Brian Luckhurst put on 94 for the first wicket and, with everyone chipping in usefully, they managed to set Australia 223 to win. Deprived of the early loss of Snow, who broke his right hand on the boundary fence, Illingworth marshalled his bowlers and fielders expertly, in addition to playing his part by dismissing Ian Redpath and Keith Stackpole. When play resumed the next day with Australia 123/5, Illingworth chose to open the bowling himself and gained the prize wicket of Greg Chappell, stumped by Knott as he was lured down the pitch. Thereafter D'Oliveira and Underwood made light work of the tail to give England victory by 62 runs, and Illingworth was chaired from the field by his players, the first man to regain the Ashes in Australia since Jardine. 'Ray handled everything so well on that last morning that there was never any danger of us losing,' recalled Underwood. [92]

His methods weren't always approved of by his manager or the MCC hierarchy, and the celebration banquet at Lord's was a funereal affair, but, as E.M. Wellings wrote in *Wisden*, he did a magnificent job and was consistency itself with both bat and ball. 'Illingworth's side in 1970/71 were mentally the toughest English side I played against,' recollected Greg Chappell. 'He subjected us to mental intimidation by aggressive field placings and physical intimidation by constant use of his pace attack. Winning to Illingworth was something he expected of himself and demanded of his team.' [93]

After Australia, the summer's Tests against Pakistan and India proved something of an anti-climax. Played for the most part in unseasonal weather, in front of sparse crowds, the cricket lacked inspiration despite both countries offering stiffer resistance than on previous visits. With Pakistan totally dominating the first Test at Edgbaston and England having the better of a rain-ruined game at Lord's, everything depended on the decider at Headingley. In a taut, low-scoring contest, Illingworth once again proved the man for a crisis. When Pakistan began the final day needing a further 206 for victory with all their wickets in hand, he decided to open the bowling himself and immediately removed Aftab Gul and Zaheer Abbas, their leading batsman, with his first two balls before dismissing Mushtaq Mohammad cheaply. A magisterial 91 from opener Sadiq Mohammad restored Pakistan's hopes, but at 184/5 Illingworth threw the ball to D'Oliveira and he responded by dismissing Sadiq and Intikhab Alam in the course of five balls. He then took the new ball and Peter Lever finished the game with three wickets in an over, leaving England winners by 25 runs.

Slightly fortunate to beat Pakistan, they had their comeuppance against India captained by Ajit Wadekar. After a close finish at Lord's, they were robbed of a win in the second Test at Old Trafford by bad weather, a game notable for Illingworth's second Test century. They should have won at the Oval but, having established a first-innings lead of 71, their batsmen then gave up the ghost. Bowled out for 101 by leg-spinner Bhagwat Chandrasekhar, India needed 173 to win, a target that took them 101 overs to complete, with Illingworth bowling at his miserly best and handling his field placings with masterly precision. When they eventually won by four wickets, they made cricket history by winning a Test on English soil for the first time, in contrast to Illingworth who lost his first game in 20 Tests as captain.

He continued at the helm the following year against Ian Chappell's Australia, despite having turned 40. In a low-scoring series, England won the first Test at Old Trafford and Australia redressed the balance at Lord's with their opening bowler Bob Massie taking 16 wickets.

At Trent Bridge, Illingworth made a rare error by inserting Australia on an excellent batting strip, and it needed a defiant rearguard action on the last day to avoid defeat. He came into his own, however, on an under-prepared wicket at Headingley, which was much to the liking of Underwood. Illingworth gave him valuable support, but his main value concerned his batting. His eighth-wicket partnership of 104 with Snow swung the game in England's direction, giving them a first-innings lead of 117, and with Underwood near unplayable in Australia's second innings they won by nine wickets to retain the Ashes. According to Woodcock, 'Illingworth's handling of the whole operation was shrewd and efficient. His batting, bowling, fielding and field placing all showed him for what he is – an outstanding competitor on the big day.' [94]

The final Test at the Oval was a classic. In a game which fluctuated throughout, Australia needed 242 to win. Early in their innings, Illingworth was engaged in a rare tussle with Stackpole and Ian Chappell when he slipped in the bowler's footmarks and twisted his ankle. Helped off in agony, he was unable to play any further part in the game, a serious loss to a side that regarded him as something of a cult figure. They became a tribe without a head, noted Woodcock. It was as though they were looking to the balcony for the next move. Had he remained out in the middle it is possible that the outcome might have been different, but as it was England eventually lost by five wickets.

Opting out of the winter tour to India and Pakistan, Illingworth subjected his captaincy to a trial of strength with his replacement Tony Lewis in the form of a Test trial at the beginning of the next season. He won back his crown, with Lewis appointed his deputy, but after the latter failed twice in the first Test against New Zealand, he withdrew from the team because of injury and didn't represent his country again.

Against Bevan Congdon's New Zealand, England were flattered to win the series 2-0, but their luck ran out against a formidable West Indies side under Rohan Kanhai. They were soundly beaten in the first Test at the Oval, which led to the dropping of Snow after one of his less successful games. He was later to write that he viewed his omission as a political move, forced on Illingworth at a time when he was struggling to hold on to the England captaincy. 'With the pressure going for me to be dropped, Ray eventually gave way when the selectors met to choose the side for the second Test against the West Indies. His own position was under fire and Ray felt it better to save the showdown argument over my presence until the time came to name the touring party for the MCC visit to the Caribbean that winter. He was hoping to be the captain, and he wanted me in the side.' [95]

England drew a bad-tempered game at Edgbaston and were trounced at Lord's. Losing the toss on an excellent wicket, Illingworth was condemned to field first with an ailing attack, and for the first time he looked helpless, powerless to stop the carnage as his bowlers were dispatched to all parts of the ground. The West Indies declared at 652/8 and dismissed England cheaply twice to win by the enormous margin of an innings and 226 runs.

The result spelled the end of the Illingworth era. Prior to the final Test, the assumption was that he would take the team to the West Indies that winter, but their capitulation at Lord's forced a rethink. Now that some of the shine had come off his leadership, his age and his fading powers as an all-rounder, especially his bowling, came into the reckoning. Perhaps more damning was the attritional cricket that England had played that year, especially in comparison with the West Indies, and the need for something more dynamic in the Caribbean.

Illingworth continued to lead Leicestershire to unprecedented success, winning the county championship in 1975, and after his retirement in 1978 he returned to Yorkshire as manager. With the county experiencing a period of great turbulence, much of it centred around the divisive figure of Boycott, he resumed his playing career in 1982, and the following year he led them to victory in the John Player League (JPL) while finishing bottom of the championship.

Falling out with Boycott and his supporters, he left in 1984 to pursue a career in cricket punditry on radio and television. In 1994 he succeeded Dexter as chairman of selectors, combining this with that of manager in 1995/96. Respected for his knowledge of the game, he found it difficult to relate to the modern-day player, and after a period of limited success he resigned in 1997.

An old-fashioned captain who led a team of salty professionals, Illingworth is justly recalled as one of England's most esteemed captains, winning six series as opposed to two lost, and he became the first captain since Jardine to regain the Ashes in Australia. Elevated to the purple at an advanced age, the additional responsibilities spurred him to greater heights and he positively revelled in the challenges of leadership, lifting his own game, fighting hard for his players' interests and receiving great loyalty in return. Knott spoke for many of them when he declared Illingworth to be the best captain he played under, chiefly because he gave him the feeling that they could win in any situation, while D'Oliveira wrote that no captain got more out of his men.

Although their form of attritional cricket didn't always make for spectacular viewing compared to the dynamics of the modern game, Illingworth's side contained plenty of grit and determination. This was seen in the way that the lower order often rode to the rescue in a batting crisis, with Illingworth himself invariably at the heart of the resistance. His captaincy had its greatest impact in tight games such as Headingley 1969, Sydney 1971 and Headingley 1971 and probably no England captain was ever held in such awe by the Australians as much as he was, which is no mean achievement.

Tony Lewis

TONY LEWIS was born in Swansea on 6 July 1938. The family moved to Neath during the Second World War and he attended Neath Grammar School for Boys, representing it at both rugby and cricket. At the age of 17, he made his debut for Glamorgan, the same year as he was chosen as a violinist for the National Youth Orchestra of Wales.

At Cambridge, he gained a rugby blue and captained the cricket eleven in 1962, a year in which he scored over 2,000 runs. It was a feat he repeated in 1966 when he was 12th man for England against the West Indies at the Oval.

In 1967 he took over the captaincy of Glamorgan and led them to the county championship two years later by playing with real adventure and flair. Although his early promise as a batsman never quite materialised, his powers of leadership made him an obvious replacement for Illingworth for the tour to India and Pakistan in 1972/73. 'All who know him like him and they do for the best reasons,' wrote Woodcock. 'He is a friendly, honest, straightforward cricketer, who loves the game and is the same person to all people.' [96]

With no Illingworth, Boycott, Edrich and Snow on board, this was an MCC side who lacked experience but contained a number of players, such as Dennis Amiss, Keith Fletcher and Tony Greig, keen to make their mark. Although new to the set-up – he was the last man to captain England on a Test debut – Lewis had gained experience of the subcontinent when touring Pakistan with a Commonwealth XI in 1967, and he'd also captained a strong MCC side to the Far East in 1970. Approaching the tour and its myriad demands in a positive spirit, he cultivated a more relaxed style than previous MCC tours and fostered a real camaraderie within the squad.

Entering the Test series as underdogs against an Indian side whose spinners posed a real threat, England had the best of all starts at Delhi, bowling them out for 173. Despite Chandrasekhar's 8-79, they managed to gain a narrow lead of 27 but a target of 207 for victory on a slow turner would test their resolve. Coming to the wicket at 70-3 on the penultimate evening, Lewis, who'd failed to score in the first innings, saw out the final overs with opener Barry Wood.

Although Wood was out immediately the next morning – Christmas Day – Lewis didn't buckle. He and Greig batted with great composure against the spinners to see England through to a six-wicket victory, the captain finishing with 70*. It was the best of all Christmas presents and the team celebrated at the British High Commission by singing carols.

In the second Test at Calcutta the England bowling and fielding was once again excellent, but their batting fell by the wayside and they lost by 28 runs.

At Madras they again batted badly, aside from Fletcher in the first innings and Denness in the second. Needing only 86 for victory, India struggled throughout and lost six wickets in reaching their target. One of them involved their captain Wadekar, who edged Chris Old to Greig at slip, only to be given not out. Incensed by the ruling, Greig charged down the pitch to make his case and others expressed dissent before Lewis called them to order. Meanwhile the umpire, who'd been unsighted by the bowler, consulted his colleague at square leg and gave Wadekar out.

Convinced that this incident was the inevitable result of both teams trying to con the umpire, in particular the numerous bat and pad appeals by fielders clustered around the bat, Lewis went to see Wadekar afterwards and said, 'Shall we play cricket for the next two Tests, or shall we cheat?' 'Let's play cricket,' Wadekar replied. Before the next game, Lewis called a team meeting to say that under his captaincy there would be no pressure on the umpire to get decisions. His edict didn't meet with universal approval but both teams adhered to the agreement, and for the rest of the series harmony prevailed.

The fourth Test was elevated by a classic century from Lewis – the first of the series by either side – but both that game and the following one at Bombay were drawn, giving India the series 2-1. Had England batted better at Calcutta and Madras, they could equally have emerged as victors. While his future prospects as an England captain remained unclear because of his inconsistent batting – two substantial scores against India were boosted by two fifties in the three drawn Tests in Pakistan – Lewis's leadership passed muster in every other capacity. *The Sun*'s Clive Taylor wrote in *Wisden*: 'He was enterprising, liked as well as respected by his players and very conscious that his job involved more than just deciding tactics on the field.' [97] Tactics wasn't his greatest strength, according to Underwood, but he was charming, lively and approachable and the 1972/73 tour was the most enjoyable he went on. Pat Pocock also admired his social graces, not least at the ceaseless round of receptions, and, although finding him a touch autocratic regarding field placings, he noted the improvement after they'd sat down to discuss it. 'In fact, Lewis did such a good job of rallying the players at critical stages of the tour that it was generally agreed by both the press and the team that despite the ultimate result it was the happiest tour they had known.' [98]

At the beginning of the 1973 season Lewis went head to head with Illingworth in the Test trial at Hove and ended up becoming his deputy for the first game against New Zealand. 'I felt Lewis was unlucky to lose the captaincy so abruptly,' wrote Amiss, 'but, examining the situation logically, it made sense to me that if we were picking the best available captain then Illingworth had to be reinstated.' [99]

In the first Test, Lewis failed in both innings, and although chosen for the next game he had to withdraw because of chronic knee trouble. He never played for England again and he retired the following year.

Thereafter, he pursued a varied and successful career, most notably in journalism and broadcasting. He was, for many years, the *Sunday Telegraph*'s rugby and cricket correspondent and fronted Test matches for the BBC. He was also chairman, president and trustee of Glamorgan, president of MCC, chairman of the Welsh Tourist Board and the first chairman of the MCC World Cricket Committee.

Mike Denness

MIKE DENNESS was born in Bellshill, Lanarkshire, on 1 December 1940. His father worked for W.D. and H.O. Wills, the tobacco company, and was a keen sportsman who played cricket with Ian Peebles, the former England leg-spinner.

At Ayr Academy Mike played in the same rugby XV as Ian McLauchlan, a future Scottish rugby captain, and Ian Ure, a future Scottish football international, and in 1958 he represented Glasgow at stand-off against Edinburgh in the inter-city schools rugby match. His cricket also blossomed at the Ayr club, and in 1959 he became the first schoolboy to represent Scotland.

Through the good offices of E.W. Swanton, who spoke at the Ayr centenary dinner, Denness made his first-class debut for Kent in 1962, and in 1964 he formed a highly profitable opening partnership with Brian Luckhurst.

He marked his debut for England against New Zealand at the Oval in 1969 with an unbeaten half-century in the second innings, but he was dropped after the first Test against the Rest of the World the following season. He did, however, play a leading part in Kent's championship win in their centenary year, captaining the side in Cowdrey's absence.

Appointed his successor in 1972, Denness led a talented side to six one-day trophies over the next five years, his friendliness and integrity helping create an excellent team spirit. These qualities, coupled with his calmness under pressure, particularly in the one-day game where he kept to set patterns and his elegant stroke-play won him the vice-captaincy to Lewis on MCC's tour to India and Pakistan in 1972/73. He played several useful innings without suggesting he was true Test class, and when Illingworth returned to the captaincy the following summer Denness was omitted from the side. Badly beaten by the West Indies, Illingworth was finally discarded, and, with Lewis unavailable to lead in the Caribbean that winter because of injury, the prize went to Denness. 'He is not, I am afraid, an adventurous captain,' wrote Woodcock. 'But he is an unselfish one, which is very much in his favour.' [100]

Denness's assignment was a formidable one. Unable to persuade the selectors to pick Snow, he was nearly deprived of the services of Boycott. Desperate to lead England, Boycott greatly objected to Denness's appointment, thinking he was his inferior both as a batsman and a captain. 'I had the gravest misgivings about touring under Denness,' he wrote in his autobiography. 'It was a mistake. Looking back, it was one of the worst England tours I have made and Mike Denness was the worst England captain I have played under.' [101] When Denness sent him an olive branch by asking whether he would take charge of the nets on tour, Boycott rejected it, explaining that such responsibility rested with the captain or the vice-captain Tony Greig. Thereafter relations remained frosty. Denness wrote: 'On a number of occasions I went knocking on his door to sit down and have a chat with him in the evening but he was always "far too busy". As the senior man he never contributed anything. I had a feeling that he was constantly undermining me.' [102] Fletcher recalls Boycott coming to him one day and suggesting that the senior players stage a coup against Denness, a suggestion Fletcher dismissed as cynical. While critical of Denness's failure to listen to advice, he told Boycott that they were in the middle of a series and they should concentrate on winning it.

In the first Test at Port of Spain, England batted poorly in their first innings to be bowled out for 131, and they toiled in the field as the West Indies, led by 142 by Alvin Kallicharran, built up a handsome lead. His dismissal after the last ball of the day – run out by Greig as he walked back to the pavilion from the non-striker's end before the umpire had called time – sparked such uproar that it required prompt action. Denness was criticised for not immediately withdrawing the appeal, but he took his stand on the laws of the game. It needed hours of discussion between officials, the two captains and the umpires before it was eventually agreed that Kallicharran should be reinstated.

The decision didn't meet with the approval of the majority of the England team, already low on morale. Facing a deficit of 261 on first innings, they received the best of all starts with an opening stand of 209 between Boycott and Amiss. Denness then added 119 with Amiss for the second wicket before he was foolishly run out for 44. His dismissal triggered a dramatic collapse as England's last nine wickets fell for 64 runs. They lost by seven wickets and they appeared to be heading for another defeat in the second Test at Kingston. Trailing the West Indies by 230 runs on first innings, they began the final day still 12 behind with five wickets left, only for Amiss to rescue them with a memorable 262*.

England's reprieve in no way shielded Denness from the growing reservations about his captaincy from both the press and the players. A humiliating ten-wicket defeat by Barbados brought matters to a head. Woodcock wrote that in 25 years of touring he'd rarely seen MCC play so badly. 'On Saturday evening, after a day's play in which MCC had lost every trick, Denness sat alone on the players' balcony with his pads on gazing into space. For ten minutes he sat there, his solitude somehow symbolic. What he needs at the moment, to rally the players, is a greater gift of communication than he appears to have.' [103] 'A shy man, unwilling to impose himself and sometimes apparently unable to communicate, he was the type of reclusive captain who could not help us in our predicament,' wrote Willis. [104]

Besides his unwillingness to consult, Denness lacked a strategic plan for his bowlers. Off-spinner Pocock recalled that, after being hit for six and four by Keith Boyce in the first Test, Denness came down the pitch and, taking his arm, said, 'I'm talking to you for appearances.' When Pocock told Denness he was making him look daft, he replied, 'Just appearances, Percy,' and he walked back to his mark.

As England prepared for the third Test, Denness caused further ructions by proposing that Boycott should bat at number four, partly to protect him from the West Indian new ball attack – they'd troubled him with the short ball – but mainly to stiffen the fragile middle order. Although not sold on the idea, Boycott went along with it but it proved a failure. Not only did the wait to bat fray his nerves, he made only ten and 13, while Denness failed as an opener. On Boycott's insistence, the experiment wasn't repeated.

England once again escaped the noose at Bridgetown thanks to a sixth-wicket stand of 142 between Fletcher and Knott in their second innings, and after a rain-affected draw at Georgetown, they returned to Port of Spain for the final Test. Boycott had underperformed to date, but he came good when it mattered. His two innings of 99 and 112 and Greig's 13 wickets went a long way towards England winning a hard-fought game by 26 runs to square the series.

Although Denness's captaincy had looked more assured in the final Test, Clive Taylor wrote in *Wisden* that his performances, both as captain and as a player, lacked conviction. There may well have been truth in Boycott's bitter observation that his batting had kept Denness in his job. Thinking that the criticism of him had been excessive, the selectors felt inclined to persevere with him. Captaining MCC against the Indians, he scored a century and then made consecutive centuries against them in the second and third Tests as England ran out overwhelming winners.

His success guaranteed him an extended lease against Pakistan, and in a drawn series blighted by poor weather Denness did nothing spectacular, but he was appointed captain to tour Australia that winter.

Although MCC arrived there in confident mood, the team lacked class. Snow had once again been unaccountably omitted, Boycott had withdrawn from Test cricket for multiple reasons and Denness was badly afflicted by a kidney infection. Although his captaincy became more collegiate and assertive than in the West Indies, neither his own form nor that of the team augured well for the first Test at Brisbane. It was there, on an uneven pitch, that England were first subjected to the withering pace and hostility of newcomer Jeff Thomson, in tandem with Dennis Lillee. Despite an heroic century from Greig, England were badly beaten by 166 runs and they lost the services of Amiss and Edrich to injury for the next Test. Confronted with these casualties, it was Denness's idea to send for Cowdrey as a replacement. In retrospect, for all Cowdrey's gallantry, it was asking too much of a 42-year-old to face such a battering, but whether anyone would have done better is debatable.

On a lightning-fast pitch at Perth, England again succumbed to the pace and bounce of the Australian quicks and lost by nine wickets. Denness in particular looked technically vulnerable, and after four consecutive failures the vultures were gathering.

Although England managed to draw the third Test at Melbourne, it brought him no personal relief with scores of eight and two. With the Ashes on the line at Sydney, Denness felt that he'd become too much of a liability and, against the advice of manager Alec Bedser, he opted to stand aside for vice-captain Edrich. It was a courageous decision, and one that filled him with misery once the match started, but it made little overall difference to the result. England were once again outplayed and the Ashes returned to Australia.

With Edrich out of action for the next Test because of cracked ribs, Denness reclaimed his place, his confidence restored by a run of good scores in Tasmania. Confronted with a drying wicket at Adelaide, he chose to field first and had Australia in trouble at 84/5, but he missed a trick by failing to bowl Titmus in partnership with Underwood when the ball was turning. As the conditions improved, Australia recovered to 304 all out and the crisis passed. Denness batted well for 51 in England's first innings, but they could only manage 172 and they went on to lose the match by 163 runs.

They finally came good in Melbourne. In seaming conditions, they dismissed Australia for 152 and went on to win by an innings. Denness hit 188 against an attack deprived of Thomson and Lillee for all but six overs and followed up with another large century against New Zealand. Reviewing his performance in Australia, the *Evening Standard*'s John Thicknesse wrote in *Wisden*: 'Denness set an energetic example in the field and promoted a better team spirit than was the case in the West Indies; mainly because he showed a greater readiness to listen to advice. There were times nevertheless when field-placings were being made by those other than the captain; but even with hindsight it is doubtful whether an England side could have been selected that might have given Australia a run for their money, no matter who the captain was.' [105]

With opinions divided over his future, Denness led England to the semi-final of the World Cup at home and was given the captaincy for the first Test against Australia at Edgbaston. Under pressure from his batsmen, unwilling to face Lillee and Thomson in the conditions, he inserted his opponents under cloudy skies, but his decision backfired when the ball didn't swing and England were later caught on an uncovered wicket open to the elements. They lost by an innings and Denness, who failed twice with the bat, submitted his resignation before the axe fell. He never played for England again.

As an outsider from Scotland, Denness never seemed entirely comfortable in England colours. A good enough player to score four Test centuries, he struggled against the more powerful attacks and was forced to stand down in Australia because of a lack of runs. A sound rather than inspiring captain, he lacked the personality to fully win over his players and to adequately fill Illingworth's shoes. He was, however, a man of the highest integrity and he showed great dignity during his travails in Australia. 'My overall verdict was that Mike did a good job for England both on and off the field,' recalled chairman of selectors Bedser, 'and it would be manifestly unfair to remember his term of leadership by his one final disaster. He deserves much better.' [106]

After he lost the England captaincy in 1975, he suffered a further setback when he was sacked as captain of Kent the following summer, a year in which they'd won two trophies. It was a shabby way to treat such a loyal and distinguished servant of the club. He joined Essex and played an important part in their rise to glory. After his retirement in 1980, he coached the second eleven for three years and worked in finance, insurance and public relations. He also acted as an ICC match referee from 1996 to 2002, was chairman of Kent from 2001 to 2004 and its president from 2011 to 2012. He died in 2012, aged 72.

John Edrich

JOHN EDRICH was born in Blofield, Norfolk, on 21 June 1937, the son of a farmer and the youngest member of a Norfolk cricketing dynasty. His four cousins, Geoff, Brian, Eric and Bill, all played first-class cricket, the last-named becoming one of England's finest post-war batsmen.

Educated at Bracondale School, Edrich played for Norfolk as a 16-year-old, a dogged left-handed opener with the most immaculate defence. After several matches for the Combined Services, he made his debut for Surrey in 1958 and the following year he hit seven centuries, forming a highly prolific opening partnership with Micky Stewart.

In 1963 he won his first Test cap against the West Indies, but despite a maiden century against Australia the following year and an undefeated 310* against New Zealand in 1965, he didn't cement his place till the tour to the West Indies in 1967/68. For the next three years he was England's leading scorer, and in Australia in 1970/71 his batting was central to their Ashes triumph.

Although limited in his range of strokes and heavy on the eye, Edrich compensated with his iron self-discipline and courage, but the very qualities which defined his batting didn't make for great leadership. Appointed captain of Surrey in 1973, he lacked the common touch and his strict, austere style won him few supporters in the team. An attempted dressing-room coup to remove him at the end of his first season was foiled by the committee and Surrey's success in the Benson and Hedges Cup in 1974 strengthened his position.

After nearly two years out of the Test side, Edrich returned to form against India and Pakistan in 1974 and was appointed as vice-captain to Mike Denness in Australia that winter. It proved the most gruelling of tours, with the fast-bowling combination of Lillee and Thomson a constant thorn in England's flesh. Edrich sustained a broken hand in the first Test which forced him to miss the next game, but he returned for the third Test and was captain in the fourth Test when Denness voluntarily stood down because of poor form.

In front of large and rowdy crowds at Sydney, it proved to be a tough baptism, although he had taken over the captaincy from the injured Illingworth against Australia at the Oval in 1972. Losing the toss and fielding first, he put insufficient pressure on debutant opener Rick McCosker, who went on to score 80. Despite dropped catches, Australia were pegged back to 310/7, but Greig was over-bowled to the exclusion of Titmus and their last three wickets put on 95 runs.

A dogged 50 from Edrich and a scintillating 82 from Knott saved England from the follow-on, but Australia built remorselessly on their lead of 110 before declaring at 289/4. They began soundly but lost three quick wickets on the final morning. More importantly, Edrich ducked into his first ball from Lillee and was hit in the ribs. He doubled up in pain and was helped off the field before going to hospital for a precautionary X-ray, which confirmed broken ribs.

He returned to a great ovation at 156/6 and defended gallantly for two and a half hours, but, despite the stoical efforts of Willis and Geoff Arnold to stay with him, they lost with 43 balls to spare. Had the rest of the batsmen displayed the same resolution as Edrich, the match could have been saved.

He missed the Adelaide Test but returned for the final one at Melbourne to finish top of the averages. He enjoyed a highly productive series against Australia at home in 1975, but after enduring a fearsome battering from the West Indian quick bowlers at Old Trafford the following year his Test career came to an end.

He continued to play for Surrey till the end of 1978, and in 1977 he scored his 100th first-class century.

After retirement from cricket he became marketing director for a bank in Jersey and, briefly, a Test selector in 1981 and an England batting coach in 1995. Although diagnosed with a rare form of incurable leukaemia in 2000, he has successfully resisted it with a course of injections of mistletoe extract.

Tony Greig

TONY GREIG was born in Queenstown in the Eastern Cape on 6 October 1946, the son of a Scottish former RAF squadron leader who won the DFC and DSO, personally presented to him by King George VI. He moved to South Africa with the RAF, met his South African-born wife there and stayed.

Educated at Queen's College, Greig captained the cricket, rugby and tennis teams, and retained a lasting gratitude to the school for the way they handled his epilepsy, which was first diagnosed when, as a 14-year-old, he collapsed during a tennis match.

Bloodied by Border in the Currie Cup at the age of 19, Greig was recommended to Sussex by his coaches at school and he marked his championship debut for them in 1967 by scoring 156 against Lancashire.

Although he played for England against the Rest of the World in 1970, he had to wait until 1972 before his official Test debut against Australia at Old Trafford. (He qualified for England by dint of his Scottish father.) An instant success, he was arguably the world's leading all-rounder between 1972 and 1977, his most spectacular contributions invariably coming when the situation most demanded them.

Six feet and seven inches, handsome and highly competitive, Greig was a blond Adonis who brought a much-needed flair to a staid England side with his belligerent hitting, his attacking bowling and his magnificent fielding. Never short of confidence, he loved the cut and thrust of the big occasion, coaxing his team-mates, niggling his opponents and entertaining the crowd.

On MCC's tour to the West Indies in 1973/74 he scaled new heights of attainment, scoring centuries in successive Tests and taking 13 wickets in the final one, enabling England to square the series; in Australia the following winter he was the only Englishman, Alan Knott aside, able to withstand the hostility of Dennis Lillee and Jeff Thomson.

He could carry his competitiveness to excess. In India in 1972/73 he was admonished by manager Donald Carr for excessive appealing; and in the West Indies his running out of Alvin Kallicharran in the first Test after the final ball of the day had been played was deemed unworthy of a fine cricketer – one of the main reasons why he lost the vice-captaincy to Edrich.

Nevertheless, for all his volatility, Greig's courage and charisma made him the obvious man to succeed Denness following England's drubbing in the first Test against Australia in 1975. As captain of Sussex since 1973, he had raised morale with his enthusiasm, empathy and will to win. Despite his South African background, his passion for England wasn't in question. (When appearing on BBC's *Desert Island Discs* in 1976, he chose, as his first two records, 'There will always be an England' and 'Scotland the Brave'.) He wanted players who would sweat blood for their country and the faith he placed in David Steele, the grey-haired artisan from Northampton, was amply rewarded by his astonishing success against Australia which gained him cult status. It seemed appropriate that the two of them should come together on the first morning of the Lord's Test when England were reeling at 49/4. Together they put on 95 and after Steele was out for 50, Greig continued to captivate a full house with a dashing 96. He returned to a rapturous reception.

The next day he carried the fight to the Australians in the field with his verbal aggression, his habit of halting his quick bowlers in their approach to make field changes and his overt triumphalism whenever a wicket fell. At one stage England had Australia wilting at 133/8, but 99 from Ross Edwards and 73 from Lillee took them to 268, a mere 47 behind England's 315.

With Edrich hitting 175, Greig set Australia 484 to win, and although he harassed them with close fielders, they easily saved the match.

England continued their resurgence at Headingley by dismissing Australia for 135 to gain a first-innings lead of 153, but once again the old enemy refused to lie down. Facing a target of 445, they'd reached 220/3 on the fourth evening before vandals sabotaged the pitch, forcing the abandonment of any further play.

In the final Test at the Oval, Australia reasserted their supremacy by making 532/9 declared and forcing England to follow on, but, led by Edrich, Steele and Bob Woolmer, they batted resolutely on a bland surface to earn themselves a draw.

After their travails in Australia, Greig had restored pride in English cricket, but his confidence, while infectious, could spill over into hubris. On the eve of their home series against the West Indies the following summer, he vowed to make them grovel. His remark, insensitive at the best of times, only succeeded in rousing his opponents to fury, especially the fast bowlers who found that extra yard of pace whenever he came to the wicket.

For all his bravado, Greig often pursued a defensive strategy, opting for hardened warriors who would sell themselves dearly. Hence the dramatic recall of the 45-year-old Close, 27 years after his first game for England, and a first cap for the 34-year-old Brearley to line up alongside other battlers such as Edrich and Steele.

Fielding first on an overcast morning in the first Test at Trent Bridge, Greig exposed himself to criticism by his failure to attack his opponents with the new ball and not bowling Underwood till the final hour. His lack of ambition was music to Viv Richards, who made 232, but on an easy-paced pitch the match petered out into a draw.

Lord's promised rather more once England gained a first-innings lead of 68, but with neither side showing the urgency required, another draw resulted.

With Brearley cast aside after two Tests, Greig bizarrely asked the veteran Close to open with the 39-year-old Edrich at Old Trafford. On a lethal wicket, the England batting was overwhelmed by the pace attack of Andy Roberts, Michael Holding and Wayne Daniel, and they lost by 425 runs. Close and Edrich top scored in the second innings but only after they were subjected to as brutal spell of intimidatory bowling as anyone could recall. Neither played for England again.

With 38 runs in five innings, Greig was a captain under pressure, but two magnificent innings at Headingley restored England's honour in an absorbing game they narrowly lost.

He was unable to repeat the feat at the Oval where, on a flat wicket, the gulf between the two sides was all too obvious. In broiling heat, Richards's majestic 291 was the cornerstone of his side's 687/8 declared, and although Amiss replied with 203, Holding's magnificent bowling proved too much for his team-mates. Numbered among his 14 victims was Greig twice, yorked in both innings for 12 and one, much to the delight of the many West Indian supporters who hadn't forgotten his grovel remark. 'His image as a sporting idol has become a little tarnished,' wrote Woodcock. 'The captaincy has taken its toll of him. It does of almost anyone.' [107] Although lumbered with a team of shire horses against one full of thoroughbreds, Greig's eccentric tactical grasp hadn't helped. At the Oval he'd replaced opening bowler Bob Willis after just two overs, despite taking the wicket of Gordon Greenidge, and replaced him with Underwood, and he delayed taking the new ball for 25 overs. In the West Indies' second innings, he lacked any kind of plan as their openers rattled up 182/0 in two hours.

Without a win in eight Tests as captain and his own form suffering, the selectors considered replacing him with the cerebral Brearley for the upcoming tour to India. Brearley, however, had yet to prove himself at the highest level and so they compromised by making him vice-captain, hoping that some of his tactical ingenuity would rub off on Greig. It proved a shrewd move since Greig loved to talk about the game, and the advice he gleaned from him, along with Fletcher, Knott and manager Barrington, was put to good effect in India.

After two years of unremitting pace, broken bones and low scores, England's shell-shocked veterans gave way to youthful recruits such as Graham Barlow, Derek Randall, John Lever and Roger Tolchard, heralding a vast improvement in the fielding.

From the first day of the tour to the last, Greig was the central figure. Idolised by the natives on his previous trip for his humour and showmanship, he looked to extend that honeymoon by charming one and all. At his initial press conference, he won glowing reviews for declaring that Indian umpires, recently the bane of the touring New Zealand team, were the best in the world, flattery that worked to his side's advantage over the coming weeks.

A consummate communicator, unlike so many of his predecessors, Greig was totally at ease with the media, and while a journalist's dream for his availability and candour, he in turn used their copy to serve his team's interests.

He was also adept at handling the crowd. They responded enthusiastically to his idea of getting the team, kitted out in their MCC blazers, to salute all sections of the stadium before each Test, and he kept them entertained during a game by giving them a wave, doffing his cap or diving for cover if a firecracker exploded. He was also meticulous about signing autographs and went out of his way to embrace strangers, making them feel special.

On a long, hard tour such as India, where the absence of facilities in the more remote areas forced the players to make their own entertainment, a positive team spirit was essential. It was to Greig's credit that he was able to achieve this. Like Illingworth, he cared about their welfare and ensured that they were given single rooms during the Tests. While insisting that everyone made an appearance in the team room each evening, he respected the wishes of those who preferred their own company to a night out on the town, and he made sure that the supporting cast received as much attention as the lead roles. Team discussions were open to all and Greig was good at accepting advice.

He also provided a personal touch, consoling those who were homesick or out of form. 'I could have cried,' he told a grateful Brearley, after the latter had run himself out in the first Test.

From his previous tour to India, Greig had noted how the home batsmen were much more vulnerable to pace than to spin and concluded that they should rely on fast bowling as their main weapon of attack, not least against the tail. According to Brearley, his policy proved highly effective. 'Lever, Willis and Old fired away, while Underwood kept the batsmen quiet – as well as taking wickets – at the other end.' [108]

In the first Test at Delhi it was debutant Lever's ten wickets, along with Amiss's 179, who was primarily responsible for England's innings win.

The seam bowlers were again rampant at Calcutta by dismissing India for 155 in their first innings. England began unsteadily on a sub-standard wicket, and when Greig came in at 90/4 the match was evenly poised. He and the reserve wicketkeeper Roger Tolchard, an inspired selection because of his ability to play spin, survived to stumps, by which time they had cut the deficit to 19. That night Greig contracted a nasty fever, but despite a high temperature the next morning he insisted on continuing his innings in blistering heat. Accepting Barrington's advice that it was a grafting wicket, he and Tolchard set out to occupy the crease, eschewing their natural attacking instincts. Together they put on 142 for the fifth wicket, and after Tolchard left for 67 Greig continued his marathon vigil, finishing the day on 94 with England 147 to the good. He was eventually out for 103 in over seven hours, which in these conditions proved a real gem. Trailing by 166, India collapsed yet again and lost by ten wickets.

He was again to the fore at Madras, sharing a century partnership with Brearley after England had lost their first three wickets for 31. Once more, the Indian batting failed dismally, all out for 164 and 83 respectively, to lose by 200 runs. England had taken an unassailable 3-0 lead in the rubber, but their victory was somewhat tainted by rival captain Bishan Bedi's allegation that Lever, India's main tormentor, had used strips of Vaseline gauze – placed above his eyes by Bernard Thomas, the team physiotherapist, to stop sweat pouring into them – to help swing the ball. It was a wounding accusation to make against a most honest cricketer to help divert attention away from his team's abject performance, but fortunately the scandal soon blew over and Lever was officially exonerated.

Until now, Greig's panegyric to the umpires had paid off handsomely, since the marginal decisions had gone their way, but at Bangalore in the fourth Test their luck ran out. On a turning wicket, the England batsmen, unnerved by the umpiring, played with little conviction and were soundly beaten, and at Bombay they were indebted to an undefeated half-century from Fletcher to secure a draw.

With his all-round performances and his inspirational leadership, Greig had not only become the first England captain since Jardine to win in India, he'd also made the captaincy his own. The BBC's cricket correspondent, Christopher Martin-Jenkins, wrote that while Greig had still much to learn about tactics, he led the team very well. 'Test cricket is all about pressure, and Greig understands this instinctively. It is difficult to think of a player who, both with bat and ball, strives so immediately and constantly to establish his presence, to let his opponents know that he is master and that he is going to dictate the terms.' [109]

To fast bowler Mike Selvey, 'Greig's strength as England captain was not in his tactical acumen, or even man-management skills. Instead, it was rooted deep in charisma like none since Denis Compton was Brylcreeming two decades before, and unmatched since, except by the remarkable Ian Botham. To a man, his players would do anything for him.

'Certainly, he was without question the most inspirational captain under whom I played.' [110]

After a brief visit to Sri Lanka, the team travelled to Australia for the Centenary Test. Although England lost by 45 runs, exactly the same margin of victory as the match in 1877, Greig helped make it the memorable occasion it was by going all out for victory after Randall's marvellous 174.

He returned a hero, but the plaudits soon turned to vitriol when news surfaced of his leading role in helping Australian media magnate Kerry Packer launch his rebel World Series Cricket (WSC) by signing up many of the world's top players. Within days, he'd lost the England captaincy and so much of the respect he'd commanded, not least because of the surreptitious manner in which he'd gone about it. 'However plausibly Greig may claim that what he is doing is for the good of English cricket,' wrote Woodcock, 'no one is likely to be convinced that he has acted less than miserably as the reigning captain.' [111]

Greig played under Brearley in the official home series against Australia in 1977, his farewell to Test cricket before concentrating on promoting WSC in Australia. He captained the World XI, and when peace broke out he joined Channel Nine as a commentator, becoming something of an institution with his distinct accent and ebullient style. Although never receiving an official honour, there was a reconciliation of sorts with his honorary life membership of MCC in 1998 and his invitation to deliver the Cowdrey Spirit of Cricket Lecture in 2012. He died later that year, aged 66.

Mike Brearley

MIKE BREARLEY was born in Harrow on 28 April 1942 to a father good enough to have played cricket in one game for Yorkshire before the war and two games for Middlesex afterwards. A pillar of the Brentham Club in Ealing and a respected teacher at the City of London School, Horace Brearley played a leading influence in his son's development, instilling in him his strong competitive instincts. 'My father is a Yorkshireman,' Brearley told the *Sunday Times* in 1972, 'and I think I've got something of his attitude. I like to try to win.' [112]

Besides being a scholar of some repute, Brearley excelled in all sports at City of London School and he played in the first eleven for five years.

He continued his gilded path at Cambridge, gaining a first-class degree in Classics and an upper second in Moral Sciences, as well as becoming the university's highest-ever run scorer and captaining the Blues with rare maturity.

On the back of his success at Cambridge and Middlesex in 1964, he was chosen for the MCC tour to South Africa that winter but failed to make the grade. After a disappointing season in 1965, he opted for a career in academia at Cambridge and the University of Newcastle. For five years he played little first-class cricket – aside from leading an MCC under-25 tour to Pakistan in 1966/67 – until he returned in 1971 to captain Middlesex. For some time, the county had become mired in mediocrity and Brearley's remit was to pour some new wine into old bottles. His innovative approach won him few friends among the county's old guard such as Titmus, Parfitt and Murray, but once they had retired he was able to shape a team of promising youngsters in his own image.

Resenting being typecast as an intellectual, Brearley, unlike many of his predecessors, possessed that priceless ability to relate to all types. The years spent researching psychology had given him a profound understanding of other people and he enjoyed the challenge of bringing the best out of his players by engaging with them both individually and collectively. He later wrote: 'I wanted a team of 11 people who were all potentially captains and thinking like captains, thinking about the game, others' and their own.' That makes life a bit more difficult. You get arguments and debates. But to get a team together, that is vital.' [113]

By standing up to powerful characters, fighting for the interests of his team and reaching out to the younger players, Brearley created the right spirit. He also proved a master strategist, espousing a more attacking approach and resorting to the unorthodox when necessary. From the moment he took the field, Brearley liked to stamp his authority on all parts of the game. A believer in a balanced attack, he was always looking to seize the initiative by shuffling his bowlers around and encouraging them to bowl different lengths. Setting his fields precisely, he kept making adjustments, especially when the bowler required them, and he possessed that knack of doing precisely what the opposition least wanted him to do.

As Brearley consolidated his authority, so his batting began to improve, and in 1976 he made his Test debut against the West Indies. He lasted only two matches, but Middlesex's championship success that summer helped his appointment as vice-captain to Greig on MCC's tour to India. Although his batting rarely sparkled, his advice and support were much appreciated and when Greig was unceremoniously discarded on return because of his leading role in establishing WSC, Brearley was his obvious successor.

Pitted against Greg Chappell's Australians, he passed his initial trial by winning the Prudential Trophy and was invited to captain England in the first two Tests. Dismissing England cheaply in the first innings, Australia looked set for a big lead until Brearley pegged them back and he then batted manfully in testing conditions. A century from Woolmer and 91 from Greig took England to safety before the bowlers inflicted some late damage on their opponents.

England went one better with a convincing win at Old Trafford, following which Brearley was appointed for the rest of the series. The third Test at Trent Bridge marked the return of Boycott from a three-year Test exile and the debut of Ian Botham. Both excelled in a gripping match and Brearley led the victory charge on the final day with a crisp 81 in England's seven-wicket win.

At Headingley, Boycott scored his 100th century in front of his home supporters, and with Botham again among the wickets, England won by an innings, completing their first hat-trick of victories over Australia on home soil since 1886. Brearley had won his spurs, not least by the deft way in which he'd kept Packer and non-Packer players united in the England set-up. In a season of turbulence and upheaval, his moderation and common sense established him as a force for stability.

Deprived of the Packer players such as Greig, Knott and Underwood, he led an inexperienced side to Pakistan and New Zealand that winter, but after two drawn Tests in Pakistan, he was forced to return home with a broken arm, leaving his vice-captain Boycott in charge. Boycott's time as captain wasn't a success, and Brearley was welcomed back with open arms for the home series against Pakistan. With Botham now a dynamic force with both bat and ball, the tourists offered little resistance and England won comfortably.

New Zealand were no stronger, but Brearley experienced a run famine all season, and after a double failure in the first Test against them the critics began to fret about his future. According to Alex Bannister of the *Daily Mail*, the selectors could carry him for the moment but could they afford to have him captain in Australia when he was short of Test class? 'But such is Brearley's present form, or lack of it,' wrote Woodcock, 'that if he were not the captain he would be out of the side, and the days are past when that is an accepted practice. Because England are at ease under Brearley and play the better for being so, it is much to be hoped that he will, as it were, pull through.' [114]

His players remained rock solid behind him and after he reached a pedestrian fifty in the second Test, batting now at number five, they celebrated in style on the pavilion balcony. The crisis had passed and, with New Zealand comprehensively beaten 3-0, Brearley was duly chosen to lead in Australia.

With the home side badly depleted by the loss of many players to WSC, England started as favourites and won the first two Tests easily enough, despite the absence of any runs from Brearley.

His nightmare run continued in the defeat at Melbourne, his first as England captain, and once again the debate about his place in the team resurfaced. 'Can a man who is neither holding his catches nor scoring runs justify his place in the side?' wrote *The Guardian*'s Paul Fitzpatrick. [115] Comparisons with former captain Denness, who dropped himself after scoring 65 runs in the first three Tests on the previous tour of Australia, were made, and Brearley, with an even worse record, did consider his position, but, bolstered by the wholesale backing of his players, he vowed to keep going.

England's batting had been fragile all series, but little excused their abject batting on the opening day of the crucial fourth Test at Sydney. All out for 152, their out-cricket was equally insipid as Australia reached 56/1 by stumps. At the instigation of fast bowler Mike Hendrick, Brearley called the team together and quietly berated them for their slipshod performance and demanded a wholehearted effort on the morrow. They duly responded with a plucky display in the suffocating heat, and, with Brearley handling his bowlers with typical canniness, Australia slipped from 126/1 to 247/7 by the close.

Dismissed for 294, the home side's lead of 142 looked all the more formidable once Boycott was out to the first ball of the innings. Brearley and Randall proceeded with care throughout the afternoon session and only began to play a few shots after tea. Brearley was out for 53, but Randall went remorselessly on to make 150. England were all out for 346 on the last morning and, on a turning wicket, their spinners, Geoff Miller and John Emburey, aided by Brearley's masterly field placings, preyed on the nerves of the Australian batsmen, bowling them out for 111 to retain the Ashes. England had come back from the dead and Brearley, the architect of their revival, was lauded by the critics, *The Observer*'s Scyld Berry calling his leadership the difference between victory and defeat.

They won the last two Tests easily enough to take the series 5-1, and Brearley's standing within his team was elevated to unprecedented heights. They not only respected him for his tactical expertise but also for his ability to relate to one and all. According to wicketkeeper Bob Taylor, Brearley was the only man who could handle Boycott and Botham properly, 'the former by quiet cajolery and Botham through a mixture of leg-pulling and firm leadership'. [116]

A fellow opener and grafter, Brearley respected Boycott's single-minded approach to batting and made due allowances for his mercurial personality. Even when Boycott spoke out against Brearley or boasted about his superior batting, Brearley didn't overreact to his jibes. He treated him fairly, sought out his views and was sensitive to the fact that he'd never felt appreciated. 'His attitude was balanced and honest and I don't think you can ask for more; certainly, I never did,' Boycott wrote in his autobiography. 'I suppose at the end of the day I felt that Mike understood me. He did not always agree with me but he did not try to change me. If I wanted extra nets, he would be the first to make the arrangements; when I appeared undemonstrative on the field he never mistook it for lack of interest.' [117] Acknowledging his natural approach, which made co-operation logical, Boycott reckoned he would have been an even better player had Brearley captained him more frequently.

The suggestion that Brearley, 13 years Botham's senior, was fortunate to captain him at the start of his Test career when he was at his most eager and productive contains some truth. According to John Lever, 'Brearley realised at a very early stage in Botham's career that, for all his massive talent and boundless self-confidence, the youngster desperately needed someone to believe in him. And Brearley showed Botham that he did by giving him his head and never trying to restrain his natural attacking instincts.' [118]

Off the field, Brearley liked Botham's friendliness, boyish humour and zest for life and admired his commitment to the team, not least his personal support when he was short of runs. Even their contrasting lifestyles presented no problem, since Brearley was relaxed about his players' private lives provided they performed on the field. 'I don't ever remember having to speak about his behaviour after hours,' he later recalled, 'although it's true I might not have known what was going on.' [119] In the opinion of spinner Phil Edmonds, Brearley and Botham were close because they didn't pose a threat to each other. 'Beefy needed to dominate a dressing room physically, whereas Brears wanted to shine intellectually. Brears relied heavily on Both's animal strength and they respected each other enormously.' [120]

As long as he was getting the best out of Botham, Brearley felt able to cut him some slack, not least at net practice, a ritual Botham always disliked, especially once the Tests had started. Yet for all the banter and high jinks, Brearley would pull rank when necessary. There were explosive spats on the field when he refused to give Botham the third slip he craved, or when Botham failed to bowl to the field that he had given him. At Sydney, during the 1979/80 Test series, it was Botham's impulsiveness with the bat that landed him in trouble. An irresponsible swipe against Greg Chappell in the second Test, after a plucky 43 by the night-watchman Underwood had played England back into the game, earned him a stinging rebuke from Brearley. Opener Graham Gooch noted that in the verbal battle between the two of them there would only ever be one winner. At the lunch interval on the final day of the England–Australia Test at Edgbaston in 1981, Taylor recalled Botham's reluctance to bowl again. As they were about to go out and field, Brearley saw him putting on his Nike tennis shoes and told him to get his bowling boots on. When Botham once again expressed reluctance, Brearley's voice changed and repeated his order, which Botham complied with. 'A lesser captain would have ducked down to him and Beefy would have got away with it,' Taylor commented. [121] 'I don't know what it is, but I took stuff from him that I'd clip other guys round the ear for,' Botham later admitted. 'There is something about Brears. He knows how I feel and what I am thinking. He makes better communication with players than any other captain I've known.' [122]

The one exception to Brearley's adroit management was Edmonds, with whom he had a heated altercation during the Perth Test when he objected to Edmonds's casual approach to 12th-man duties. Originally friends and allies against the old guard at Middlesex, they found each other's company stimulating, but as time went on their relationship began to unravel, their mutual regard giving way to mutual contempt. He [Brearley] had this need to dominate the dressing room intellectually, Edmonds later recalled, 'And I always spoke out.' [123]

His constant barbs to Brearley's suggestions did him no favours, Brearley declaring that he was the most difficult person he ever captained. 'For some reason, Phil could always wind Mike up,' commented Taylor. 'Phil seemed to think that Mike wasn't the only man in the squad with a Cambridge degree and he would be rather assertive about that. Mike would sometimes fly off the handle at Phil, even though a man of his intellect and psychological depth should surely have realised that Edmonds was just trying to rile him. I suppose every man has his blind spots and Edmonds was certainly one with Mike.' [124]

As Edmonds's stock continued to plummet, he increasingly felt slighted by Brearley and there would be quarrels about field placings and the way Edmonds was bowling. Not surprisingly, after their set-to in Australia, his appearances for England under Brearley were strictly limited.

After leading England to the final of the 1979 World Cup, Brearley continued to underperform in the four-Test home series against India – which England won 1-0 – but the media were now more concerned as to whether he would be available for the winter tour.

Following on from the outbreak of peace between the Australian Board and WSC, a hastily arranged itinerary, in which Australia played three Tests each against England and the West Indies and a triangular limited-overs tournament, was devised. The details hadn't been settled before England flew out and when Brearley expressed reservations about some of the experimental playing conditions in the triangular tournament, he was immediately slated for being obstructive.

His popularity didn't increase when he placed every single fielder, including the wicketkeeper, on the boundary to stop the West Indies winning the first one-day international (ODI), and thereafter he became a perennial target for abuse. The hostility didn't seem to affect his batting, since he enjoyed one of his most productive series as an England player, but it might well have contributed to the general fatigue which slightly diminished his captaincy. After England had lost all three Tests, he admitted that he'd been too relaxed with certain players and that he hadn't spent enough time with them off the field. Boycott and Willis criticised the lackadaisical approach to practice and *Wisden* reported that Brearley wasn't as positive as he might have been in countering the many problems.

On returning home, he announced he wouldn't be available for any further overseas tours, and with the selectors deciding on an immediate change of leadership they went with his recommendation of Botham. It proved to be an ill-fated choice because Botham not only struggled to motivate his players, he also suffered an alarming decline in his own form. After 12 matches without a win, his time in charge came to an inglorious end against Australia at Lord's in 1981 and an SOS went out to Brearley. He agreed to lead the side for the next three Tests, later extended to four, and was welcomed back with open arms by the players. With Australia one up in the series, he had his work cut out, and for three and a half days of the third Test there appeared to be little that he could do to prevent another defeat. On a typical Headingley wicket, Australia, with some luck, scored 401/9 declared before Lillee, Terry Alderman and Geoff Lawson went to work on the England batsmen. Forced to follow on 227 behind, they were heading for oblivion when Botham, partnered by Graham Dilley, Old and Willis, played one of the most remarkable innings in Test history. His 149* not only restored his self-confidence, it also allowed England to dream of the impossible. Over drinks the night before the denouement, Brearley agreed to Willis's suggestion that he should bowl fast and straight in the second innings and told him not to worry about no-balls, a recent fault which had caused him to reduce his pace, for, given the nature of the pitch, Willis possessed the pace and bounce to run through the opposition.

Before they went out to field, Brearley called for more aggression and more encouragement for the bowlers. The Australians, needing 130 for victory, would be the nervous ones, he stressed, and on that pitch anything could happen.

His words seemed more in hope than expectation, as Australia proceeded comfortably to 56/1, before Brearley, at Willis's request, switched him to the Kirkstall Lane End, which gave him the slope and the breeze. The effect was dramatic. Quickly into his stride, Willis bowled with fearsome hostility, and within the course of six overs either side of lunch he took six wickets.

With Old taking the crucial wicket of Allan Border, Australia slumped to 75/8. Lillee and Ray Bright then added 35 in four overs with some swipes, forcing Brearley on to the defensive, but, critically, he held his nerve. With a mere 21 needed, he told Willis, on advice from Mike Gatting, to keep bowling straight at Lillee and, four balls later, Lillee chipped a straight half-volley to mid-on where Gatting held an acrobatic catch. When Willis capped an astounding performance by uprooting Bright's middle stump, he'd bowled England to a miraculous victory by 18 runs, only the second time in Test cricket that the side following on had gone on to win. 'Willis bowled fantastically,' recalled Graham Gooch, 'but it was Brearley who instilled that will to win in us.' [125] 'Brearley made the right bowling changes, field placings, squeezed the runs,' concurred David Gower. 'He knew what he was doing. We didn't question him.' [126]

After a summer of economic hardship and social discontent, manifest by inner-city riots, Headingley helped raise national morale and the wedding of Prince Charles to Lady Diana Spencer days later only added to the euphoria. This robust patriotism was on display throughout the fourth Test at Edgbaston, particularly on the unforgettable final day when Brearley once again provided the alchemist's touch. In a taut, low-scoring contest, England were indebted to their lower order for setting Australia any kind of target. Although Brearley kept their batsmen in check, they seemed to be edging towards the 150 they needed when he played his trump card. At 115/5 he recalled Botham, sensing that he had a psychological hold over the Australians. Brushing aside his reluctance to bowl,

Brearley told him to run in hard and, urged on by a baying crowd, Botham acted entirely to script by taking the five remaining wickets for one run in 28 deliveries. While his magnetism administered the final knock-out blow, he acknowledged the great part played by Brearley and his astute field placings. 'It was brilliant captaincy,' recalled former Australian captain Richie Benaud, 'an exhibition showing Brearley had correctly gauged the strength and weakness of the opposition, which is one of the vital things in cricket leadership. I have seen a lot of captains unwilling to take with their minds the risk which they know in their hearts is worth the gamble. Brearley was never like that even in defeat and he deserves full marks for it.' [127]

Botham went on to play another brilliant innings at Old Trafford, enabling England to win a third successive Test and retain the Ashes. When Brearley finally bowed out of international cricket with a fifty in the drawn game at the Oval, he could reflect on a proud unbeaten home record in 18 Tests as captain, and that his 58.06 percentage success rate in 31 Tests as captain is exceeded only by W.G. Grace and Douglas Jardine among England captains who led in more than ten Tests. Facts, of course, don't tell the whole story. 'The statistics suggest that he is one of the great England captains,' wrote Illingworth, 'the luckiest would be nearer the truth' [128] – a tart observation that contained an element of truth. Brearley never captained against the mighty West Indies and many of his 18 victories were gained against depleted sides in the Packer era.

Furthermore, he had an all-rounder of exceptional ability in Botham to win him games which might otherwise have been lost. Yet while Botham was good for Brearley, it is also true to say that, as 1981 showed, Brearley brought the best out of Botham and Willis, both of whom had lost their lustre over the previous year. His advice, encouragement and support allowed them to play their natural game and his composed optimism enabled the rest of the team to believe in miracles when they might have given up the ghost. According to Boycott, Brearley's reputation for man-management was no myth. He had no hesitation in rating him the best captain with whom he played. It was an opinion shared by the majority of his England team-mates. Illingworth, it is true, had his supporters, but even Edmonds, for all his disagreements with Brearley, placed his leadership on the highest of pedestals. 'There are so many things I admire, and like, about Brears. In purely cricketing terms, he is the best captain I have ever seen. The tremendous thing was the way in which we were always trying to achieve something positive in the field when Brears was in charge. Even when the situation warranted a defensive action, it was positive defence, with a constructive aim in mind. We were not meandering about aimlessly, as has happened with some England captains.' [129]

In 1982 Brearley marked his final season with Middlesex by leading them to another championship, their fourth in seven years. He then changed direction by training as a psychoanalyst, becoming in time the president of the British Psychoanalytical Society. He has also written on cricket as an occasional columnist and author, most notably his *The Art of Captaincy*, published in 1985 to much acclaim, and served MCC as president, trustee and committee man, in particular as chairman of the World Cricket Committee from 2011 to 2017.

Geoff Boycott

GEOFF BOYCOTT was born in Fitzwilliam, Yorkshire, on 21 October 1940. Both his father and paternal grandfather were employed in the local pits and his father suffered severe damage to his spine in a pit accident, which brought about his premature death.

Keen to escape the narrow confines of a mining community – although he lived with his mother until her death in 1978 – Boycott used his talent for cricket, first nurtured in the backyard of his home, as a passport to better times. Acknowledging his genuine ability, his family found the money they could ill-afford to pay for his weekly coaching sessions at the former Somerset leg-spinner Johnny Lawrence's indoor school at Rothwell. The journey involved three long bus journeys and a mile's walk to reach it, often in bitter weather, but Boycott never complained, especially since Lawrence was an esteemed coach.

By the age of 13, he was playing league cricket for Ackworth and, at 15, he captained his school team, Hemsworth Grammar, a cut above the other boys. Fiercely determined to become a cricket professional, he left school at 17 to work as a clerical officer at the Ministry of Pensions for the next five years. He continued his cricket at Barnsley with Dicky Bird, later a world-class umpire, and Michael Parkinson, the future television presenter, as team-mates, but while impressing everyone with his dedication and mental toughness, his future greatness wasn't yet apparent.

A move to Leeds enhanced his prospects and, after some sterling performances in the Yorkshire second eleven, he made his debut for the first team in 1962. The strength of his ambition set against the fierce competition for places merely reinforced his fixation for practice, and in 1963 his geese turned to swans. The Cricket Writers' Club made him Young Cricketer of the Year, and in 1964 he won the first of his 108 England caps against Australia, his maiden century coming in the final Test at the Oval.

For the next decade, he was England's first-choice opener, aside from his controversial one-match omission in 1967 for scoring 246* against India too slowly. On tour to the West Indies in 1967/68, and in Australia in 1970/71, he rarely batted better, but his greatness as a player came at a cost. To friend and foe alike, he remained a problematic individual – moody, selfish and obsessive – his bombastic self-confidence concealing a streak of deep insecurity. For all his tactical acumen, his failure to relate to his team-mates blighted his captaincy of Yorkshire between 1971 and 1978 and compromised his chances of captaining England. When Denness was appointed successor to Illingworth in 1973, Boycott's disillusion was such that he rarely cooperated with him on tour to the West Indies, and after a double failure against India in the first Test in 1974 he went into voluntary exile for three years. He used this time to concentrate on Yorkshire before returning in triumph against Australia in 1977 with a century in the Trent Bridge Test. He followed this up with another in the Headingley Test – his 100th century – in front of his home crowd, undoubtedly his proudest moment. His reward was the vice-captaincy of England's tour to Pakistan and New Zealand that winter, a weakened side because of the Packer defections, and when captain Brearley broke his arm in an inconsequential match in Pakistan, his dream of captaining England had at last come true. He initially won the support of his players by vigorously backing their opposition to the home side playing their Packer players in the third Test at Karachi, to the point of threatening a strike. Although the Pakistan board backed down and the match went ahead, it ended in a tedious draw.

From Pakistan to New Zealand, where some very different conditions taxed England's inexperienced batsmen, placing a greater onus on Boycott to succeed. On winning the toss in the first Test at Wellington, he inserted his hosts and bowled them out for 228. England replied with 215, of which Boycott made 77 in over seven hours, hardly an innings to inspire his players. Set 137 to win on a sub-standard wicket, Boycott went early, whereupon the floodgates opened as the team were brushed aside for 64, their first-ever defeat against New Zealand. Gatting, who wasn't playing in the match, recalls his first experience of what a disgruntled Boycott could be like. 'It was not pleasant. He was having a bad trot himself, and when other batsmen failed in Wellington he accused everybody of playing like schoolkids. He didn't shout, but he was brutally blunt.' [130]

When Boycott was out cheaply in the next match against Young New Zealand, he took his frustration out on Gatting and Paul Downton, the young reserve wicketkeeper. 'We'd teamed up to play golf, and were looking forward to it,' recalled Gatting, 'but instead we had to bowl that afternoon at a grim Boycott in the nets. He had us running in, knackered, for nearly two hours, along with an assortment of schoolkids, so it wasn't much practice for him anyway.' [131]

England won the second Test at Christchurch despite, rather than because of, Boycott's captaincy. Geoff Cope, his Yorkshire team-mate, recalls that he delayed the toss and when he returned to the pavilion Lever asked who was playing. There was silence, and Boycott started putting his pads on so they found a scorecard to discover who'd been selected. 'Then he got out lbw. He sat in a corner with his hands on his knees, pads on. Two hours later he was still there.' [132]

With Botham making a superb maiden Test century, England scored 418 and gained a first-innings lead of 183. Time, however, was short, and Boycott's failure to accelerate proved highly detrimental to the interests of the team. Increasingly frustrated by his approach, Botham came to the wicket and deliberately ran him out, a dismissal that sent Boycott into total despair. Sitting on a bench in the corner with a towel over his head, he showed no interest in the side, and when Edmonds asked him whether he should pad up, Boycott replied that Willis, the vice-captain, was responsible for the batting order.

The next morning, despite being 279 ahead on a sporting wicket, Boycott's refusal to declare provoked mutiny in the ranks. It needed the forceful intervention of manager Barrington and Willis to make him finally see sense. He later took credit for England's win after Willis and Botham dismissed New Zealand for 105 in three hours.

With the third Test ending in stalemate, the team returned home having unearthed little new talent, aside from Botham's great leap forward as a dynamic international all-rounder. While Boycott's abrasive style brought the best out of Edmonds in a way that Brearley could never do, and youngsters such as Randall, Lever and Gatting all benefitted from his technical expertise, his captaincy failed to inspire. Willis felt he was too cautious and defensive and, according to Botham, 'Geoff Boycott could never be a successful captain of England, because he could never command the respect of the players. He was too self-centred. He has sold his soul for his average – a sorry epitaph.' [133]

His captaincy also lacked the diplomatic touch. As a perfectionist himself, Boycott expected the best possible conditions in which to practise and when, by his reckoning, his hosts failed to deliver, he had no hesitation in saying so. At Temuka, venue for the match against Young New Zealand, the cricket journalist Don Mosey recollected that the rural community had gone to great lengths to welcome the England team, yet the pitch and general hospitality failed to measure up with Boycott. His comments greatly offended his hosts. His blunt outspokenness also led to ruptures with manager Ken Barrington, especially his aggressive press conference after England's defeat in the first Test when, in response to unflattering comparisons with Brearley, Boycott launched into a full-scale assault on the New Zealand press.

Increasingly, captain and manager began to go their separate ways, conferring only when necessary. The effects of this strained relationship were to be felt when the team returned home. Barrington requested a personal meeting with the authorities at Lord's, at which he spelt out his reservations about Boycott's captaincy, and when the England side to play Pakistan that summer was announced, Brearley was back as captain. 'When he took over after I broke my arm,' Brearley later wrote, '[Boycott] won little except the recognition that he was not the man to captain England.' [134]

Within months of losing the England captaincy, Boycott was deposed as Yorkshire captain. He continued to play for his country until 1982, before masterminding a rebel England tour to apartheid South Africa, which effectively ended his Test career. His final years with Yorkshire were scarred by rancour and division following the committee's attempt to dismiss him in 1983. He finally retired in 1986, aged 45, and became a respected, if outspoken, cricket commentator on radio and television. He was knighted in 2019 for services to cricket.

The Age of
Instability: 1980–89

B REARLEY'S success looks all the more impressive when compared to the fate of his successors during the 1980s. At a time when England had David Gower, Graham Gooch, Mike Gatting, Ian Botham, John Emburey, Phil Edmonds and Allan Lamb in their prime, it seems incredible to think that their record should be such a dismal one, with only 19.2 per cent of their games ending in victory, the worst of any decade bar the 1940s when England was recovering from the ravages of war. None of the seven captains post-Brearley in this decade was able to bring any consistency/stability to the team. The rigours of county cricket, the surfeit of injuries, the chaotic selection system, two rebel tours to South Africa, the hedonistic lifestyle and the casual approach to practice all played their part, alongside the deficiencies of many a captain.

Following the failure of the veteran Keith Fletcher to impose himself on England's tour to India in 1981/82, he was sacked by the new chairman of selectors Peter May, and Bob Willis became the first fast bowler to captain England since Gubby Allen. It said much for Willis's staying power that he remained a leading wicket-taker during his two years in charge, but the effort he expended on his bowling compromised his captaincy, and after a dismal tour to New Zealand and Pakistan in 1983/84 he was relieved of his responsibilities.

He was replaced by David Gower who was a throwback to the Golden Age with his debonair charm alongside his elegant batting and chivalrous approach to the game. His batting helped him win the Ashes in 1985, the prelude to presiding over a calamitous tour to the West Indies the following winter when he suffered a second 5-0 whitewash by his opponents. It wasn't merely the margin of defeat which grated, but also the manner in which it came about, especially the slipshod approach to practice, and for this Gower was deemed responsible. He lasted only one further match in charge before he was discarded for his vice-captain, Gatting, only then to be restored to favour against Australia in 1989. It proved to be an unhappy second coming as England lost 4-0 to Australia, and even the phlegmatic Gower was rattled by the intense press scrutiny. At the end of a disastrous summer, he wasn't only replaced as captain but was also omitted from the team to tour the West Indies.

In contrast to Gower, Gatting was a man from the ranks with a bullish personality and a fierce determination to win. Despite losing his first two series against India and New Zealand in 1986, his stock rose considerably when retaining the Ashes in Australia, but, with Botham's powers very much on the wane, England lost to Pakistan both at home and away in 1987. The series in Pakistan followed an acrimonious one in England, and Gatting's simmering discontent with the officiating boiled over in an unseemly confrontation with umpire Shakoor Rana in the second Test at Faisalabad. He was now on borrowed time, but his dismissal came over some trumped-up tabloid charge about his private life, lamentably handled by both the selectors and the TCCB. It was the beginning of a shambolic summer in which England fielded four captains against the West Indies, culminating in Gooch, whose leadership prowess wasn't rated by the new chairman of selectors, Ted Dexter, hence his return to Gower for the Australian series in 1989 following the veto of Gatting by the TCCB on the ground that he hadn't done sufficient penance for his past misdemeanours.

With the ousting of Gower for a second time, Dexter felt he had little choice but to return to Gooch. It proved to be a defining moment in the history of the captaincy because after all the upheavals of the previous decade a period of stability was now imperative.

Ian Botham

IAN BOTHAM was born in Heswall, Cheshire, on 24 November 1955, but was raised in Yeovil, Somerset, where his father worked for Westland Helicopters. A precocious teenager at Buckler's Mead Comprehensive School, his cricketing talent was such that he played for Somerset colts aged 13. Leaving school at 16, he worked for two years on the Lord's ground staff, where his lowly status fired his rebellious instincts. Never short of self-belief, he bristled at the lack of recognition in his potential and left there all the more determined to prove his critics wrong.

In 1974 he began a one-year contract with Somerset and, joining a gifted group of youngsters such as Viv Richards, Peter Roebuck and Vic Marks, they prospered under the firm but inspirational leadership of Close. After three years of steady progress, he made a dream debut for England against Australia at Trent Bridge in 1977, taking five wickets in the first innings. He took another five in the next Test at Headingley, a match which saw England regain the Ashes.

With Greig now departing England for WSC, Botham emerged as his heir apparent, and on tour in New Zealand that winter and back home the following summer he captivated the crowds with his exhilarating performances with both bat and ball.

He played a leading part in the retention of the Ashes in Australia in 1978/79 and continued to prosper under Brearley's leadership. When appointed to the selection committee on the tour to Australia the following winter, he impressed Brearley with his technical grasp, his commitment to the team and his leadership in the minor games, while his stunning all-round performance in the one-off Jubilee Test against India at Bombay further illumined his star.

On their return home, Brearley announced that he was no longer available to tour, and, although he stated his willingness to stay on for the summer series against the West Indies to help his successor settle in, the selectors opted for an immediate change. Unwilling to appoint an outsider not worth his place in the team or contemplate a return to Boycott, they fell in with Brearley's recommendation and appointed the 24-year-old Botham, despite his lack of experience in leadership. The decision wasn't unanimous. Close, Botham's mentor at Somerset, felt that he shouldn't be burdened with such a responsibility at his age, particularly against a side as powerful as the West Indies, but his was a minority voice in a country which acclaimed Botham's heroic stature.

Initially appointed for the two ODIs, his match-winning batting in the second game at Lord's gained him the leadership for the Test series. He began in encouraging fashion with 57 in the first Test at Trent Bridge, a game England narrowly lost by two wickets. Thereafter the gap between the two sides widened and only bad weather prevented the West Indies from winning any more games, but the longer the summer progressed, the greater Botham's retreat from the Olympian peaks. He ended the summer with a duck in the Centenary Test against Australia at Lord's and his failure to make a game of it only added to the crescendo of criticism against him, which included gratuitous attacks on his expanding girth and his family.

Although the selectors stuck with him for the winter tour to the West Indies, an arduous assignment grew ever more taxing, when, shortly before their departure, he was arrested on an assault charge in Scunthorpe – he was later found not guilty – bringing him further unwelcome publicity.

From the beginning of the trip, England were plagued by bad weather, inadequate practice facilities and inefficient travel plans, but while Botham remained determined throughout, he failed to appreciate the needs of each player. His captaincy was instinctive, often superb, but his judgement of character and treatment of others was poor, noted Gooch. 'I believe he didn't really understand what the players needed as individuals, he lacked that knack of fine tuning that coaxes that extra couple of per cent out of someone.' [135]

His relaxed lifestyle and aversion to practice didn't sit easily with those of a more disciplined bent. Boycott wrote of his lack of maturity: 'Terrorising the dressing room, half dislocating the odd shoulder and sitting on somebody's chest may be okay for a player of elephantine stature, especially with a captain at hand to call a halt when it threatens to get out of hand. It is no behaviour for a captain who will later have to call for greater discipline and sense of responsibility from his players.' [136]

These divisions were apparent to Viv Richards. 'He was not supported well enough as captain by some of the senior guys. You didn't need to be in the same dressing room to find that out. You could see that just from looking at the way they responded to him. There were some clashes. Beefy was too casual in some ways.' [137]

Following a delayed start to the first Test at Port of Spain, Botham inserted the West Indies, and their openers, Gordon Greenidge and Desmond Haynes, responded with a partnership of 168, the foundation of their side's 426/9 declared. England then collapsed to 178 all out and followed on 248 behind, but with interruptions for bad weather and the pitch still in good condition, they had high hopes of saving the game. Ever the optimist, Botham pronounced bullishly that if his side were to lose heads would roll. His words came back to haunt him when England lost by an innings and Botham holed out to Richards's gentle off spin at a critical stage. His partner Boycott wrote: 'I could not believe it and neither could Richards; he almost went berserk with delight. Botham had played the wrong shot in our situation and the wrong shot on that pitch, where the uneven bounce made it difficult to time a forcing stroke in the air.' [138]

The party flew to Guyana without vice-captain Willis, who retired home with injured knee ligaments, depriving Botham of a much-valued source of advice. After the cancellation of the Test there, caused by the government's objection to the presence of Willis's replacement

Robin Jackman, with his South African connections, they moved on to Barbados and more trouble. Not only did they suffer the grievous loss of assistant manager Barrington, who died of a heart attack in the middle of the third Test, they also lost by 298 runs. Although they showed great spirit to draw the final two games, Botham was made the scapegoat for their 2-0 loss. His personal form – 73 runs at an average of 10.42 and 15 wickets at 32.80 – had plummeted, which in turn had undermined his authority as captain. Worn down by an avalanche of personal criticism, and reluctant to accept advice from his team-mates, Botham cut an increasingly aloof and troubled figure. 'I've never seen him like that, he was withdrawn and negative,' wrote his friend Trevor Gard, the Somerset wicketkeeper who met up with him in Antigua during the fourth Test. 'It looked as if it was all getting on top of him.' [139] Jackman recalled how he was summoned to his room at the end of the tour. 'I had never before seen this colossus of a man so broken. I never thought I would see Ian Botham openly shed a tear but he did that night and I was privileged to be the one that he sought out to provide solace.' [140]

According to Boycott, Botham suffered in the West Indies – and England suffered as a result – from his lack of experience and technical skill as a captain on the field, not least some of his field placings. 'Nobody – not even a player as highly talented as Botham – can expect to cram into three Test years the experience and worldliness which most county captains take ten years or more to sharpen into a fine edge.' [141]

Given Botham's fall from grace, the selectors were minded to dispense with his services as captain for the forthcoming series against Australia, but with a lack of obvious alternatives they appointed him on a match-by-match basis. Having lost the ODIs 2-1, he was then appointed for the first Test at Trent Bridge, a low-scoring match which England lost by four wickets, mainly because of their fallible catching. Brearley, from his vantage in the press box, noted Botham's reluctance to bowl on a pitch tailor-made for him and his failure to impose himself on the game.

Increasingly resentful of all the criticism, he again appeared listless in the second Test at Lord's. Wicketkeeper Taylor remarked how he couldn't get the players going in the warm-ups and nets. In a dull game that ended inconclusively, Botham was out for a pair and he walked back to the pavilion on the final day in stony silence without even a consoling hand from the MCC members. In his 12 matches as England captain, he'd scored 276 runs at an average of 13.80 and his 35 wickets had cost 32 apiece. No wonder he now felt like falling on his sword, but the selectors had already decided to depose him. It was his misfortune that he'd been handed the captaincy at such a young age and that all of his matches in charge were against the West Indies and Australia. Yet, equally, the very qualities that made him such a charismatic all-rounder rather conspired against his capacity for leadership. 'Right to the very end, Ian never quite learned the art which Mike Brearley perfects, of making individuals feel good in themselves and also part of a motivated unit who expect to win,' wrote Gooch in his diary. [142] According to Botham's most recent biographer Simon Wilde, 'Like Geoff Boycott before him, Botham had wanted the England captaincy and yet when it came to it his personality, like Boycott's, proved unsuited to the challenge.' [143]

Once liberated from the England captaincy, Botham returned to his brilliant best with his match-winning exploits against the Australians. For the next few years he remained one of the world's leading cricketers, before injury and additional weight reduced his effectiveness. He resigned the Somerset captaincy at the end of 1985 after two years in office and left the county the following year in protest at the dismissal of his good friends Richards and Joel Garner. He spent several years at Worcestershire before finishing his career at Durham. He retired in 1993 and went into the media as a commentator and analyst for Sky Sports. He was knighted in 2007 for services to charity and cricket.

Keith Fletcher

KEITH FLETCHER was born in Worcester on 20 May 1944. His parents were Londoners who had taken refuge with relatives after being bombed out of their home. In 1947 the family moved to Cambridgeshire. At the age of 13 he opened the batting with his father for the local village, Caldecote. Two years later he played club cricket for Royston, Jack Hobbs's old club, where he scored his first century. Recommended to Essex, he made his debut for them aged 17, and in no time he became their leading batsman, impressing with his range of shots and immaculate timing.

Selected for the England under-25 tour to Pakistan in 1966/67, he was first capped against Australia at Headingley in 1968. Preferred to the Yorkshire slip specialist Phil Sharpe, he incurred the derision of the home crowd by dropping several hard chances at slip and failing to score in the first innings.

A painfully shy person who felt out of place in the England dressing room, it took him five years to establish himself at Test level and even during his prime years of 1973/74 he rarely played with the same fluency he displayed at Essex. Vulnerable to the pace of Lillee and Thomson in Australia in 1974/75, he was dropped the following summer and was lost to Test cricket, aside from a brief return on the tour to India and Australia in 1976/77, until his appointment as captain in succession to Brearley in 1981.

In many ways, to pick a 37-year-old as captain who hadn't played for England for nearly five years seemed a retrograde step, but his record at Essex and his experience in India were major considerations in his favour.

Always a shrewd tactician whose advice was highly valued by captains such as Lewis and Greig, Fletcher had proved himself at Essex by turning a team of laughing cavaliers into a highly professional unit, their first championship arriving in 1979. Adept at seizing the initiative and promoting a winning mentality, Fletcher, like Brearley, knew how to get the best out of his men by treating them as individuals, by his constant encouragement and by keeping them amused with his quirky humour.

Inheriting Brearley's mantle was no easy inheritance, but Fletcher was leading a side that had beaten Australia so memorably the previous summer and contained a nice mixture of youth and experience. They began promisingly, winning three of their first four games, including the first ODI, only then to come unstuck in the first Test at Bombay. On a poor pitch, they erred by playing an additional bowler at the expense of their batting and allowing some flawed umpiring to get the better of them, the result being that they played with little conviction in either innings and lost by 136 runs.

The umpiring continued to haunt Fletcher in the second Test at Bangalore. Given out caught at the wicket for 25 when he swept Ravi Shastri, the left-arm spinner, his disillusion was such that he used his bat to knock off the bails as he turned for the pavilion. *Wisden* called it 'an unworthy reaction from someone who had been at pains to tell his team to accept the umpiring for what it was'. [144] Accepting his misdemeanour – the only on-field one in his career – Fletcher apologised to the president of India's Board of Control, but the media gave the incident maximum publicity and it made a terrible impression on Peter May, the incoming chairman of selectors.

On a lifeless wicket, the Bangalore Test drifted to a draw and, confronted with India's negative tactics now that they were one up, Fletcher appreciated that his batsmen needed to show more aggression in order to give the bowlers time to force a result. Prior to the third Test he informed a press conference that Boycott and Chris Tavare, his two most cautious batsmen, had been instructed to be more positive at the crease. His comments made headlines in the papers back home, and when Boycott received one such copy he took exception to them, especially since Fletcher had never spoken to him about such matters. While many players would have dismissed the story as journalist licence, Boycott wasn't quite so appeased, especially since he was in a depressed state at the time. Having upset the Indian government of Indira Gandhi by playing in South Africa in contravention of the Gleneagles Agreement of 1977, which discouraged sporting links there, he'd been advised by the manager Raman Subba Row to stay off politics, advice which caused some tension between the two of them. He also fretted about his position at Yorkshire, the primitive accommodation up country and some of the travelling arrangements, all of which posed a threat to his health and general wellbeing.

When Boycott confronted Fletcher about his comments at the press conference, Fletcher insisted that he'd been misquoted, but Boycott, armed with a tape recording of the exchange, felt able to prove his point and force Fletcher to publicly apologise. The incident did nothing to improve his already taut relationship with captain and manager. Although Fletcher tried to accommodate Boycott's fads, Boycott refused his requests for tactical advice, did little to help the youngsters and detached himself from the team more than normal. His century at Delhi, otherwise another immemorable draw, saw him become the leading run scorer in Test cricket, a long-held ambition, but any upsurge in his spirits proved to be ephemeral.

The fourth Test at Calcutta turned out to be his last for England. Claiming to be unwell, he didn't field in India's second innings and went off to play golf without permission from the management. His egregiousness outraged his team-mates, and when ordered to apologise by Subba Row and Fletcher he requested a return home, a request the management agreed to. Within days of his return, he was putting the finishing touches to the England rebel tour to South Africa, which involved several of his team-mates in India.

Calcutta provided England's best chance of victory. Having gained a lead of 40 on first innings, an enterprising 60* by Fletcher in the second innings gave his bowlers six hours to bowl out India on a pitch where the ball was turning and keeping low. Smog, however, delayed play for 70 minutes the next morning, much to Fletcher's consternation, and he and four other players sat down in the middle in protest after the umpires had taken the players off for bad light.

With two lifeless pitches producing two more drawn games, England lost a series for the third winter running. A comfortable victory in Sri Lanka's inaugural Test did little to ease the disappointment of a tour which abounded in turgid cricket. While Fletcher was a popular captain who scored useful runs, his leadership had been surprisingly lacklustre, especially England's dilatory over rate (India's was no better). According to Scyld Berry, he failed to fully motivate his men and get them to play above themselves; and to Taylor, his success on the field with individuals was tempered by his lack of conviction at team meetings when he just stated the obvious. Brearley, covering part of the tour for the *Sunday Times*, thought that selection was awry, for having played an additional bowler for the first Test when, on a dubious pitch, they should have strengthened the batting, they then settled on a four-man attack for the next three Tests on lifeless wickets when they were one down in the series.

On returning home, Fletcher was offered £45,000 to play in South Africa but declined, placing his loyalty to the England captaincy above the lure of the rand. Given their respectable performance in India and the lack of an obvious alternative, Fletcher expected to retain the captaincy for the summer Tests against India and Pakistan. It was thus a considerable shock when he received a telephone call from May to tell him that the selectors had decided to make a change. He did not provide any criticism or explanation, although it later transpired that Fletcher's dissent at Bangalore and his negative leadership played a major part. When he put down the phone Fletcher felt as drained and depressed as he'd ever felt. Craving solitude, he took off in his car to mull over the reasons behind his dismissal. For weeks he couldn't come to terms with the fact that he was no longer captain and he continued to harbour resentment at the way he'd been treated, especially since he'd turned down South Africa.

Fletcher continued to captain Essex to further glory before ceding the captaincy to Gooch. After his retirement from the first-class game in 1988, he captained the Essex second eleven prior to becoming England coach between 1993 and 1995, a position in which he failed to do himself justice. After being summarily dismissed, he returned to Essex to become first-team coach and then manager of their under-15 side.

Bob Willis

BOB WILLIS was born in Sunderland, County Durham, on 30 May 1949. His family moved to the Surrey village of Stoke D'Abernon, near Cobham, when he was six and he was educated at the Royal Grammar School, Guildford, where he excelled as a goalkeeper as well as at cricket. Determined to be a fast bowler from an early age, he progressed through Stoke D'Abernon Cricket Club and the Surrey under-age sides before making his first-class debut for the county in 1969, taking 17 wickets in five matches.

Although in and out of the first team in 1970, his explosive pace won him good reviews and when injury forced England fast bowler Alan Ward to return home from Australia prematurely in 1970, the six foot five Willis was called up as a surprise replacement. He soon justified his presence in Illingworth's Ashes-winning team by bowling intelligently and fielding brilliantly in the final four Tests. Overnight fame, however, didn't guarantee him a regular place in the Surrey championship team of 1971, prompting his departure to Warwickshire at the end of that season.

Forced to sit out the first half of the next season while he qualified, Willis was soon among the wickets and contributing to Warwickshire's championship success. Despite missing part of 1973 because of injury, his bowling earned him a recall in the final Test against the West Indies at Lord's. He bowled with plenty of fire and appeared ready to step into Snow's shoes as England's strike bowler, until injury once again assailed him. He missed much of the 1975 season while he recovered from operations on both knees, but driven on by sheer willpower he marked his return to Test duty by taking eight wickets against the West Indies at Headingley in 1976.

Although highly successful against India in 1976/77, he ran out of steam in the Centenary Test at Melbourne and was rebuked by captain Tony Greig for his lack of fitness. He accepted the reprimand in good faith and undertook a far more rigorous training regime. It proved a pivotal moment in his career, since he turned into a great fast bowler, his ungainly action no impediment to the speed and bounce he extracted.

A fierce opponent of Kerry Packer, Willis became a loyal and perceptive vice-captain to Brearley in Australia and although further knee trouble cut short his tour to the West Indies in 1980/81, he once again overcame setbacks with his magnificent 8-43 against Australia at Headingley in 1981.

That winter he went to India as Fletcher's vice-captain, and, when Fletcher was discarded on return, the selectors, faced with even fewer viable alternatives in light of the bans imposed on the South African rebels, chose Willis, an establishment loyalist, as his replacement. He confessed to feeling flabbergasted and it is easy to see why.

No fast bowler had captained England since Gubby Allen and his captaincy of Warwickshire had been limited to two curtailed seasons, but he had been an influential vice-captain on four tours to four different England captains. On the 1977/78 tour to New Zealand, he'd promoted Botham when quick runs were needed in the second Test and all but compelled Boycott to declare first thing the next morning; in Australia a year later he had counselled Brearley against dropping himself because of poor form; and in the inaugural Test in Sri Lanka, he berated the team to good effect after a sloppy session in the field, since they went on to win comfortably. 'There is no doubting his courage, his determination or his humour, and he is uncompromisingly opposed to the shabbier aspects of the game,' wrote Woodcock. 'For all that, it is difficult not to have reservations about his appointment. Though currently fit, his record in that respect is not good.' [145] Fitness aside, Woodcock's main reservation about Willis concerned his lack of tactical feel, a theme he kept returning to during his two years in charge.

Against Sunil Gavaskar's India in the Lord's Test, Willis had a dream start to his captaincy, taking nine wickets in England's seven-wicket win.

The second Test was badly affected by the weather and the third Test at the Oval was an unlimited run feast. Willis's delayed declaration on the final day upset some, but one up in the series and unsure about bowling out India on such a plum surface, he placed discretion above valour.

A sterner challenge awaited him from Imran Khan's Pakistan, a talented but mercurial side whose raucous appealing and sledging brought a rawer edge to proceedings. England won a finely balanced match at Edgbaston and Pakistan triumphed in style at Lord's when a neck injury forced Willis to stand aside in favour of Gower. His bowling was greatly missed.

He returned for the decider at Headingley, another close-fought match in which the marginal decisions went England's way in their three-wicket victory. Given their weakened state caused by the absence of several of the South African rebels, Willis could look back on his first summer in charge with quiet satisfaction. Aside from his 'intransigence' in allowing the Oval Test against India to peter out, *Wisden* commended him for his 'capital start to his late and unexpected accession to the England captaincy'. Only the mercurial ways of their batsmen, 'and England's determination, personified in Willis's own unstinting efforts, prevented Pakistan from winning the series'. [146]

With the absence of several players, notably Gooch and Emburey, their chances of beating Australia appeared remote, especially now that Greg Chappell was back to captain them. After an encouraging draw in the first Test at Perth, England were soundly beaten at Brisbane, undone by the pace of Lawson, and it was the threat he posed in the third Test that prompted Willis to commit the most notorious error of his captaincy. Inclined to bat first on a typical Adelaide wicket, he was talked into fielding by his batsmen, who disliked the prospect of facing Lawson with the new ball. No sooner had Willis made the decision than he came to regret it, since Australia experienced few terrors to finish the day at 265/3. 'I have seldom felt so angry about a day's cricket,' he wrote in his diary that evening, 'but most of the anger is directed at myself for not being strong enough to insist. Now I am faced with trying publicly to justify a decision I thought absurd.' [147]

Facing Australia's first innings of 438, England could only manage 216 in reply, and even a century by Gower when they followed on couldn't prevent an eight-wicket defeat.

On Lamb and Botham's prompting, England resolved to become more assertive thereafter and, galvanised by Tavare's aggressive 89 at Melbourne, they looked a more competitive unit. Australia led by three runs on first innings, but 65 from England opener Graeme Fowler and stiff resistance from the lower order set the home side a challenging 292 to win.

A hostile spell by fast bowler Norman Cowans took England to the brink of victory but, with 74 still needed, Allan Border and last man Jeff Thomson refused to lie down. As they carefully accumulated, Willis was roundly criticised for spreading the field and giving Border easy singles so that they could bowl at Thomson. They continued in similar vein the next morning until, with only four more wanted, Willis gave the ball to Botham. He did the trick first ball by having Thomson caught by Miller at slip, much to the delight of the team.

Their spirit continued into the final Test at Sydney, but several crucial umpiring decisions went against them, the most heinous occurring in the opening overs when Willis ran out opener John Dyson by some distance, only for the batsman to be given not out. Dyson went on to make 79 in Australia's 314, which gave them a first-innings lead of 77, but on a turning pitch they began tentatively in their second innings.

Had the spinners, Miller and Eddie Hemmings, bowled better, they could well have been match-winners, but their line and length were too erratic and Willis admitted that he'd kept them on too long. A fine 137 from Kim Hughes condemned England to chase an improbable 460 to win, but a valiant rearguard action, most notably from night-watchman Hemmings, enabled them to draw.

Always a worrier as a player, Willis became increasingly intense as captain with a strong commitment to his players. Forced to shoulder the main burden of the attack and lacking a reliable partner at the other end, he expended so much energy on his bowling that he struggled to provide enough tactical guidance. While others such as Taylor and Gower directed operations in the field, he stood at mid-off, arms folded, looking expressionless. Richie Benaud called it captaincy by committee.

According to Fowler, Willis had very much a mechanical approach to the game. When he ran nets, bowlers had to bowl off their full run-ups and batsmen had to treat it like a Test match. Those who smashed the ball would incur his displeasure, as would those who underperformed in fielding practice. A great trier himself, Willis expected nothing less than total endeavour from his charges and he became increasingly exasperated with those who fell short, especially some of the younger players. Even Randall, a model professional, rebelled against an attempted curfew by the management towards the end of the tour, but, that aside, he thought Willis very fair and selfless. 'Bob's greatest triumph on a long and difficult tour was that he kept the party in harmony even when results weren't good,' recalled Botham. [148]

Following the World Cup in England in 1983, New Zealand stayed on for a four-match series, posing a greater test than many of their predecessors. Hostile bowling by Willis was largely responsible for England's easy win at the Oval, but despite another Herculean effort in the second Test at Headingley – the last of his nine wickets giving him his 300th in Test cricket – it was New Zealand who triumphed, their first win in England.

England returned to winning ways at Lord's and Trent Bridge. Whatever Willis's tactical limitations, he'd rarely bowled better, as his 20 wickets at 13.65 signified, the best return on either side. He was duly asked to carry on for the winter tour to New Zealand and Pakistan, one tour too many as it proved.

After having the better of the first Test at Wellington, England fell totally apart at Christchurch. On a suspect wicket, they bowled abysmally, allowing the home side to score 307, before their batsmen performed equally badly, dismissed for 82 and 93, the first time that an England side had been bowled out in both innings for fewer than 100. Willis was scathing about his side's display and once again decried the lack of pride and professionalism in some of the younger players who seemed too attached to the bright lights. Their humiliation helped substantiate allegations in the *Mail on Sunday* that certain members of the team had smoked dope.

After a turgid draw at Auckland, giving New Zealand their first Test series victory against England, the weary tourists departed for Pakistan and found themselves playing a Test within less than three days of arrival. In conditions very different to New Zealand, the batsmen, Gower aside, failed to master the mysteries of Abdul Qadir's wrist spin and, although Pakistan batted recklessly when chasing 65 for victory, they were fully deserving of their three-wicket win. It proved to be Willis's last match in charge. A viral infection forced his premature return home and, with Gower thriving on the additional responsibilities with scores of 152 and 173* in consecutive Tests, both drawn, it was clear that his time had come.

Although never a great tactician, and too inclined to indulge Botham, Willis's courage and willpower won him a loyal following from his players even if some of them failed to meet the standards he demanded. Despite the additional burdens which he now carried, he continued to be England's premier bowler and set an admirable example in his approach to the game, never stooping to criticise umpires in public. While unsuccessful on the two tours he led, he won his three series at home and, overall, he won more Tests than he lost.

After his retirement from cricket in 1984, Willis worked in events and hospitality before becoming a forthright cricket commentator, mainly for Sky Sports. He died in 2019, aged 70.

David Gower

DAVID GOWER was born in Tunbridge Wells on 1 April 1957. His father, an excellent sportsman, was for many years in the Colonial Service and home for David's first six years was the British administered territory of Tanganyika.

After prep school at Marlborough House in Sussex, Gower followed his father to King's School, Canterbury, playing three years in the eleven and captaining it in his final year.

Having made his debut for Leicestershire in 1975 – his father was now registrar of Loughborough Colleges – Gower quit his law course at University College, London, after a year to concentrate on cricket. Blossoming under the tutelage of Illingworth at Leicester, his progress was such that he won his first Test cap against Pakistan at Edgbaston in 1978. Pulling his first ball for four, he began with consecutive fifties and immediately won a devoted national following for his exhilarating stroke-play. His maiden Test century arrived later that summer against New Zealand at the Oval, and the next year he went one better with a double century against India at Edgbaston.

In 1982 he was appointed vice-captain to Willis and led England for the first time against Pakistan at Lord's, a match they lost by nine wickets, and when illness forced Willis out of the tour to Pakistan in March 1984, Gower celebrated his promotion with two large centuries. Much less autocratic than Willis, he looked to create a vibrant team spirit by promoting trust, encouragement and individuality.

Appointed captain in his own right against Clive Lloyd's West Indians that summer, his start couldn't have been a more thankless one, since his opponents were one of the most formidable teams in cricket history. From the opening overs of the first Test, it was men against boys. Batting first on a damp pitch at Edgbaston, England were skittled for 191 with debutant opener Andy Lloyd sustaining a horrendous blow on the side of the head by a ball from Malcolm Marshall. He spent more than a week in hospital and never played Test cricket again.

After the West Indies compiled a mammoth 606, the home side once again had no answer to Marshall and Garner and lost by an innings and 180 runs. During the West Indian innings, Gower's captaincy had come under fierce scrutiny, especially his over-reliance on Botham's bowling, a criticism that surfaced throughout his captaincy.

With Willis about to reach the end of the road, the temptation to rely on Botham and his mystical powers was all too irresistible, despite the increasing wear and tear to his body. His 8-103 gave England a narrow first-innings lead at Lord's and a second-innings century from Lamb consolidated their position. With the West Indians tiring on the fourth evening, the batsmen accepted the umpire's offer to come off for bad light, a decision that prompted much criticism of Gower, since he was inside the dressing room watching Wimbledon on television rather than directing proceedings from the balcony. The next day it all proved rather academic, since the West Indies, challenged to score 342 for victory, won by nine wickets with 11.5 overs to spare against some ragged England bowling, most notably by Botham.

Another heavy defeat at Headingley meant that Gower became the first England captain to lose the first three Tests of a home series since Johnny Douglas against Warwick Armstrong's Australians in 1921.

England began promisingly at Old Trafford by taking the first four West Indian wickets cheaply, but Greenidge, with another double century, put his team out of reach. Facing a West Indian total of 500, Lamb was the only batsman to offer extensive resistance with his third century of the series. He was still two runs short of three figures when numbers ten and 11 were dismissed, but as the players were leaving the field Gower appeared on the balcony to wave them back. Batsman Paul Terry, who'd earlier retired with a broken arm, returned to the middle to allow Lamb to complete his century, but he was then told to stay put to try and make the 21 additional runs to avoid the follow-on, a hopeless task, since Terry was in no state to defend his wicket.

As England slid to an innings defeat, the one minor consolation was Gower's only half-century of the series. Beaten again at the Oval and losing 5-0 to one of the greatest teams in cricket history, Gower, adopting a cheerful pose, didn't complain about his lot all summer. Yet, mitigating circumstances aside, there were reservations about his captaincy. Aside from his over-indulgence of Botham, there was, according to Lamb, too much of a defeatist mentality in the team, and when veteran off-spinner Pat Pocock was recalled to the England team after eight years, he told Gower he'd never known such a shoddy attitude.

With Gower's leadership credentials still a matter of debate, he was given the chance to prove himself in India that winter. The absence of Botham, taking a winter off, paradoxically helped Gower establish his authority over a young team which included a number of good friends. He plumped for the return of the feisty Phil Edmonds and the inclusion of Gatting as vice-captain, a great boost to the latter's confidence, since, Brearley aside, it was the first time he felt somebody genuinely wanted him in the side.

Within hours of their arrival at Delhi, the team woke up to the news that the Indian prime minister, Indira Gandhi, had been assassinated, sparking off a bloodbath. They sought refuge in Sri Lanka and returned ten days later in good spirits, only then to be dealt another devastating blow. On the eve of the first Test at Bombay, Percy Norris, the British deputy high commissioner of Western India, was assassinated on his way to his office the day after he'd entertained the team in style. Shocked and concerned about their safety, the majority wanted to go home, but manager Tony Brown, having sought official advice from the relevant bodies, resolved that the tour should proceed with some minor alterations to the itinerary. Gower's unruffled calm helped soothe frayed nerves and, once again, the team found additional strength in adversity.

The immediate onset of the first Test helped distract attention from external events. In an absorbing game, England were mesmerised by the leg breaks and googlies of 19-year-old Laxman Sivaramakrishnan who took 12 wickets in the match, aided by some eccentric home umpiring. They lost by eight wickets but took heart from Gatting's first Test century and they refused to develop a siege mentality like Fletcher's side three years earlier. Gower told them they could still win the series, playing down the threat from Sivaramakrishnan – quite accurately – and decreed that there should be no dissent towards the umpires.

A solid 160 from rookie opener Tim Robinson gave England a 111-run lead in the second Test at Delhi and when the match seemed to be drifting to a draw on the final day, Gower had other ideas. In a rare display of anger, he berated his players for their pessimism and assured them that victory was still in their grasp. Shunning the opportunity to take the new ball, he plumped for the relentless accuracy of spinners Pocock and Edmonds, who, aided by precisely set attacking fields, forced India into acts of wilful indiscretion. Taking the last six Indian wickets for 28, England scored the 125 needed in two hours to win by eight wickets, a great pre-Christmas tonic.

After a dull draw at Calcutta, England played exceptional cricket at Madras to win by nine wickets, and a captain's innings by Gower just when his team needed it ensured a draw at Kanpur. By winning the series 2-1 they became the first team from any country to win a series in India coming from behind. Besides developing a great team spirit, Gower brought the best out of Gatting, Edmonds and Fowler in a way that other captains had failed to do by accepting them for their ability. When he visited Edmonds to discuss his ragged bowling at the beginning of the tour, Edmonds cut him short, assuring him that he would be alright. 'You must expect a man like Edmonds to assert his individuality every now and then,' Gower later remarked.

'A wise captain will accept that as part of the man. Every now and then, he will lose a little balance and control, but if you want to use his talents, you must let that go. Of course, he is a loner, with his headphones and his books, but so long as his contribution is fine – in team meetings and on the pitch – then I am happy.' [149]

With Botham refreshed after a winter off and the South Africa rebels such as Gooch and Emburey available again, England looked stronger than an Australian side weakened by the retirement of Greg Chappell, Rodney Marsh and Dennis Lillee. After three Tests there was little between the two sides as the 1-1 scoreline indicated, but England had much the better of the fourth Test and concluded in style with crushing victories at Edgbaston and the Oval. Both games were a triumph for Gower, who scored 215 in the former and 157 in the latter, batting at his best. According to Gooch, 'The key to David's captaincy that summer was his own confidence with the bat and his ability to pressurise the Aussies in the field, with runs to spare.' [150]

As he stood on the Oval balcony, basking in Ashes glory, Gower looked forward to the winter tour to the Caribbean, declaring that the West Indies would be quaking in their boots. The words were uttered in jest, but there was a feeling that England, unlike 1984, could now give them a run for their money. Their hopes soon turned to ruin as events conspired against them.

Days before their departure, Gower's mother died and, left with all the responsibility of sorting out her affairs, he arrived late and deflated. Opting to miss the first game, he was badly compromised by photos of himself and Botham relaxing on board a yacht while the team slumped to an embarrassing defeat against the Windward Islands, the weakest of the provincial sides in the Caribbean.

Dire practice facilities in Antigua, their early base, gave Gower and Botham the perfect excuse to avoid long net sessions, but their constant aversion to practice not only set a bad example to the rest of the team, it also gave the impression they lacked pride in their performance.

Botham's pervading influence once again proved a thorn in Gower's side. Something of a law to himself, it wasn't such a problem when he was winning games for England off his own bat, but his halcyon days were behind him, and in the West Indies he was reduced to bland mediocrity. He further upset morale by inadvertently encouraging the less reputable sections of the tabloid press to shadow the team at every step, so they could file lurid stories about their personal lives.

Before the series began, Gower declared that the West Indies had the firepower but England had the expertise. The first part of the statement proved rather more valid than the second. They were badly shaken in the first ODI when Gatting's nose was broken by a vicious delivery from Marshall, forcing him to return home for an operation. By the time he returned several weeks later, his team-mates were heading for another whitewash. In the first Test at Kingston, England were bundled out for 159 and 152 on a lethal wicket, their confidence shattered by the venom of the West Indian attack, especially debutant Patrick Patterson.

They were badly beaten at Port of Spain and when they lost at Bridgetown in little more than three days before a large English contingent, the disillusion was palpable, a feeling exacerbated by Gower's decision to hold voluntary nets the day after the defeat and his failure to turn up himself.

While England were losing the fourth Test at Port of Spain with more abject batting, Gower was spending much time persuading Gooch to play in the final Test in Antigua. Throughout the tour the latter had been subjected to political pressure orchestrated by the Antiguan deputy prime minister Lester Bird because of his views about South Africa, and although he reluctantly agreed to go to Antigua his moroseness had done little to raise spirits. 'When David came back from Antigua, he was as low as I have ever seen him,' recalled his agent Jon Holmes. [151] A popular calypso song at the time, 'Captain, the Ship is Sinking', blared out from the stands throughout the Test to remind him of his plight.

On a lifeless wicket, England showed greater resilience than in the previous games, with Gower, their best batsman in the series, scoring 90 in the first innings, but while disconcerted by another defeat he raised a laugh afterwards by remarking that the ship was well and truly sunk and lying 20 fathoms deep. 'This is something like the 30th tour I have reported in the past 36 years,' wrote Woodcock, 'and never have I seen such a lack of what the modern player so prides himself on possessing – professionalism.

'It has seemed at times as though discipline and firm leadership are considered to be of no account. In fact, they were never more needed.' [152]

Wisden was equally scathing in its assessment of the tour. 'Much went wrong, too, that with firmer captaincy and management might not have. In cold fact, England never had a hope. That they could and should have done better, few who saw them would dispute. Their lack of commitment was reflected in their attitude to practice, a department in which West Indies showed them up to be amateurs.'

Having paid tribute to Gower's batting and personality, its correspondent then questioned his leadership by calling him a dilettante. 'Regrettably, it was not only that he had no faith in practice – a weakness exacerbated by Ian Botham's presence – but sometimes he seemed even to lack interest.' [153]

Humbled by his team's drubbing in the West Indies, Gower was put on stay of execution by his appointment for the two ODIs and the first Test against India, and was told by Peter May, the chairman of selectors, to be more assertive in the field. Irked by the edict, Gower responded by having T-shirts printed with 'I'm in Charge' on them. After drawing the ODIs one each, England, without Botham who was suspended for an admission of drug taking, lost the first Test by five wickets, their sixth loss in a row, sealing Gower's fate. He came off the field to hear that he'd lost the captaincy to his deputy, Gatting. Later that summer another blow came his way when Leicestershire decided to dispense with his services as captain.

Gatting remained in office till he was undone by a sex scandal during the first Test against the West Indies in June 1988, the summer in which England had four captains, the last of whom was Gooch.

Despite Gooch's promising start, his powers of leadership were questioned by the new chairman of selectors, Ted Dexter. Swayed by the views of manager Micky Stewart, he looked to restore Gatting to the captaincy, but his choice was vetoed by the chairman of the TCCB's cricket committee, Ossie Wheatley, who recalled his disciplinary lapses in Pakistan 18 months earlier. It was now that Dexter, with Stewart's reluctance, fell back on Gower.

'I'd like the job back. But it goes against precedent,' had been Gower's parting shot when replaced by Gatting and, unaware of his second-choice status, Gower was delighted to be back in charge after three years away. According to Simon Barnes, he returned a more experienced and mature person. 'His face is a good deal less cherubic and his banter is a fraction less pronounced. This old defensive mechanism has been toned down a little.' [154]

Gower began on the right footing by beating Allan Border's Australians in the three ODIs, but it was a brief ray of sunlight before the gathering storm. Ignoring his own instincts, he inserted Australia in the first Test at Headingley and went into the match without his spinner, Emburey. Australia, a stronger and meaner side since their previous visit four years earlier, amassed 601/7 declared before bowling out England on the final afternoon, an embarrassing collapse which provoked a ferocious backlash from the press.

The knives were again out at the Saturday evening press conference in the Lord's Test as England stared defeat in the face. Sensing an intimidating atmosphere, a tense-looking Gower was unusually terse in his answers before finally losing his cool when quizzed why Australia's last four wickets had compiled 263 runs and why had he bowled Neil Foster from the Pavilion End. He suddenly stood up and walked out of the press conference, saying, 'That's it, boys. I'm off,' a breach of etiquette which earned him a wigging from Dexter. The fact that Gower was off to the theatre to watch *Anything Goes* exposed him to further ridicule. His eloquent century on the Monday restored some of his reputation, but it couldn't save England from another defeat.

A rain-affected draw at Edgbaston was merely a temporary reprieve before they met their Waterloo at Old Trafford. Australia won by nine wickets to regain the Ashes, but their achievement was overshadowed by confirmation of another England rebel tour to

South Africa, to be captained by Gatting and including three men playing in the current Test.

As the season progressed, the pressure on Gower intensified. He became more remote, rarely consulted with his bowlers and was caught by the television cameras flicking a double V-sign towards a lone barracker on the Saturday of the Old Trafford Test.

With England in disarray, the team had all but given up. Spinner Nick Cook, recalled for the fifth Test at Trent Bridge, said it was like walking into a morgue, and opening bowler Devon Malcolm, making his debut, was shocked at the amateur approach. Aside from the shortage of practice, there was no discussion of the opposition at the eve-of-Test dinner and no team talk in the dressing room. 'Turning up the day before a Test match and expecting to switch on the tap may well have worked for a brilliant batsman like David, but it was no way to prepare the majority of players for representing their country.' [155]

From the Australian perspective, Geoff Lawson recalled it as the only Test he played in when he didn't have to break a sweat. England were once again badly beaten and only rain prevented further ignominy at the Oval.

Given the malaise infecting English cricket then, there were limits to what any captain could achieve, but Gower's leadership had once again been found wanting. 'Gower is a charming man and a charming cricketer,' concluded Brearley. 'But he is not a leader.' [156]

'David was a deep thinker about the game but he thought of it more as an individual sport,' wrote Micky Stewart. 'He didn't see the team ethic as essential in the way I did or as Mike Gatting did.' [157]

'The players let David down badly in 1989,' noted Gooch, 'but he seemed to let things drift too often and didn't set the right example. He was too remote and appeared to have his mind elsewhere too often. He is the least snobbish of blokes and excellent company but when he captained us in 1989 he struggled to get the best response from the players eventually.' [158]

In light of such a dreadful summer, Gower not only lost the England captaincy, but also his place in the side to tour the West Indies, a contentious omission given his continued prowess with the bat. He was recalled against India the following year and scored two centuries against Australia on tour that winter, but his lack of sympathy for the work ethic of captain Gooch saw him jettisoned once again. He played in only three more Tests and, following his retirement at the end of the 1993 season, he moved into the media, becoming in time Sky Sports Cricket anchor and commentator.

Although Gower's image of debonair insouciance was often mistaken for indifference, his relaxed style of leadership, while a positive boost to some, prevented him from imposing his will or motivating others when the team were struggling. 'Perhaps I wasn't always firm enough with those who needed guidance,' he wrote in his autobiography. 'Maybe that was a failing.' [159] Had he been captain in an earlier era when cricket was played primarily for enjoyment, his languid style might have proved more effective, but in the troubled 1980s when the game had become ruthlessly professional something more disciplined was needed, even though the pendulum was to swing too far in the other direction.

Mike Gatting

MIKE GATTING was born in Kingsbury, Middlesex, on 6 June 1957, the son of an airport fitter with Handley Page who also worked as a steward in the local sports club. From the earliest age sport dominated his life, and that of his brother Steve, later a professional footballer for Arsenal and Brighton and Hove Albion, their various jousts nothing if not competitive.

During his time at John Kelly Boys' High School in Cricklewood, Gatting played cricket for the Middlesex Schools and Brondesbury, one of the top clubs in London, impressing his seniors with the power of his stroke-play and his deep appreciation of the game.

In 1972 he first played for Middlesex second eleven, helping them win the under-25 competition in 1974, and he made his first team debut in 1975.

He topped the Young England batting averages on their tour to the West Indies in 1976 (he was also a useful medium-paced bowler) and his reward for scoring 1,000 runs in his first full season in 1977 was his selection for England's tour to Pakistan and New Zealand that winter. He failed in all three of his Test innings and didn't play again until his recall against the West Indies in 1980.

For the next four years he was in and out of the England side, his lack of runs reflected in his lack of acceptance in the dressing room. The turning point came when he was appointed vice-captain to Gower on the tour to India in 1984/85. Amid the wreckage of the England batting in the first Test at Bombay, Gatting's 136 in the second innings stood out, its quality recognised by the England cricket writers who rose to him as he returned to the pavilion.

He followed this up with a double century in the fourth Test at Madras and, playing under a captain who rated him, he soared ever upwards. Even a broken nose sustained against Marshall in the first ODI on the 1985/86 tour to the West Indies spared him much of the obloquy hurled at his team-mates for their feckless attitude. Defeated 5-0, Gower's lackadaisical leadership was now on the line, and, following England's defeat against India in the first Test at Lord's in June 1986, he was deposed in favour of Gatting.

A cheerful, open-hearted and amiable personality, Gatting brought the struggles of his upbringing to his captaincy. Fiercely competitive – although entirely honest in the way he played the game – he practised hard, gave everything in the middle and expected the same from his players. Those who shirked a challenge would be loudly admonished, but beneath the passion and the bluster there lay a more sensitive side who cared deeply for his men. He treated his bowlers with respect, gave a voice to the younger players and displayed flexibility towards the mavericks.

As a tactician, he knew the game backwards and followed in the Brearley tradition of playing positive cricket, qualities which helped him lead Middlesex to three championships.

His start as Test captain could hardly have been less propitious. Losing the toss on an unpredictable wicket at Headingley, England bowled poorly, enabling India to dictate the course of a match they went on to win by 279 runs.

The third Test at Edgbaston was altogether a more even affair. Gatting played a true captain's innings of 183* and, had he made more use of Emburey on a turning wicket, England might well have sneaked a win instead of having to settle for a draw.

India were followed by New Zealand, a side far stronger now than their amateur outfits of the 1950s and 60s. After drawing the first Test at Lord's, England, desperately missing Botham's bullish magnetism, caved in all too easily to Richard Hadlee at Trent Bridge, losing by eight wickets.

The return of Botham for the final Test at the Oval lifted all those around him, including the captain. Taking a much firmer grip in the field, Gatting then batted with commendable gusto as he and Gower shared a partnership of 223, which set up a potential winning position before rain washed out most of the final two days.

Following the lack of leadership on the previous tour to the West Indies and the recent installation of Bob Simpson as coach of the Australian side, the TCCB appointed Micky Stewart, the former captain of Surrey, as England's first cricket manager. Responsible for preparation and discipline, he immediately struck up a close relationship with Gatting and together they brought a greater rigour to the nets, fielding practice and tactics. In addition to his organisational skills, Stewart also won appreciation for his personal advice and encouragement, while Gatting ensured that the junior members of the party were in no sense neglected.

Although both men were keen to instil a stronger work ethic to the team, they knew they had to tread carefully with the old stagers, Gower, Botham and Lamb, all of whom were free spirits. Acknowledging the importance of winning them over, they took them into their confidence, listened to their advice and tolerated their exotic nightlife. In return, Botham responded positively to Gatting's request that he work with the younger bowlers, all of which helped create an excellent team spirit. 'It was one of the happiest and most enjoyable tours I'd been on,' wrote Botham, 'and Gatt deserves a lot of credit for that. If hard work was needed, he wasn't afraid to ask for it, but for the most part he was content to let his senior pros choose their own workload in training and practice.' [160]

This new-found professionalism wasn't immediately apparent during the early matches when their pitiful performance attracted all-round ridicule and prompted talk of a resounding Australian victory. The approach of the first Test, however, concentrated minds in the England camp, especially among their leading players who thrived on the bigger stage.

Sympathetic to Gower's lack of form, Gatting volunteered to take the number-three slot and his fighting 61 on the opening day helped his team win the early skirmishes. They finished that evening on 198/2, the perfect bridgehead for Botham to make piercing inroads the next day with a spectacular century that destroyed Australian morale.

The home side could only manage 248 in reply to their opponents' 456 and, forced to follow on, they fared little better at their second attempt, leaving England victors by seven wickets.

Boosted by a rare win at Brisbane, England continued their domination at Perth. Australia were once again forced to follow on and only a painstaking century from captain Border saved them from another defeat.

The absence of Botham due to injury weakened the England attack at Adelaide. On the most placid of surfaces, Australia ran up over 500, but centuries from Chris Broad and Gatting guaranteed the tourists a draw.

Amid English-type conditions on the opening morning of the Boxing Day Test at Melbourne, Gatting not only inserted Australia, but also picked Gladstone Small ahead of Neil Foster once opening bowler Graham Dilley declared himself unfit. His choice was amply vindicated, since Small broke the back of the Australian batting with five cheap wickets.

Having dismissed the home side for 141, England then built a match-winning lead, with Broad scoring his third century in consecutive Tests. Batting again, 208 in arrears, Australia's spirit appeared to have deserted them and before teatime on the third day the England dressing room was awash with champagne as they celebrated the retention of the Ashes with the singer-songwriter and avid cricket fan Elton John.

A narrow win by Australia in the final Test at Sydney didn't detract from a highly successful tour, enhanced by the winning of both one-day competitions. Nothing during Gatting's captaincy came close to emulating this triumph as his road thereafter became ever steeper.

A home series against Imran Khan's Pakistan promised much. England were the better side in the first two Tests and they could have won the fourth Test, but they were outplayed in the decisive third Test at Headingley. Batting first on winning the toss, they were

31/5 after an hour and never recovered. Bowled out for 136 and 199, they lost by an innings.

Recalling their fate at Headingley, Gatting, on winning the toss at Edgbaston, chose to insert Pakistan and was pilloried by the press as they made hay in the sun. Responding to their total of 505, Gatting redeemed himself by scoring 124 to put his side narrowly in front, and when Pakistan collapsed on the final afternoon an England victory seemed quite a probability.

Requiring 124 in 18 overs, they began with a flourish but panic set in during the later stages and they finished 15 runs short with three wickets left.

In the final Test Pakistan reasserted their superiority at Headingley by batting first on a plumb Oval wicket and amassing 708. England – following on 476 behind – were indebted to a defiant 150* from Gatting and 51* from Botham to save their blushes.

The latter stages of the game had been played in a rancorous atmosphere after umpire David Constant had given Botham not out when on 20, an atmosphere all too palpable throughout the series. Constant, a polarising figure on the previous Pakistan tour to England, once again upset the tourists, the repercussions of which were to be far-reaching on England's 1987/88 tour to Pakistan.

With Gower taking a winter off, Botham playing for Queensland in the Sheffield Shield and Lamb omitted, this was a rather different England side from the one that gallivanted around the West Indies and Australia during the previous two winters. Although their absence helped restore some internal discipline, it deprived the party of some much-needed perspective when things began to go awry.

With Pakistan still seething over their treatment by England's umpires, and the TCCB's rejection of their request that Constant shouldn't stand in the Tests, they were in no mood to accommodate their opponents' wishes over choice of officials. Ignoring all three of their World Cup umpires, the Pakistan board appointed Shakeel Khan for the first Test and he proceeded to antagonise England with a number of contentious decisions, including the dismissal of opener Broad in the second innings, given out caught behind to a ball he missed by some way. Broad's refusal to leave the crease earned him a reprimand from the England management but nothing more, and at the end of the game, in which they lost by an innings, bamboozled by Pakistan's talismanic leg-spinner Abdul Qadir, Gatting denounced the umpiring, comments which attracted disapproval in a *Times* editorial.

Unwilling to compromise, the Pakistan board, without consulting England, appointed Shakoor Rana, a divisive figure, for the second Test and he was soon niggling Gatting as his team took control on the second day. A minor breach of cricketing protocol was allowed to escalate into a full-blown crisis when Shakoor, employing some expletive-ridden language, accused Gatting of cheating, which prompted the England captain's furious finger-wagging retort.

Outraged by Gatting's response, Shakoor refused to continue officiating until he received an apology, but with Gatting loathed to give one, the whole of the third day was lost as fruitless negotiations dragged on interminably.

As footage of Gatting's confrontation with Shakoor was broadcast around the world, their altercation divided opinion back home. Many ex-players, familiar with the vagaries of Pakistan umpiring, sympathised with Gatting, but not Dexter. Blaming England for the crisis, he said that cricket couldn't be played unless everything the umpire said and did was accepted. A further editorial in *The Times* opined that Gatting, by giving in to frustration, had destroyed the game's most precious code, and in the same paper Simon Barnes accused England of double standards.

'By open dissent, and by implicit support of open dissent from captain and team management, England abandoned the principles of fair play they claimed they were defending. In effect, they said that if a Pakistani refuses to walk, it is because he is a cheat; when an Englishman refuses to walk, it is because the umpire is a cheat.

I dare say the umpire was in the wrong, but, with Gatting's rant, he and England have forfeited all claim to moral rightness.' [161]

Instructed by the TCCB to apologise unconditionally to Shakoor, Gatting reluctantly obliged with the tersest of notes, and when the game resumed bad weather consigned it to a draw. The third Test also ended in stalemate, giving Pakistan the rubber 1-0. 'Yet, at the end of the most acrimonious cricket tour of modern times,' wrote Alan Lee, the cricket correspondent of *The Times*, 'the hard truth was that, whatever the extraordinary nature of the provocation, England had performed poorly and behaved reprehensibly.' [162]

Their general conduct barely improved on tour to Australia and New Zealand after Christmas. In the Bicentenary Test at Sydney, Broad was fined for smashing his stumps on dismissal and in New Zealand there were several cases of dissent when decisions went against them.

With the series ending nil all, it meant England had gone 13 matches without a victory and Gatting's failure to stamp out the egregiousness of his players raised doubts about his future as captain.

With the TCCB on his back, not least for the forthcoming serialisation of his autobiography detailing events in Pakistan, which contravened his tour contract, Gatting was placed on probation, appointed merely for the first two Tests against the West Indies. England batted stoically to earn a draw in the first Test at Trent Bridge, but their efforts were overshadowed by events off the field. On 9 June two tabloid newspapers published a story that during the game Gatting had invited a barmaid to his room at the team hotel and spent the night with her. The selectors, while accepting his word that nothing untoward had occurred, still deemed his behaviour irresponsible enough, especially in light of their recent strictures about player discipline, to relieve him of the captaincy for the second Test. According to Brearley, the treatment of Gatting was despicable, since any indiscretion on his part was dwarfed by the failure of the authorities to stand up to what he perceived to be the prying nastiness of the modern media.

While the press lay siege to Gatting and his family, he withdrew from the team for the second Test, and although he returned for the third Test his heart wasn't in it. He declared his unavailability for the rest of the series and appeared in only one game against Australia the next year. At the beginning of that rubber, the selectors had wanted to reinstate him as captain, but their choice was vetoed by Ossie Wheatley, the chairman of the TCCB cricket committee, who hadn't forgiven him for his altercation with Shakoor Rana. His reasoning failed to impress Gatting, who, disillusioned with the leadership of English cricket, led a controversial rebel tour to South Africa in 1990. His defiance incurred a three-year ban from Test cricket and, although he returned to the England side on their 1992/93 tour to India, his days as captain were over.

Gatting's time as captain will always be remembered for his altercation with Shakoor Rana and the lurid allegations about his private life which brought about his downfall. Perhaps a more interesting question is why a man so liked and respected as a captain should have presided over such a disappointing record as England captain with only two wins in 23 matches? At times he appeared at the mercy of his underperforming players; equally on other occasions he allowed his lingering resentment about Pakistan umpires and TCCB administrators to infect his team. Perhaps it was his misfortune to have played in the wrong era. His natural decency and honest endeavour deserved something better.

On retirement from Middlesex in 1998, Gatting coached the team for two years before becoming ECB managing director of Cricket Partnerships. He was president of MCC in 2013/14 and has been chairman of the World Cricket Committee since 2017.

John Emburey

JOHN EMBUREY was born in Peckham, south London, on 20 August 1952, the son of a *Sunday Times* print worker. Learning his cricket in the street, he switched from medium pace to off spin at Peckham Manor Secondary School under the guidance of cricket master Mike Gunton.

After three years playing for the Surrey youth teams between 1968 and 1971, Emburey's failure to win a contract with them greatly disappointed him. Recommended to Middlesex by Surrey coach Arthur McIntyre, he made his debut for the first eleven in 1973 and quickly impressed captain Brearley, but with spinners Edmonds and Titmus in harness, his opportunities proved strictly limited. Disillusioned with his lot, he was contemplating leaving at the end of the 1976 season, only to learn of Titmus's departure to become Surrey's coach.

Quickly stepping into his shoes, Emburey won his county cap the following year and in 1978 he celebrated his England debut – against New Zealand at Lord's – by taking a wicket in his first over.

By 1982 Emburey was England's leading spinner, but his participation in the rebel tour to South Africa that year not only earned him a three-year ban from Test cricket, it also cost him the vice-captaincy of Middlesex, the only member of the rebel team to be punished by his county. His demotion rankled, especially when Gatting beat him to the Middlesex captaincy following Brearley's retirement.

He returned to England's ranks against Australia in 1985 and enjoyed his two most successful years in Test cricket before the effects of the one-day game began to curb his powers as an attacking off-spinner.

Since 1983 Emburey had been a popular vice-captain of Middlesex and he led them shrewdly when Gatting was absent, drawing on advice he'd gleaned from Brearley. In 1986 he became England's vice-captain and played a vital mediating role in Pakistan in 1987, advising the team against abandoning the tour when they felt let down by the TCCB in their stand against umpire Shakoor Rana.

Always craving the England captaincy, he willingly accepted the role of caretaker captain for one match after Gatting was deposed in June 1988. Without a victory in their previous 13 Tests, Emburey faced the toughest of assignments when he led the side out against the West Indies at Lord's. On an overcast morning they made the best of all starts, reducing their opponents to 54/5 at lunch, but a sixth-wicket stand of 130 between Gus Logie and Jeffrey Dujon set them on the road to recovery and ultimately a comfortable win.

Emburey's one-match tenure was extended to the third Test at Old Trafford, an unhappy occasion for both him and his team. Bowled out for 135 on the first day, he opened the bowling himself, and his enterprise was nearly rewarded when Richie Richardson was dropped by wicketkeeper Paul Downton. It was the nearest he came to leaving his mark on a match which England, with abject batting, lost by an innings. At a time when his bowling was no longer Test standard and with the next match on a seamer's strip at Headingley, he gave way to Chris Cowdrey as captain, a cause for regret since he'd done little wrong in his two matches in charge.

After reappearing for England against Australia the following year, Emburey joined Gatting's rebel tour to South Africa in 1990, the one player to go on both rebel tours. Even after serving another three-year ban, he was recalled to the England side for the tour to India in 1992/93 and made his final Test appearance against the West Indies in 1995, aged 42.

After his retirement from first-class cricket in 1996, he coached Northamptonshire, Middlesex and Ahmedabad Rockets. He is currently a scout for the ECB.

Christopher Cowdrey

CHRISTOPHER COWDREY was born in Farnborough, Kent, on 20 October 1957, the eldest child of Colin Cowdrey, one of England's greatest cricketers.

Encouraged by his father's gentle guidance, he learned the rudiments of the game in their garden first at Bickley, then at Limpsfield, replete with a hard net and a bowling machine.

At Wellesley House Prep School and Tonbridge School, Cowdrey suffered the inevitable comparisons with his father as he shaped up nicely. Chosen for the Tonbridge first eleven at 14, he overcame a difficult start to make rapid progress, culminating in an exceptional final season when he scored 966 runs at an average of 80. He was also a charismatic captain, one of the very best in the school's history, combining tactical flair and aggression with the Cowdrey will to win.

In 1976 Cowdrey captained a talented and unbeaten young England side to the West Indies, the year before he made his debut for Kent, aged 19, against the Australians. Within weeks he scored his maiden first-class century, but it was to be another six years before he added another.

Although his attacking batting, useful seam bowling and brilliant fielding made him a one-day specialist, Cowdrey averaged 56 in the championship in 1983 and impressed enough the following season to be picked for England's tour to India. His figures in the five Tests were modest, but his charm and joie de vivre made him an indispensable part of a tour of this kind. England won 2-1 and Cowdrey returned to a new challenge of captaining Kent.

It proved a tricky inheritance as Tavare, his predecessor, had been sacked in contentious circumstances and Cowdrey had several challenging years restoring unity to the dressing room. His salvation came with the arrival of a dynamic chairman of the cricket committee, Jim Woodhouse, in 1987. He quickly became a good friend and together they worked closely to restore morale, not least by lending a friendly ear to the players. A bad start to 1988 was transformed by the appointment of the former Australian Test player John Inverarity as coach at short notice, and a combination of inspiring captaincy, brilliant fielding and an excellent team spirit turned an ordinary side into a victorious one. By mid-season they were leading the table and, as England faltered against the West Indies, the calls for Cowdrey to assume the leadership grew ever louder. After losing the second and third Tests, Emburey's two-match stint as captain was terminated and Cowdrey was appointed in his place to provide a fresh impetus. The fact that the chairman of selectors, Peter May, happened to be his godfather merely added an extra twist to the story.

Cowdrey's elevation generated enormous publicity – he and Colin were the second father and son combination to lead England, emulating Frank and George Mann – and raised inflated hopes about what he could achieve. On arriving at Headingley, the venue for the fourth Test, the gateman didn't recognise him and wouldn't let him into the ground. It was a portent of things to come. In England's first innings, Cowdrey was out without scoring and, although he did well to restrict the West Indies' first-innings lead to 74 – both Gooch and Gower complimented him on his captaincy – it proved more than enough. On a seaming wicket, England were no match for Marshall, Curtly Ambrose and Courtney Walsh in their second innings. All out for 138, they lost by ten wickets and Cowdrey's scores of nought and five, along with five innocuous overs, gave substance to those critics who claimed he wasn't Test class.

He returned subdued to Canterbury for Kent's match against Sussex. A nasty blow on the foot was serious enough to pose doubts about his availability for the fifth Test. Cowdrey hoped to be fit but, unlike Allan Lamb, he was given no time to recover by manager Micky Stewart. Gooch took over the captaincy and Cowdrey was led to believe that he wouldn't be welcome in the dressing room so he didn't attend. He returned to fitness with a century against Derbyshire, only to hear from a spectator that Gooch had kept the captaincy for the one-off Test against Sri Lanka. The decision to ditch him without any explanation from May or Stewart shattered Cowdrey. When he complained about his shabby treatment to *The Sun* days later, his outburst landed him in trouble with the TCCB for speaking out without official sanction. He was fined £500 for his pains, and to add insult to injury Kent missed out on the championship by one point.

In retrospect 1988 proved the pinnacle of Cowdrey's career. Kent's fortunes went sharply into reverse and he handed over the captaincy to Mark Benson in July 1990. With increasing doubts about his fitness, he was released by Kent at the end of 1991 and after a year playing for Glamorgan he retreated into the media, broadcasting for *Test Match Special* and *TalkSport*. His son Fabian briefly played for Kent, becoming the fourth Cowdrey to play for the county side.

The Hour Before Dawn: Captaincy in the 1990s

THE appointment of Micky Stewart, the ex-Surrey captain and manager, as England manager in 1986 was an acknowledgement that the national team needed to adopt a more professional approach and that the captain needed help in carrying out his manifold responsibilities. Stewart consolidated his position by retaining the Ashes in 1986/87 and, although his methods didn't always win the support of the players, they were certainly a sign of things to come.

With the appointment of Gooch as captain in September 1989, Stewart found a ready soulmate and together they set out to replace the champagne culture of the 1980s with something more austere. Practice, fitness and preparation became their panacea for success and by immediately transforming their fortunes in the West Indies, a series they were unlucky to lose 2-1, Gooch became the unlikely saviour of English cricket. His batting exploits throughout the summer of 1990, not least his scores of 333 and 123 against India at Lord's, further raised his esteem and, although his leadership became increasingly inflexible, especially in his relationship with

Gower, he remained indispensable. As results began to fade and Gooch became more careworn, he was urged by Stewart to stay put, but a crushing Ashes defeat in the summer of 1993 convinced him that he'd run his race. His voluntary departure after four years in charge became the model for most of his successors.

Michael Atherton faced a daunting inheritance on taking over from Gooch for the final two Tests against Australia, but runs in both games and a welcome victory at the Oval gave him political capital to choose a youthful side to tour the West Indies. Despite his bravura batting, England still lost 3-1 and a number of players didn't impress Ray Illingworth, the incoming chairman of selectors who'd been given the power of veto in the composition of the team.

Never short of self-confidence, Illingworth proved to be as forthright a chairman as he'd been captain, and when his traditional views clashed with Atherton's more forward-looking agenda, he invariably carried the day – helped by the latter's brush with ball-tampering against South Africa in 1994. Diminished by his folly, Atherton was forced to abide by Illingworth's choice of Gatting and Martin McCague to tour Australia that winter (neither justified their selection) and throughout the trip he was hampered by his chairman's criticism of his leadership.

Following defeat in Australia and the dismissal of coach Keith Fletcher, Illingworth took over his duties, further blunting Atherton's authority, not least in South Africa in 1995/96 when his ongoing spat with fast bowler Devon Malcolm undermined team morale. Atherton's position improved when Illingworth ceded the coaching duties to his friend David Lloyd, but, with the demands of county cricket conspiring against the interests of the Test side, he struggled to motivate a collection of underperforming and self-absorbed individuals. With results remaining poor and his own form hampered by chronic back pain, he quit at the end of England's tour to the West Indies in March 1998.

After a brief interlude by Alec Stewart, the captaincy passed to Nasser Hussain in July 1999. Beaten in his first series by New Zealand, which sent England to the bottom of the *Wisden* World Championship and booed by the crowd at the end of the Oval Test, he couldn't have endured a tougher baptism, but fortunately for him help was on the way.

Graham Gooch

GRAHAM GOOCH was born in Leytonstone on 23 July 1953 and experienced a typical East End upbringing with working-class parents, trips to the seaside and tight-knit communities. Leaving school at 15, he did a four-year apprenticeship in engineering, which enhanced his appreciation of playing sport for a living.

His love of sport was fostered by his father who used to play cricket for East Ham Corinthians. Graduating through Ilford Cricket Club, and the Essex system, Graham made his county debut in 1973 and, two years later, he was playing for England against Australia, aged 21. Caught on a rain-affected wicket at Edgbaston, he began with a pair and was dropped after one further game.

Inured by his travails, Gooch returned to county cricket all the more determined to succeed at international level. His switch to opening in 1978 not only made him more disciplined, it also earned him a Test recall and he marked it with a half-century against Pakistan at Lord's. He continued to score prolifically as an opener, not least in two series against the West Indies in 1980 and 1981, but in 1982 he incurred a three-year Test ban for leading the first rebel tour to apartheid South Africa.

After three years plundering county attacks, he returned to Test duty against Australia in 1985, scoring a magisterial 196 in the final game at the Oval, but he endured a torrid trip to the West Indies that winter, not least for the concerted opposition among some local politicians to his South African connections. Never a great one for touring, he opted out of the England tour to Australia in 1986/87 and didn't play against Pakistan the following summer because of a severe loss of form. A century for MCC against the Rest of the World in the MCC Bicentenary match at Lord's helped him on the road to recovery and a successful World Cup in India and Pakistan re-established his position at the top of the England order.

His sheer class was manifest during the summer of 1988 when he averaged 45 against the West Indies' awesome pace quartet, by far England's leading batsman. He also captained them in the final Test at the Oval, and against Sri Lanka at Lord's, at the end of a shambolic summer in which three other captains, Gatting, Emburey and Cowdrey, had been discarded.

His prosaic lifestyle and lugubrious manner had never suggested leadership material, although back in 1980/81 Botham had wanted him as his vice-captain in the West Indies when the incumbent, Willis, was forced home prematurely because of injury. In 1982 he'd captained the England rebels in South Africa and in 1986 he led Essex to the county championship in his first season in charge, only to return to the ranks in 1988 because of a shortage of runs the previous year.

Relieved of the captaincy, he began 1988 in prime form, and when Keith Fletcher dropped out of the side to make way for a younger player Gooch stepped up once again, a more mature person. He began to enjoy captaincy and when the England selectors came knocking at his door, he was more than happy to oblige. He rallied a demoralised team, made 84 in the second innings and, although they eventually lost by eight wickets, he won credit for restoring their self-respect.

He went one better with a convincing win in the one-off Test against Sri Lanka and he obtained a release from his contract with Western Province so that he could captain England in India that winter. His change of heart and the presence of other South African rebels in the squad upset the Indian government enough to cancel the tour.

Having gained the England captaincy, Gooch was in no mood to lose it, but his hopes were stymied by the appointment of Ted Dexter as the new chairman of selectors. The previous summer Dexter, in his role as a *Sunday Mirror* journalist, had disparaged his leadership credentials, especially his lack of charisma, and so, not surprisingly, he wasn't retained as captain. Dexter and manager Micky Stewart wanted to reinstate Gatting, but when Gatting was vetoed by the TCCB because of his altercation with umpire Shakoor Rana, they opted for Gower. It proved a poisoned chalice since England were outplayed by Border's Australians and Gower didn't survive the humiliation. With Gatting ruling himself out of further contention by leading another rebel tour to South Africa, there seemed little alternative to Gooch. The reaction to his appointment was underwhelming. The doyen of cricket writers, E.W. Swanton, wrote that he'd found no one who regarded Gooch as a natural leader, either in terms of personality or tactically, but this was to underestimate him.

A great admirer of Fletcher's captaincy at Essex, Gooch, on succeeding him, drew heavily on his advice, especially regarding the positioning of fielders, and he won respect for his dedication, his supreme physical fitness and his sheer weight of runs. He found a great ally in Micky Stewart and together they preached the virtues of hard work, discipline and self-respect. England's participation in the Nehru Cup, a one-day tournament staged in India that autumn, proved an ideal opportunity to impart their new work ethic and to promote team spirit. They undertook further physical fitness training and specialist coaching at Lilleshall National Sports Centre on return, so that by the time they left for the Caribbean in January a quiet confidence pervaded the party.

The excellent spirit remained throughout the tour. They trained hard, they ate out together and discussed tactics. As past form would dictate, the home side started overwhelming favourites, but they underestimated their opponents and their new-found sense of pride. Adhering to a four-man pace attack, England looked to frustrate the West Indian batsmen by bowling to a tight off-stump line and wearing down their bowlers with painstaking batting.

Their tactics worked to perfection in the first Test at Kingston. Bowling with pristine accuracy, the England attack, led by Angus Fraser, dismissed their opponents for 164, and, thanks to 132 from vice-captain Lamb, they gained a first-innings lead of 200. The West Indies promised something better in their second innings, only to collapse against Gladstone Small and Devon Malcolm, leaving England jubilant victors by nine wickets. Such a stunning success against all the odds delighted everyone and vindicated Gooch's work ethic.

Despite enduring a frustrating time in Guyana watching the rain come down, England continued to astound with their dream start in the third Test at Port of Spain. Inserted by Gooch, the home side were soon reeling at 29/5 and, although Gus Logie hit 98, 199 was hardly a match-winning total.

England replied with 288 and with Malcolm again the destroyer with 6-77, giving him ten wickets in the match, they required 151 to win. Despite losing Gooch with a broken hand, they made it through to lunch at 71/1 and victory seemed a mere formality when a storm deluged the ground. By the time the match resumed at 4.05pm, the West Indies' desultory over rate in deteriorating light combined to thwart England of a well-merited victory. Not only that, they would be without their captain and Angus Fraser for the rest of the tour.

Under Lamb, they gave a stoical display in the fourth Test at Bridgetown, taking the game to the final hour, before being pulverised into submission days later in Antigua to give the West Indies the rubber 2-1. Had Gooch been able to play, it might well have been different.

'Gooch acceded to the captaincy in an unfortunate manner for he was nobody's first choice,' declared *Wisden*. 'But he confounded all preconceived notions about his limitations and emerged as the most influential figure of the tour. He was obsessive about his own physical fitness and his own mental preparation. He believes intensive training vital to the extension of his career, and from his self-motivation came the spur for other, younger and less gifted players to approach their game the same way. Gooch repeatedly commanded an unfailing respect among his players, and earned it by his quiet, individual counselling, his caring touch and his thoughtful tactics. In his own way, he was the most impressive England captain since Brearley.' [163]

Gooch returned to the captaincy for the summer Tests against New Zealand and India in triumph, not only beating both sides 1-0, but also playing the best cricket of his life. Against India, in the first Test at Lord's, he scored 333 and 123, then followed that up with another century at Old Trafford and 85 and 88 at the Oval. The return of Gower added stability to the batting, and England set off for Australia hopeful of regaining the Ashes they'd lost so abjectly in 1989. It wasn't to be.

From the opening days of the tour the same sense of purpose and camaraderie that had galvanised England in the West Indies was absent, and indeed the longer it progressed, the less effective the regimented approach became. An infected hand injury that side-lined Gooch for a month didn't help. The tourists looked ragged in their early matches, and in the first Test at Brisbane they threw away a narrow first-innings lead with a spineless batting performance in their second innings to lose by ten wickets.

It was a similar story in the second Test at Melbourne, except that Gooch was now back. Having established a lead of 46 on first innings, Gooch and Wayne Larkins consolidated nicely with a second-wicket stand of 86. At that point Gooch was out, the signal for a seismic collapse against Bruce Reid, the last nine wickets falling for a mere 47 and Australia went on to win by eight wickets.

Frustrated by his team's collapse at Melbourne, Gooch remained in high dudgeon at Sydney when Australia exploited England's woeful fielding to make 518. Never one to hide his feelings, he gave his players a fearful dressing down, thereby alienating Gower, who thought that Gooch had been far too negative.

Determined to make his point, Gower, a centurion in the previous Test, then batted to the manor born for 123 and, with Michael Atherton also making a century, England gave as good as they got. Declaring 49 behind on the fourth day, they claimed two wickets before stumps and on the final day the bowlers, led by spinner Phil Tufnell, worked their way through the Australian batting. With four hours left, they hovered uneasily on 166/7 before tail-ender Carl Rackemann dug in, defying England for 102 balls. During that time Gooch, in what he later called his greatest tactical error as captain, over-bowled his spinners at the expense of the quicks. When he eventually recalled Malcolm, he bowled Rackemann in his first over but by then it was almost too late. Left to make 255 in 28 overs, Gooch and Gower went for glory, but inevitably the stardust faded and the match was drawn.

After this brief revival at Sydney, it was back to mundanity with defeat against New South Wales and an inconsequential game against Queensland at Carrara on the Gold Coast. It was there that Gower posed the first major challenge to Gooch's captaincy.

In contrast to the self-contained Gooch, who led something of an austere lifestyle, Gower was the laughing cavalier whose free spirit favoured the flamboyant over the utilitarian. The most elegant of batsmen, he relied on his unique talents, most notably his precious gift of timing, to perform on the biggest stage. Never one for physical training and net practice, he fretted under the regimented approach of Gooch and Stewart and made little effort to conform. When questioned about his lack of commitment, Gower pointed to his overall record for England and his success on the tour so far, which ran to nearly 350 runs after three Tests.

It was during their game against Queensland that Gower looked to restore a touch of levity to a group of players low on morale. Leaving the ground without permission, he and team-mate John Morris hired two Tiger Moth aircraft from a nearby airfield and, flying low, buzzed the ground to salute Robin Smith's century. Their prank and their later return to the airfield to pose for pictures incensed the England management, which fined them £1,000 each, a sanction which Gower thought unduly severe. 'That Gooch, Stewart and Peter Lush, the tour manager, felt in all seriousness that Morris and I should be sent home tells you all you need to know about their po-faced approach to life,' he wrote. [164]

According to wicketkeeper Jack Russell, Gower was a complex character who needed handling with sensitivity, but Gooch couldn't do that. 'If Goochy's man-management had been better, David would have come around, and been visibly supportive. But there was to be no meeting of minds.' [165] Relations remained distant in the fourth Test and when Gower was out to a casual chip, caught at long leg, one of three men posted for the shot, his stock fell further in his captain's estimation.

With Gooch leading the way with 87 and 117, England managed a draw at Adelaide, but in the final Test at Perth they fell apart, losing by nine wickets. Disillusioned by more feckless batting and fielding, Gooch didn't mince his words at the post-match press conference, questioning his players' pride and commitment. He had every right to be disappointed by them, but, according to Lamb, his methods didn't work for everyone. 'This was the tour which finally convinced me that Gooch and Stewart got it wrong by over-doing the daily grind of nets and training when we weren't playing.' [166] 'For England in Australia, the diet was cricket morning, noon and night,' wrote John Thicknesse in *Wisden*, 'and for too many of the players it was indigestible.' [167] 'That 1990/91 tour of Australia took a lot out of Graham Gooch as captain,' commented Russell, 'and I don't think his standing was ever the same again.' [168]

Frustrated by his failure to motivate his team in Australia, Gooch reluctantly agreed to continue in office against Viv Richards's West Indians, still boasting a formidable bowling attack. In the first Test at Headingley, played in seaming conditions, England did well to gain a first-innings lead of 25, only then to struggle yet again in their second innings. At 124/6 they seemed destined for defeat, but Gooch was there still and, batting with growing authority, he played one of the great Test innings. 'Carrying his bat for 154 in a total of 252 puts Gooch on a pedestal above anything he or any of his contemporaries have done,' wrote Robin Marlar of the *Sunday Times*. 'Church bells have been rung and sermons preached for less.' [169]

Requiring 278 for victory, the West Indies lost by 115 runs, giving England their first victory at home over their opponents since 1969.

After a draw at Lord's, the West Indies won the next two Tests by exposing the frailties of the home batting. Graeme Hick, a failure in his first Test series, Lamb and Russell gave way to Botham, Tufnell and Alec Stewart at the Oval, changes fully vindicated by the result. Batting first, England made 419 before Tufnell lured the West Indies to their doom. Following on 243 behind, they proved of sterner mettle in their second innings, but not enough to prevent a five-wicket England victory, which enabled them to share the rubber.

Once again, Gooch, England's man of the series, deserved all the accolades that came his way. His 174 in the victory against Sri Lanka capped another memorable summer and persuaded him to lead England in New Zealand that winter, prior to the World Cup held in Australasia. With Tufnell in peak form and the fielding a great improvement on the previous tour, they won the three-Test series 2-0, and with a better slice of fortune they could well have won the World Cup rather than been runners-up.

Returning from what he'd assumed would be his last overseas tour, Gooch looked forward to leading his country against Pakistan that summer. The tourists were a highly talented if volatile group of players under their controversial captain Javed Miandad, and in another contentious series between these two sides Gooch won plaudits for his statesmanlike approach.

After the first Test was blighted by bad weather, the second Test at Lord's was a classic. Magnificent bowling by Wasim Akram and Waqar Younis posed severe problems for the England batsmen in both innings, but scoring 138 for victory looked beyond Pakistan when they slumped to 95/8, before Wasim and Waqar steadied the ship and steered it calmly into port.

Bad weather marred the third Test but Gooch's magisterial 135 at Headingley, along with seamer Neil Mallender's bowling, helped England to a six-wicket victory.

They were unable to repeat their success in the deciding Test at the Oval, where once again Wasim and Waqar proved too good for them. Pakistan won by ten wickets to take the rubber 2-1, and while there was no disgrace losing to such a competitive outfit, the critics were beginning to mount. Brearley wrote: 'The fact is that Gooch leads by example; by hard work, encouragement and by his own magnificent batting. But he still lacks the ability to respond subtly to the conditions, and his attitude to spinners borders on contempt.' [170]

In retrospect Gooch wished that he'd given up the captaincy there and then rather than agree to lead England in India that winter, partly to help his good friend Keith Fletcher, who'd replaced Stewart as England coach (as the position was now called). Even before the tour began, the selectors provoked outrage by omitting Gower and Jack Russell, their best wicketkeeper.

Although his dislike of the one-day game was well known, Gower's pedigree had shown little sign of abating when he'd returned to the England side against Pakistan that summer. Moreover, he remained a supreme player of spin and he had the added attribute of being a left-hander, but in the end 8,000 Test runs counted for nothing, his exclusion ostensibly due to his age, despite the fact that Gooch himself and Emburey were considerably older and Gatting was the same age.

Gower and Russell's omissions were the most heinous in a sequence of selectorial blunders, which included the elevation of leg-spinner Ian Salisbury from a net bowler to full-time member of the squad and a place in the first Test ahead of the other spinners Emburey and Tufnell; the inclusion of reserve wicketkeeper Richard Blakey in the final two Tests against India; and the omission of Atherton for the second Test, whose demotion also necessitated the promotion of Robin Smith to opener to cover for the late withdrawal of Gooch, laid low by food poisoning.

Aside from the usual challenges of touring the subcontinent, the team were confronted with an Indian Airlines strike which compelled them to undertake long, tiring rail journeys on what was already an exhausting itinerary. And for Gooch there were the added distractions of a marital separation on the eve of his departure, which sent him into his shell, a debilitating illness and, for once, a severe shortage of runs.

Playing lamentably throughout, England became the first team to lose all their matches in a Test series in India, each of their defeats by an embarrassingly wide margin. 'Now the cover of victory has been stolen away, and Goochism stands exposed,' wrote Simon Barnes. 'It is as limited as any other doctrinaire system.' [171]

Haunted by the defeatism of the team, Gooch was once again close to quitting, but a vote of confidence from Fletcher and the prospect of one further tilt against the Australians persuaded him to have second thoughts.

One of the most remarkable aspects of Gooch's captaincy was how the added responsibilities helped spur his batting. One bad series aside, he'd never played better and now, on the brink of his 40th birthday, he continued to stand head and shoulders above his team-mates. Despite scoring 65 and 133 in the first Test, England lost to Australia by 179 runs. According to Botham, there was no way they could save the series if Gooch continued as captain. 'With Gooch at the helm they look like a bunch of men condemned to walk up Tyburn Hill before being publicly hanged one after the other.' [172]

Having once again threatened resignation unless there was a discernible improvement in their performance at Lord's, it seemed illogical that he subsequently vowed to carry on given their ignominious defeat there. A much-changed side held their own at Trent Bridge, but at Headingley Australia's superiority was so pronounced that it finally pushed Gooch over the edge. 'Nobody would talk me out of it this time, although Keith Fletcher tried,' he later wrote. 'I was in a gloomy depression, banging the same old drum, but the players weren't reacting. Nobody was following my tune. It was time for a fresh, younger bandleader with a new approach and brighter ideas.' [173]

He wasn't being modest after the event. Brearley wrote at the time: 'A fresh mind, more open, less battered, more inspiring, is called for. The work ethic, overstressed, can fail to value sheer flair, as most notably with Gower.' [174]

Having made his decision on the second day of the match – Australia were well on their way to 653/4 declared – Gooch was demob happy thereafter, enjoying a few drinks in the team hotel bar and really going for his shots. 'It was an emotional time for him,' recalled Atherton, his successor. 'He had given the captaincy his all and it was easy to see the strain he was under. It was an indication also that the responsibilities had begun to weigh too heavily on him.' [175]

Gooch had gone some way towards restoring a sense of pride to the England cricket team. Following the upheavals of the late 1980s, he also brought stability to the captaincy and made himself indispensable by his rock-like integrity and his sheer volume of runs.

Even when he began to lose his grip during his final year, there was no question of the selectors deposing him; far from it, since Dexter, who'd once ridiculed his powers of leadership, was now pleading with him to stay.

His pleas fell on deaf ears, and rightly so because, after four years and 32 Tests in charge, Gooch had run out of road, his rigorous work ethic and personal example no longer able to lift his players to the heights necessary to live with the very best.

A creature of habit, he lacked the imagination to see that what worked for him didn't necessarily work for others, and by failing to fully recognise Gower's flights of genius, he deprived England of one of its greatest batsmen in all but three of his last 20 matches in charge. That said, it was Gooch, the ardent Thatcherite with his values of hard work and self-reliance, who encapsulated the spirit of the times, and during his time as captain a new professionalism took hold that changed English cricket forever.

Following his resignation, Gooch continued to play for England under Atherton until the end of the 1994/95 tour to Australia and for Essex until the end of 1997, by which time he'd amassed 128 centuries.

After retirement, he has remained active in the game as a broadcaster on *Test Match Special*, England selector, head coach at Essex and England batting coach.

Allan Lamb

ALLAN LAMB was born in Langebaanweg, near Cape Town, to British parents on 20 June 1954. His father was a useful club bowler and Lamb was an outstanding cricketer at Wynberg Boys' High School and Abbotts College.

He celebrated his first game for Western Province, aged 18, with a half-century against Eastern Province, and after two years of National Service he came to England in 1977 to further his career. He joined Northamptonshire by special registration in 1978 and proved such an asset that he topped the national averages in 1980.

Having served a four-year residential qualification, Lamb made his England debut against India in 1982 and for the next decade he was one of the mainstays of the middle order, his flamboyant personality making him a close friend of Gower and Botham.

In 1984 he scored three centuries against the redoubtable West Indian attack, his aggressive stroke-play the perfect antidote to bowlers who looked to batter their opponents into submission.

After a disappointing tour of Australia in 1986/87, Lamb spent a year on the sidelines before returning against the West Indies in 1988 and scoring a gritty century at Lord's.

The following year he was appointed captain of Northamptonshire and looked to invigorate them with the same positive attitude that he brought to his batting. With Gower, Botham, Gatting and Emburey all absent for the 1989/90 tour to the West Indies, he was named as vice-captain to Gooch, his effervescent personality a useful counter to the captain's natural reserve.

Warming to another crack at the West Indies, Lamb played a vital role in England's unexpected victory in the first Test at Kingston with a majestic 132. It was following Gooch's broken hand in the third Test that Lamb assumed the captaincy for the rest of the tour, his task made all the more challenging with Gooch still hovering in the background and central to all major decisions.

Renowned as something of a gambler, Lamb began true to form by inserting the West Indies on a flat wicket at Bridgetown, hoping that any early moisture would play to his bowlers' advantage. Without seamer Angus Fraser, incapacitated by a hip injury, England lacked the control of the two previous Tests, but, nevertheless, they were still in the game at 108/3 when Viv Richards strolled imperiously to the wicket. Forced out of the previous Test because of illness and subjected to endless comment about his fading powers, the West Indian captain was in no mood to submit meekly to the hostility of the England attack. No sooner did Devon Malcolm drop short, Richards mounted his charger, dispatching him for 18 in one over. Lamb withdrew him from the attack soon afterwards, a move which Malcolm thought to be premature, although this was his most inauspicious performance of the whole tour as figures of 0-142 would signify. According to the sports journalist Richard Evans, he appeared to have missed Gooch's reassuring presence. 'From a distance it seemed as if Lamb's high-pitched, staccato tones, accompanied by some less than accommodating field placings, were not quite the kind of leadership a troubled and still inexperienced fast bowler needed.' [176]

In reply to the West Indies' 446, Lamb led the fightback with a feisty 119, but England trailed by 88 on first innings. With the home side set on quick runs on the penultimate day, Lamb went on to the defensive, slowing the over rate down to ten an hour, but he couldn't prevent a declaration that evening. England, in the hour or so remaining, lost three wickets and, bravely though they resisted on the morrow, the West Indies – with Ambrose taking eight wickets – were fully deserving of their victory.

Leaving Barbados exhausted, the tourists were in no state to play another Test in Antigua two days later, especially since their injury list was mounting. So serious was their plight that Gower, who was covering the series for television, had been drafted in to play against Barbados, and Lamb wanted him to play in the Antigua Test, but his choice was vetoed by the management. It proved a serious oversight because the England batting, without Gooch, lacked depth, and on the fastest pitch of the series they were no match for the West Indian quicks.

Defeated by an innings, they lost the series 2-1. Had Gooch remained fit, the result might well have been different. 'Lamby had great talent as a batsman and worked very hard at his own game,' declared Alec Stewart, then on his first tour, 'but Gooch thought more about the overall picture and we missed his leadership.' [177]

Lamb returned home to another productive summer against New Zealand and India and he retained the vice-captaincy on the 1990/91 tour to Australia. Once again fate intervened and he found himself captaining England in the first Test at Brisbane while Gooch recuperated from a poisoned finger.

With the match evenly poised after two days there then took place one of those notorious incidents which left something of a stigma upon those concerned. Bowled out cheaply in their first innings, England fought back the next day to gain a narrow lead of 42, only then to see their batsmen struggle once again in their second innings. They reached 56/3 by the close, with Lamb one of the not-out batsmen, at which point he and Gower, who'd already been dismissed, headed for the Gold Coast some 50 miles away to have dinner with media tycoon Kerry Packer and Tony Greig at Jupiters Casino.

Although they drank sparingly and were back in their hotel by 1am, they were photographed coming out of the casino. More important, Lamb was out almost immediately the next morning, and although there was no obvious connection between his dismissal and his late night it didn't look good, especially as England collapsed to 114 all out to lose by ten wickets. The press were quick to accuse Lamb of a dereliction of leadership and *Wisden* later referred to his shocking error of judgement.

Forced to miss the next two Tests himself because of injury, Lamb was relieved of his vice-captain responsibilities at the end of the tour and within a year he'd played his last Test. He continued to captain Northamptonshire until his retirement at the end of the 1995 season.

Thereafter he set up Allan Lamb Associates Limited, specialising in corporate sporting events, and he has proved a popular after-dinner speaker.

Michael Atherton

MICHAEL ATHERTON was born in Failsworth, Lancashire, on 23 March 1968. His first cricketing coach was his father, Alan, a Bolton headmaster who, besides representing Manchester United reserves, played cricket for Woodhouses in the Lancashire and Cheshire League.

Educated at Briscoe Lane Primary School, Atherton became their first pupil to go to Manchester Grammar School. His parents struggled to pay the fees, but their investment was amply rewarded, since he flourished in that intense academic and sporting environment. In addition to his success in the football eleven, he topped the batting averages in his first full year in the cricket eleven, captaining the side in his final three years.

Having broken all kinds of school records during his time there, and receiving a solid grounding in league cricket when playing for Woodhouses, he continued his gilded ascent at Cambridge. Making his debut against Essex, the university were soon 20/7, but Atherton stood firm and scored 73, convincing himself that he could make it as a first-class cricketer. He captained Cambridge for two years and left the university a more confident, rounded personality.

Weeks after he came down, he won his first England cap, against Australia at Trent Bridge, after only 23 matches for Lancashire. He began with a duck but broke through spectacularly the following summer against New Zealand and India, scoring 753 runs in

11 innings and forming a highly successful opening partnership with Gooch.

His form fluctuated somewhat thereafter, but scores of 80 and 99 in the second Test against Australia in 1993 re-established his position at the top of the order. Once again, England failed to mount an effective challenge for the Ashes and, after they went 3-0 down at Headingley, Gooch resigned the captaincy. While Stewart had deputised for Gooch twice earlier in the year, Atherton had youth and innovation on his side. At the age of 25 he became England's 73rd captain and the first Lancastrian for 41 years, his background, intelligence and batting pedigree all pointing to his rendezvous with destiny.

A shy, rather solitary person, Atherton was an unassuming northerner who shunned the celebrity lifestyle in favour of a night in the pub, a day's fishing or a good book to read. Determined to remain his own man, he spoke his mind and made little effort to court popularity with the media. Yet behind the dour exterior there lay a more animated personality whose honesty, humour and self-effacement gained him a loyal following. While perfectly capable of admonishing a player who had fallen short, he'd invariably do this in private and he provided a sympathetic shoulder to lean on for those in trouble. David Lloyd, England's coach between 1996 and 1999, wrote: 'Many times, I saw him turn down the chance to spend an evening with the gregarious group on a tour and instead go and knock on the door of someone feeling down, drag him out for a meal and cheer him up. The team knew this but nobody else would appreciate such a side to the Atherton character.' [178]

In his first Test in charge, he won the toss and opened up with 72 but, thereafter, Australia's superiority once again reasserted itself and England lost by eight wickets. For the final Test, Atherton pressed for the recall of Hick, and Hick duly rewarded him with 80 in England's first innings. On a lightning-fast Oval wicket, the return of Malcolm, Fraser and Steve Watkin made all the difference as England emerged victors by 161 runs.

Flushed with his triumph, Atherton was given a leading say over the selection of the team to tour the West Indies. Convinced that

England needed to emulate the example of Australia in the mid-1980s by following a bold youth policy, he placed his faith in young bucks such as Nasser Hussain, Mark Ramprakash and Graham Thorpe as opposed to the old sweats such as Gower and Gatting.

Although the West Indies were no longer quite the force of old, their batting contained a genius in Brian Lara and two exceptional opening bowlers in Ambrose and Walsh. It was Walsh who singled out Atherton for a torrid examination in the first Test at Kingston, but despite being hit his refusal to buckle won him the admiration of his team-mates. 'It was hugely impressive and increased his authority as captain in the eyes of all of us in the England dressing room,' recalled Malcolm. [179]

England lost that match, and the next one at Georgetown, despite Atherton's 144, but they seemed destined to reverse their fortunes in the third Test at Port of Spain, before disaster set in. With the home side only 67 ahead in their second innings with half the side out, Hick, normally the most reliable of catchers, dropped Shivnarine Chanderpaul twice, enabling them to make a recovery of sorts. Requiring 194 to win on a wearing wicket, England endured the worst of all starts when Ambrose trapped Atherton first ball and, thereafter, he ran amok through the England upper order with a stupendous spell of bowling. His 6-24 was overwhelmingly responsible for their 46 all out, only one run more than their lowest-ever total, a crushing defeat that shattered the dressing room.

Determined not to overreact, Atherton didn't say much then, but he did let fly in Grenada after a feeble batting display against a Board XI had resulted in a heavy defeat. His words carried weight because England bounced back in Barbados with their best cricket of the tour. Opening up in front of thousands of British supporters, Atherton and Stewart put on 171 for the first wicket, establishing an early advantage they never surrendered, winning by 208 runs.

They then batted resolutely at St John's, Antigua, to secure a draw after Lara had run riot with a record-breaking 375, Atherton leading the way with 135, taking his run tally for the series to 530 with an average of 50.60. 'I had great admiration for the way Athers led from the front, instilling extra determination into us by toughening it out at the crease,' wrote Russell. 'Whatever the subsequent reservations about Mike Atherton as a tactical captain, no player on that tour of the West Indies will forget the lead he gave us. He made you want to go through barbed wire and brick walls for him.' [180]

England's fightback, however, cut little ice with the new chairman of selectors, Ray Illingworth. He was publicly critical of several leading players and having extracted an assurance from the TCCB that he would have the final say in selection, he set about laying down the law. Wholesale changes were made for the first Test against New Zealand and, when Malcolm bowled poorly, Illingworth, overriding the wishes of Atherton, omitted him for the second Test. 'That day was the lowest point of my career to date,' Malcolm later wrote. 'Getting no support from my captain made it worse, especially after he'd admitted that he wanted me to play.' [181]

England beat New Zealand 1-0 but they were completely outclassed by South Africa, who celebrated their return to Test cricket in England with a mammoth 356-run victory at Lord's. The match, however, is chiefly remembered for a ball-tampering scandal. On the third afternoon, as England struggled to stay in the match, television cameras caught Atherton rubbing something from his pocket on the ball. The third umpire witnessed the incident and informed both umpires and match referee Peter Burge. Burge summoned Atherton after close of play that evening to explain himself. Atherton assured him that he hadn't put anything in his pocket, and Burge accepted his explanation that nothing untoward had occurred.

The next morning's Sunday papers weren't so convinced, and, after they had published damning photos of the incident, Illingworth took it upon himself to investigate further. Atherton admitted to him that he had had dirt in his pocket and that he had misled the match referee. Accepting that his captain hadn't tampered with the ball and he was simply drying his hands with the dirt to free the ball from sweat so it could swing, Illingworth, anticipating a punitive sanction from the match referee, acted peremptorily by fining Atherton £1,000 for putting dirt on the ball and £1,000 for misleading the match referee. It did the trick in that Burge took no further action, but it didn't stop him describing Atherton's behaviour as infringing the spirit of cricket or stopping the media, led by the BBC's cricket correspondent Jonathan Agnew, for waging an all-out war against him. 'If the captain of England's cricket team fails to uphold the values of his society or the values to which society aspires,' declared *The Times*, 'he is unworthy of that uncommon honour which the captaincy represents. He should be replaced.' [182]

In the days after the Test, Atherton was relentlessly pursued by the press, but, after a brief wobble, his determination to stay put was boosted by the support he received from the players, the coach and the TCCB.

He also received a warm reception from the Headingley crowd when he came out to bat in the second Test. Displaying his habitual resilience, he scored a fighting 99, although his efforts were overshadowed by his comment that 'a hundred would have been the best answer to the gutter press'.

Getting the better of a draw at Headingley, England went to the Oval needing to win to level the series. The omens weren't good when, in reply to South Africa's 332, they languished at 222/7 and Atherton was fined half his match fee by Burge for expressing mild dissent at his lbw decision. Appreciating the depth of his plight, Gooch urged the team to rally behind their captain and they responded positively to his drumbeat. A spirited eighth-wicket stand of 71 between Darren Gough and Phil DeFreitas formed the backdrop to a devastating spell of fast bowling by Malcolm, his 9-57 totally decimating South Africa to set up an England eight-wicket victory. It was a much-needed boost for Atherton but any hopes this might lead to a more collegiate style of decision-making were soon dashed when it came to picking the side for Australia. Feeling himself to be in Illingworth's debt after the ball-tampering row, he bowed to his wishes, so that, while he was quite prepared to accept Gooch, he had Gatting and fast bowler Martin McCague foisted upon him rather than Fraser, who Illingworth didn't rate. 'The selection of the Ashes squad was the final proof that it was no longer the captain who had the final say,' wrote Atherton. 'Illy was the main influence. After all I'd been through in the previous weeks, I wasn't really in much of a position to argue.' [183]

On an injury-hit tour, England lost the first two Tests and were 20/3 in the third Test at Sydney, but a fourth-wicket stand of 174 by Atherton and John Crawley orchestrated a spectacular fightback, before inspired bowling by Gough dismissed Australia for 116. Building on a lead of 193 the English batsmen made steady progress in their second innings, but the run rate began to sag as Hick approached his first century against Australia. With time beginning to seep away, Atherton chose to declare, setting the home side 449 for victory, leaving Hick undefeated on 98 and in high dudgeon. 'The silence in the dressing room was deafening,' recalled Gough. 'Nobody could believe what he'd done. The spirit that had been built over three-and-a-half hard-fought and inspired days evaporated in that split second.' [184]

'In purely cricketing terms the move was entirely justified,' Atherton later wrote. 'However, it had a disheartening effect on the team precisely at a time when we ought to have been itching to get at Australia. For that reason, it is not a decision I would have taken again.' [185]

A double-century opening partnership by Michael Slater and Mark Taylor by lunchtime on the final day gave Australia an outside chance of victory, but a heavy shower freshened up the wicket and on the resumption of play it became a different game. Operating in familiar conditions, Fraser, a late tour replacement for the injured McCague, swung the game England's way with five quick wickets as Australia teetered at 292/7, but a combination of stubborn resistance by the tail and bad light foiled them at the last.

England continued their mini-revival with a surprising victory at Adelaide before they reverted to type at Perth, losing by 329 runs. In retrospect, the decision to take Gooch, Gatting and McCague proved flawed, while the presence of Illingworth for part of the tour did little to enhance Atherton's authority. According to Malcolm, 'On that tour, he seemed to lack drive, there was no killer instinct from him on the field and he didn't communicate very well with us. He gave the appearance of being fed up of being lumbered with a group of players who wouldn't have all been his preferred choices.' [186]

Losing the Ashes cost Fletcher his job as coach, much to Atherton's regret, and Illingworth assumed supreme control as manager and coach as well, in addition to his other responsibilities, a retrograde step in the eyes of the players. He took a couple of months to reappoint Atherton for the home series against the West Indies and then only for the first two Tests. Although they were badly beaten in the first Test, they came from behind to win at Lord's, with debutant Dominic Cork the hero.

An uneven pitch of variable bounce tailor-made for the West Indian fast bowlers at Edgbaston saw England overwhelmed in just over two days, much to the fury of a large Saturday crowd, some of whom abused Atherton, but, once again, they redressed the balance at Old Trafford. A match of fluctuating fortune turned England's way on the fourth morning when Cork claimed a hat-trick and they overcame early losses to win by six wickets.

Although Lara flourished on two flat wickets in the final two Tests, so did Atherton, and both matches were drawn.

Having held the West Indies to 2-2, England approached the tour to South Africa with confidence. In South Africa's wettest summer in memory, two of the Tests were ruined by rain and the home side failed to win the second Test at Johannesburg against all the odds. One hundred and sixty-seven for four at the beginning of the final day, and with fast bowlers Allan Donald and Shaun Pollock on the warpath, England's cause looked close to hopeless. The fact that they batted all day and lost only one wicket was primarily down to Atherton's heroic 645-minute 185*, one of the great rearguards of Test history.

With the fourth Test a tame draw, all depended on the decider at Cape Town. Thinking that their team had lacked the killer punch in previous games, Atherton and Illingworth opted to play five bowlers at the expense of a sixth specialist batsman, an error, since, once again, their batting lacked ballast. All out for 153 in their first innings, their bowlers fought back to have South Africa 171/9, only then to undermine all their efforts with an hour of mayhem. Throughout the tour a serious rift had developed between Illingworth and Malcolm, the man who, 18 months earlier, had destroyed South

Africa at the Oval. Frustrated by Malcolm's unwillingness to listen to technical advice and his inconsistency in the middle, Illingworth and bowling coach Peter Lever had taken to berating him in public. Dropped for the third and fourth Tests, much to his resentment, he was back in the team for Cape Town and was entrusted with the new ball in the hope of blasting out South Africa's number eleven Paul Adams. Unfortunately, his radar went missing, his four erratic overs conceding 26 runs, and with the other bowlers also off form, the last-wicket pair of wicketkeeper David Richardson and Adams added 71 vital runs.

Their stand proved the death knell of England's chances. Atherton was dismissed cheaply for the second time in the match, Thorpe was controversially run out and the last six wickets fell for 19 runs as they subsided to a ten-wicket defeat.

A 6-1 thrashing by South Africa in the ODIs followed by an abject showing in the World Cup in India and Pakistan brought the curtain down on another unfulfilling winter. 'Admittedly, Atherton is not the liveliest of leaders,' noted the former Somerset captain turned columnist Peter Roebuck. 'He can be stubborn, arrogant, dismissive and stiff. He lacks the words to rouse a flattened team, cannot match Beelzebub's roar: "Awake, arise, or be forever fallen". Nor can he put an arm around a player he does not respect.' [187] He went on to suggest that he needed a young, optimistic coach with the imagination to lift the team just at a time when change was in the air.

Worn out by its physical demands, Illingworth resigned as manager and was replaced by David Lloyd, the former Lancashire captain and coach, who was a soulmate of Atherton's. His appointment gave his captaincy something of a second wind, since England beat India at home in 1996 before losing to Pakistan, their batting once again unable to withstand the potency of Wasim Akram and Waqar Younis.

For the tour to Zimbabwe and New Zealand that winter, an edict prohibiting wives and families from joining the players upset a number of them and a wet Christmas in Zimbabwe without their loved ones offered little in the way of seasonal good cheer. England hadn't won many friends in Zimbabwe when they'd opposed their admission to full Test match status in 1992 and their dour, standoffish approach throughout their stay – not helped by substandard accommodation and facilities – further alienated the locals. Although unfortunate not to have won the first Test, their failure to beat their opponents in two games and their 3-0 loss in the ODIs only added to Atherton's woes as he battled with a serious decline in his own form. Subjected to ever greater vitriol in the press, relations between the team and the media deteriorated to such an extent that the traditional Christmas party given by the former for the latter was cancelled.

Desperate to leave Zimbabwe, England's mood lifted immeasurably once they arrived in New Zealand. A strenuous workout with the bowling machine at Hamilton did wonders for Atherton's confidence and he returned to form in the first Test with a masterly 83. With three hours still remaining, England were on the brink of victory, with the home side 13 ahead and the last pair in, but an unbroken century partnership between Nathan Astle and Danny Morrison, one of the worst batsmen in Test cricket, staved off defeat, heaping further pressure on Atherton.

New Zealand's reprieve proved merely temporary, since England won at Wellington and they triumphed again at Christchurch by four wickets, with Atherton contributing 94* and 118.

Their optimism carried over to the beginning of the season. Mark Taylor's Australians were seen off 3-0 in the ODIs and they were well beaten in the first Test by a side brimming with confidence. The tide soon turned, however, as Australia recovered their composure. England were saved by the weather at Lord's and were badly beaten in the next three Tests. With the Ashes lost once again, Atherton felt minded to give up the captaincy. Not only was he becoming completely self-absorbed by it to the detriment of those around him, but the criticism was getting to him.

Once again, England rallied at the Oval as Australia, not for the first time, tripped up chasing a small total. Their victory, ably masterminded by Atherton, gave encouragement to all those who wanted him to remain in charge. David Graveney, the chairman of selectors, Lloyd and Stewart were among those who urged him to lead England in the West Indies and, having given it some thought on holiday, he complied with their wishes. 'Perhaps my week's fishing at the end of the season had restored me and renewed my hope,' Atherton later wrote. 'Maybe the challenge still excited and energised me. Possibly I felt we had a great chance of success. Whatever the reason, it was a bad decision and one I knew I was going to regret.' [188]

With the West Indies so dependent on Ambrose, Walsh and Lara, Atherton thought England had a reasonable chance of beating them, and nothing during the early part of the tour disabused him of such hopes. After the first Test was cancelled on the first morning because of a dangerous Kingston wicket, the next two Tests were played at Port of Spain, the West Indies winning the first game by three wickets and England triumphant in the second one by the same margin.

Condemned to bat last on a turning wicket at Georgetown, England lost there by 242 runs – Atherton scoring nought and one – yet when the boot was on the other foot at Bridgetown the West Indies were saved by the weather.

At St John's, Antigua, in the final Test, England again had the worst of the conditions, especially when they were inserted on a damp wicket, and, although outplayed by their opponents, they merited a draw rather than another defeat.

Deflated by defeat and another dire series with the bat – Ambrose dismissed him six times – Atherton acknowledged that his time was up. Having advised the management of his intention to resign, he called his team together at the end of the game and informed them that he was vacating the captaincy. He thanked them for their efforts and then headed off to tell the world of his decision, leaving his team-mates in a state of shock and grief. He returned looking remarkably chipper to a dressing room which showered him with genuine affection. 'He had dealt with so much over 52 Tests and four and a half years without complaint,' wrote Stewart. 'No one had led England in more Tests or been better at leading from the front. We hadn't won enough Tests consistently enough to encourage Athers to believe that better times lay ahead.' [189]

Russell shared similar sentiments. 'We all felt we'd let him down, and I can state with complete conviction that his stock in the England dressing room was as strong as ever before he made his announcement. He's the toughest guy I ever played cricket with, and he has my total respect as player, captain and person.' [190]

For a side that could rise to great heights – Bridgetown 1994, the Oval 1994, Lord's 1995 and Edgbaston 1997 – Atherton's England remained infuriatingly inconsistent, only beating New Zealand (twice) and India amidst six series defeats. It was certainly Atherton's misfortune that he lacked a powerful attack compared to Australia, South Africa, Pakistan and the West Indies, a problem compounded by persistent injuries to leading bowlers Gough, Fraser and Dean Headley.

He was also hampered by a domestic structure which placed the interests of the counties above those of the Test team and an amateur selectorial system which chopped and changed the players with alarming regularity. To what extent this state of uncertainty contributed to player volatility, either in form or in character, is unclear, but, certainly, Atherton had more than his share of tricky customers to deal with. He did his best, not least by his courageous batting against a generation of great bowlers, but, ultimately, he couldn't inspire his men to show that same resilience, a poor reward for a proud patriot who deserved better.

Having renounced the captaincy, Atherton was happy to play under his two successors, Stewart and Hussain, and when the latter was forced to miss two Tests against Australia in 2001 he reluctantly returned to the helm. In the second of those games at Trent Bridge, England pushed Australia for much of it before the latter pulled away to win by seven wickets. At the end of a disappointing series with the bat, he retired and slipped easily into the media, becoming a highly respected journalist and broadcaster with Sky Sports. He is currently cricket correspondent for *The Times*.

Alec Stewart

ALEC STEWART was born in Merton on 8 April 1963 into a family steeped in sport. His father, Micky, played cricket for both Surrey and England, while his mother, Sheila, excelled at hockey and netball and both his siblings were accomplished athletes.

Fanatical about both cricket and football, Stewart fully embraced his father's work ethic from an early age. An outstanding wicketkeeper-batsman at Tiffin School, he also played club cricket for Malden Wanderers and for Surrey's second eleven.

In 1981 he made his debut for the county side and there, under the watchful eye of his father, who, as manager, afforded him no preference, he developed his game, his superb timing aided by the hard, bouncy wickets at the Oval.

From 1981 he spent the next eight winters playing grade cricket for Midland-Guildford, Western Australia, an experience which intensified his combative approach, not least his verbal jousting with the opposition.

In 1985 he won his county cap and, chosen for the England tour to the West Indies in 1989/90, he made his debut in the first Test at Kingston. Inclined to be a touch impetuous at first, it took him time to establish himself at this level, but a maiden century against Sri Lanka at Lord's in 1991 and two centuries against New Zealand the following winter confirmed his new-found status. On tour to the West Indies in 1993/94, he made a century in each innings in the Bridgetown Test, and over the next decade he proved himself one of England's most consistent batsmen, although all too often he had to sacrifice his preferred position as opener to take on the added responsibility of keeping wicket.

Missing out to Atherton when Gooch resigned the captaincy in 1993, he gave him his fullest support, and when Atherton called it a day in 1998 his experience, ability and the respect he commanded won him the role he'd always craved. A model professional – immaculately turned out, superbly fit and clean living – and an ardent patriot who gave everything, Stewart's regimented approach permitted little sympathy with temperamental mavericks such as Andrew Caddick or Phil Tufnell, neither of whom played for England under his auspices. But, in the main, he offered vocal encouragement in the field, supported his bowlers with the fields they wanted, and proved more sensitive than Gooch to individual needs.

Given England's lean decade against the top sides, Stewart faced a challenging assignment against Hansie Cronje's South Africa. He began purposefully at Edgbaston. Having secured a 112-run lead on first innings, his team batted adventurously in their second innings to set up a declaration, only for rain to wash out the final day.

Stewart again showed positive intent at Lord's by winning the toss and inserting his opponents. On a helpful wicket South Africa struggled to 46/4 but it went awry from then on as Jonty Rhodes hit a century and England ended up losing by ten wickets.

They were once again forced to follow on 369 behind at Old Trafford, but this time they showed more resolve. Atherton and Stewart added 226 for the third wicket, Stewart's 164 one of his finest knocks for England, and despite the middle order contributing little, the lower order kept fighting. As the last pair, Robert Croft and Fraser, saw out the final overs to deprive South Africa of victory, Stewart raced on to the middle at the end to embrace his players, knowing the psychological boost it would give the team thereafter.

At Trent Bridge, Stewart, on winning the toss, once again fielded first, a decision that seemed flawed when South Africa made 374. England replied with 336 before bowling out their opponents for

208 and Atherton, surviving a controversial caught-behind appeal off Donald, guided his side home by eight wickets.

In the deciding match at Headingley, England trailed by 22 on first innings but a painstaking 94 from Hussain in their second innings kept them in contention. Requiring 219 to win, South Africa crashed to 27/5 before a sixth-wicket stand of 117 by Rhodes and Brian McMillan gave them renewed hope. At the scheduled close they needed another 34 runs for victory with two wickets left, but an extra half hour was possible should one side claim it. With his bowlers close to exhaustion, Stewart had no wish to continue and, with South Africa dithering, unsure of the rules, he marched his men briskly off. His initiative proved well justified, since England regrouped overnight and mopped up in the morning to win by 25 runs.

To have beaten South Africa, albeit with some good fortune from umpiring decisions, enhanced Stewart's authority as his team prepared to tour Australia. Having sought the England captaincy, the burdens of leadership fell lightly upon him, especially since he and his family kept a low profile off the field. 'The playing demands didn't weigh me down either,' he later wrote. 'By then I was very experienced and knew my own game inside out and how to prepare myself, physically and mentally.' [191]

With Australia unbeaten against them for over a decade, England's underdog status was compounded by the number of injuries they sustained. Indebted to the weather for saving them at Brisbane, they were soundly defeated at Perth and Adelaide. With Stewart short of runs, he decided to relinquish the gloves to reserve wicketkeeper Warren Hegg at Melbourne and revert to opening the batting. The move paid off, since he scored 107 and 52 in a low-scoring match. Chasing 175 for victory, Australia seemed to be coasting at 103/2 before a stunning catch by Ramprakash at square leg sent back Justin Langer, sparking a middle-order collapse against paceman Dean Headley.

As the game neared its climax, both Headley and Gough were tiring at the end of an uninterrupted three hour and 50-minute stint in the field (caused partly by the early tea interval and partly by making up time for the loss of the opening day). Although Steve Waugh, the not-out batsman, claimed the extra half hour at 7.22pm against Stewart's wishes, he then made little effort to shield the tail from the strike, a fatal error as Gough dismissed Stuart MacGill and Glenn McGrath in three balls to give England victory by 12 runs.

Buoyed by their unexpected triumph, England went to Sydney in great heart. Stewart lost the toss for the fifth successive time and Australia gained a crucial 102-run advantage on first innings. They were also fortunate to see opener Michael Slater survive a blatant run out, since he went on to make 123 out of their total of 184. Facing a daunting target of 293 on a turning wicket, Stewart and Mark Butcher began boldly, but the middle order was no match for MacGill's leg spin and England lost by 98 runs. 'No player can have had a greater workload than Stewart on his first tour as captain,' declared *Wisden*. 'His leadership style relied more on remember the three lions on your chest than tactical finesse. But his strutting demeanour at least made England look purposeful, and he could not be blamed for the injuries, dropped catches and batting collapses.' [192]

Stewart retained the captaincy for the 1999 World Cup, the first to be held on home soil since 1983. He upset the ECB by siding with the players in a modest revolt over pay, and when England failed to reach the second stage of the World Cup for the first time, Stewart, amid a rising tide of disillusion, was unceremoniously thrown overboard. Perhaps he was always going to be a stop-gap captain, but his removal seemed unduly premature, a sop to media pressure reminiscent of the bad old days. He had, after all, won England's first series against a major Test side for 11 years, while his loss to Australia was no worse than Gooch and Atherton's before him and Hussain's afterwards.

Although Stewart bore no grudges about his demotion, he thought it illogical since he lost the Test captaincy on the basis of the team's failure in the World Cup. Gough wrote: 'After all the furore about the contracts and the behind-the-scenes nonsense, Lord's were after a scapegoat. The Establishment view was that Stewie had been found wanting in keeping the England players under control. That was his job. Our one-day form was the problem, culminating in disappointment in the World Cup, yet Stewart was sacked as our Test captain.' [193]

Stewart continued to play for his successor, Hussain, and, having deputised for him at Lord's against the West Indies the next year, he subsequently celebrated his 100th Test with a century at Old Trafford. He remained at the heart of the England team as wicketkeeper-batsman until his final Test against South Africa at the Oval in 2003.

In 2004 Stewart became a founding director of Arundel Promotions with management services to leading sports personalities, before his appointment as director of cricket at Surrey in 2014.

The Modern Captaincy: 1999 to the Present

THE appointment of the Zimbabwean Duncan Fletcher to replace David Lloyd as coach in 1999 wasn't merely a change of personnel, it marked the transformation of the system. Long admired for his coaching, Fletcher only accepted the job provided he had full control over the Test side, which now became possible with the introduction of central contracts in 2000, and he used this to telling effect, raising standards of fitness and practice and forging a healthy team ethic. With Hussain uncompromising in his desire for success, England rediscovered the art of winning, beating the West Indies in a rubber for the first time in 31 years, and triumphing in both Pakistan and Sri Lanka. Australia, however, continued to elude them – much to Hussain's frustration, especially on tour there in 2002/03. Well into his fourth year as captain and weighed down by fatigue, his volcanic temperament periodically erupted. Feared and respected but no longer able to motivate his players as of old, he voluntarily gave way to Michael Vaughan after the first Test against South Africa the following summer.

Relaxed and thoughtful, Vaughan proved an ideal captain, especially in getting the best out of his star players such as Steve Harmison, Andrew Flintoff and, later, Kevin Pietersen. Building on Hussain's foundations and working closely with Fletcher, he was soon leading England to glory, his greatest triumph coming in the summer of 2005 when they regained the Ashes for the first time in 16 years. In a rubber notable for its captivating cricket, his captaincy stood on a par with Brearley's, especially his willingness to attack and his composure under pressure, only then for misfortune to assail him. Afflicted by serious knee trouble on tour to Pakistan that autumn, he was incapacitated for a full year, during which time his ailing team slumped to a 5-0 whitewash in Australia under Flintoff's faltering leadership.

Returning to Test duty in the summer of 2007, Vaughan now had to contend with a new coach, Peter Moores, whose regimented style differed markedly from his own. Compelled to dance to Moores's tune and disillusioned with his own deteriorating form, Vaughan stepped down in the wake of England's defeat against South Africa in August 2008. His sudden departure days before the final Test and the selectors' wish to have one man captaining both the Test and one-day teams created a vacancy for which there were few obvious contenders. Consequently, they took a gamble by choosing Kevin Pietersen, a brilliant batsman with little captaincy experience and with a mercurial personality that polarised opinion. In a previous age he might well have survived, but in the age of the dual captaincy his fractious relationship with Moores proved to be his undoing. Convinced that he couldn't work with a coach whose training methods weren't conducive to the international arena, Pietersen relayed his concerns to the chairman of the ECB, Giles Clarke, on tour to India months later, and he then went further by threatening to resign unless Moores was removed prior to the forthcoming tour to the West Indies.

Unfortunately, news of his ultimatum became public over New Year when Pietersen was on holiday in South Africa, and when the ECB met to discuss it the fact that he didn't carry the dressing room told against him. Forced into a corner with a pistol pointed at them, the ECB stood their ground and returned fire by dismissing both captain and coach.

With English cricket in crisis and the team about to depart to the West Indies, opener Andrew Strauss was installed as the new captain and Andy Flower, one of Moores's staff, as acting coach. Their start couldn't have been more traumatic as they were shot out for 51 in the first Test at Kingston to lose by an innings. Chastened by their drubbing, Strauss was able to persuade his team to assume greater responsibility for their actions and with three centuries in the next three Tests he practised what he preached.

He continued in sublime form against Australia that summer and, against all expectation, he won back the Ashes. Working closely with Flower, by now England's director of cricket, and with an expanding support staff, they turned the team into a highly professional outfit which went eight series unbeaten, culminating in a 4-0 thrashing of India that took them to the top of the ICC world rankings. In under three years Strauss had become one of England's most esteemed captains, his success owing more to personal character than tactical insight, yet, like Vaughan in 2005, his time at the top was all too brief. Team fatigue, a loss of personal form and dressing-room friction made 2012 an especially gruelling year and Strauss, like Gooch, Atherton, Hussain and Vaughan before him, found the four-year cycle the limit of his endurance. His resignation was deeply regretted when he handed over to his vice-captain Alastair Cook.

Cook, less assertive than Strauss, took time to establish his grip over the team and it needed the exclusion of Pietersen and the retirement of several old timers following the Ashes whitewash of 2013/14 before he came fully into his own. Given a fresh lease of life by new coach Trevor Bayliss, he regained the Ashes in 2015 and won in South Africa that winter, but while England began to play a more adventurous game under his leadership their form remained patchy. Defeated 4-0 in India in 2016/17, an exhausted Cook conceded that the team needed a fresh impetus and relinquished the captaincy to his deputy Joe Root with little fanfare.

Captains are now part of a much greater support structure and possess less authority than in Brearley's day, let alone the autocrats of the amateur age, but, compared to the instability of the 1970s and 80s when their predecessors came and went with alarming frequency, they are now relatively secure in their tenure and choose the moment of their departure. What they cannot escape from is the relentless international schedule, the growing demands of the media and the intense fatigue that sets in after several years. The fact that no captain has felt able to carry on beyond the normal four to five-year cycle suggests that leadership in the modern age remains as intense as ever.

Nasser Hussain

NASSER HUSSAIN was born in Madras on 28 March 1968 to an Indian father and an English mother. His father, Joe Hussain, represented Madras in the Ranji Trophy, and when the family moved to England in 1975 he took control of an indoor cricket school in Ilford, coaching his three sons religiously. A temperamental character, he wanted the very best for his children and instilled in all of them his intense work ethic and passionate desire to succeed. 'My Dad pushed me as much as a father could,' Hussain later wrote. 'He used to drive me everywhere, to every game. If I didn't get runs or wickets, you could cut the atmosphere with a knife. He wouldn't talk to me for a couple of days. It was as serious as that.' [194] On one occasion, when Hussain, playing for Forest School, scored a century and took nine wickets with his leg spin, his father berated him for not having taken the final wicket as the last pair played out time. It was this exposure to such high expectations that helps explain Hussain's highly strung temperament as he spent the rest of his career trying to win his father's approval.

At 15 he was considered the most promising leg-spinner in the county, but as he grew he lost his flight. He turned to batting instead and became the first cricketer at Forest to score 1,000 runs in a season since 1901.

After Durham University, Hussain joined Essex in 1987 and was profoundly influenced by the winning mentality of captains Fletcher and Gooch. Two years later he rose to national prominence with 990 runs in 15 matches and he was chosen for England's tour to the West Indies that winter. Enduring a taxing time in his first three Tests, he made little impact and spent the next three years in the wilderness.

Regaining his place against Australia in 1993, he scored 71 and 47* at Trent Bridge but did little thereafter, and he remained out of contention until 1996. He marked his return with a century against India in the first Test at Edgbaston and followed up with another one at Trent Bridge.

The next year he went one better, scoring 207 against Australia at Edgbaston, and when Atherton relinquished the England captaincy in March 1998 Hussain, his vice-captain, went head to head with Alec Stewart for the succession. Still deemed too self-obsessed and confrontational – he was twice suspended by Essex for alienating his team-mates – he lost out to Stewart but, undeterred, his batting continued to progress, and when Stewart was sacked after the 1999 World Cup Hussain was appointed in his place.

A proud, passionate player who hated to lose, he wanted to stiffen the spine of his team-mates, who, he thought, had grown up soft. 'This softness comes from playing county cricket, which is all very matey and lovey-dovey,' he declared. 'No one is sledging anyone, we are all mates out there and it's about a few cups of tea and maybe a Pimms or two afterwards.' [195]

Honest to the core, Hussain brooked no excuses when they fell short, and he could be coruscating in his criticism in private, but he backed them in public. Although notoriously self-absorbed as a player himself, captaincy made him open his eyes to those around him. He won the respect of his players by embracing all types, not least the more challenging ones such as Andrew Caddick, Tufnell and Thorpe, his attitude shaped by his own troubled past as a rebel.

The key to his captaincy was his immediate rapport with new coach Duncan Fletcher, the former captain of Zimbabwe who'd won his stripes as a coach with Western Province and Glamorgan. Well respected as a meticulous organiser and deft man-manager, Fletcher liked to stay in the background and was perfectly content that his captain ruled supreme on the field. Although very much his own man, Fletcher listened quietly to what players had to say, never talking down to them, and treated them as individuals. Boosted by the introduction of central contracts, he and Hussain tried to provide a greater sense of continuity by selecting players of character and giving them time to prove themselves.

Before Fletcher took up his post at the end of the 1999 season, Hussain faced New Zealand, a middling team infused with a hard-nosed ethos. He began in positive vein at Edgbaston, where, in a low-scoring game, England overcame a first-innings deficit of 100 to win by seven wickets with night-watchman Alex Tudor scoring 99*.

His fortune deserted him at Lord's when he sustained a broken finger during his first innings of 61. England's 186 proved sorely inadequate as New Zealand eked out a big lead, and with Hussain unable to bat in their second innings they tumbled to a nine-wicket defeat.

His injury kept him out of the Old Trafford Test which England, with the help of the weather, managed to draw, meaning that all came down to the final game at the Oval. Back on parade, Hussain exuded authority in the field, not least the way he handled his bowlers. They dismissed New Zealand for 236, but, carrying an exceptionally long tail, they could manage only 153 in reply.

The England bowlers fought back to have the tourists 39/6 in their second innings, before a belligerent 80 from their charismatic all-rounder Chris Cairns kept them in contention.

Requiring 246 to win, England seemed marginal favourites when Atherton and Thorpe took them to 123/2, but once they were both out the fight went out of them as the last seven wickets fell for 19 runs. They not only lost a series at home to New Zealand for only the second time, they slipped to the bottom of the *Wisden* World Championship. As the critics attributed England's demise to the failings of a cricketing culture which bred mediocrity, a section of the Oval crowd took out their frustration on Hussain, booing him at the presentation ceremony.

With English cricket at rock bottom, Hussain could at least derive comfort from coach Fletcher now that he was on board. They chose a young, inexperienced team to tour South Africa in the hope that Andrew Flintoff, Michael Vaughan, Chris Adams, Chris Read and Gavin Hamilton, among others, could establish themselves at the highest level.

Unfortunate to be inserted on a damp wicket at Johannesburg against Donald and Pollock in the first Test, England endured a nightmare start of 2-4 and 116 all out to lose by an innings.

They were unfortunate again at Port Elizabeth, this time with the umpiring, but they escaped with a draw owing to Hussain, who followed up his 82 in the first innings with 70* in the second.

He continued his golden run at Durban with 146* in England's 366/9 declared. South Africa fell cheaply to Caddick and were forced to follow on, but a monumental 275 from opener Gary Kirsten ensured they saved the match with ease.

Two horrific batting failures at Cape Town exposed all England's old frailties and they lost by an innings, before gaining a consolation win in the rain-affected match at Centurion, courtesy of captain Cronje's generous declaration.

While many of the youngsters, Vaughan and Flintoff aside, failed to come good, the tour had at least set England on a new, upward path, with captain and coach not only forming an immediate rapport but also promoting an excellent team spirit. 'The most encouraging aspect of the tour was Hussain's impact as captain,' reported the *Daily Express*'s Colin Bateman in *Wisden*. 'Appointed the previous summer after the World Cup, he stamped his authority on a team containing his two predecessors, Michael Atherton and Alec Stewart. His batting flourished with the extra responsibility, and he was by some distance the team's best player. Often regarded as a confrontational character, intense about his personal success, Hussain handled his players with thoughtful attention to detail.' [196]

England's new-found confidence was on show against Zimbabwe at Lord's the following summer, but their victory gave way to an inglorious draw against them at Trent Bridge and an overwhelming defeat against the West Indies at Edgbaston. Compelled to miss the second Test at Lord's because of a broken thumb, Hussain watched transfixed from the balcony as Stewart once again took over.

An extraordinary game reached its climax on the third day when England, left 191 to win on a lively pitch, seemed destined for defeat till an unbroken ninth-wicket partnership of 33 between Dominic Cork and Gough saw them through to a two-wicket victory.

Confronted with a similar challenge the previous year, England would probably have buckled under the pressure, but Hussain had instilled a new resilience in the side. It was a quality he showed in abundance throughout 2000 when his batting went to pieces, his miserable Test aggregate of 92 runs in ten innings that summer culminating in a pair at the Oval. While his captaincy was clearly affecting his batting, his dearth of runs didn't affect his captaincy, which remained forceful and purposeful. Opener Marcus Trescothick was successfully blooded and the faith he placed in the temperamental Caddick was amply rewarded with the latter's rise to the front rank of the England attack. He and Gough destroyed the West Indies at Headingley – the match was over in two days – and, along with Atherton's batting, they helped England to a resounding win at the Oval, their first series win over their opponents in 31 years. 'The manner in which, as the final wicket fell, he [Hussain] slumped to the ground was a picture of an obsessively focused man close to mental exhaustion,' wrote *The Guardian*'s Mike Selvey. [197] 'No one has earned a break more.' 'His captaincy was a major factor in our success that summer, and he led from the front without the benefit of runs or being in form,' wrote Gough. 'That took some doing.' [198]

Boosted by their new-found resolve, England set out for Pakistan, their first tour there in 13 years, full of positive intent. Well prepared for the challenges there, not least facing their top-flight spinners, Saqlain Mushtaq and Danish Kaneria, on turning wickets, they were Pakistan's equals in the first two Tests. At Karachi in the deciding game, Hussain stressed the need to occupy the crease and, led by Atherton's nine-and-a-half hour vigil for 125, they finished 17 short of the home side's first-innings total of 405. He then instructed his bowlers to give nothing away and their attritional approach taxed the patience of the Pakistan batsmen to the extent that they lost their last six wickets for 30 runs.

Needing 176 to win in a minimum 44 overs, England scored freely through Hick and Thorpe, but Pakistan's blatant time-wasting caused Hussain apoplexy in the pavilion as the light faded fast. When he joined Thorpe at the crease with 20 still needed it was near darkness, but the umpires, miffed by captain Moin Khan's shenanigans, had decided to stay put and Thorpe, with a couple of edges, saw England home by six wickets. It was their first series win in Pakistan since 1961/62, and Pakistan's first-ever defeat at Karachi in 35 Tests. According to *The Sun*'s John Etheridge, writing in *Wisden*, Hussain's presence at the wicket at the end was most appropriate, since, his shortage of runs aside, he remained a towering figure. 'He was tactically sharp, refused to allow the frustrations and restrictions peculiar to touring Pakistan affect his squad, motivated them superbly and, not least, displayed commendable restraint at being given out incorrectly at least three times on the tour, twice in the second Test alone.' [199]

He continued to display his leadership credentials on tour to Sri Lanka after Christmas. Following a toxic one-day international between the two sides at Adelaide in January 1999, in which the Sri Lankan captain Arjuna Ranatunga was charged with bringing the game into disrepute, this tour was never going to be for the faint-hearted. The provincial games proved an early warning of the storm to come, and with two inexperienced officials in charge of the first Test at Galle both teams were warned by the match referee to conduct themselves in the right spirit. His words had little effect as England were undone by the Sri Lankan spinners, egged on by some hysterical appealing and some rank bad umpiring.

Following another double failure with the bat, Hussain was close to his wits' end, unable to sleep properly and stalking the corridors of the team hotel in the early hours. Stiffened by the support of his team, he warned them off a siege mentality post-Galle. At Kandy, in a poisonous atmosphere exacerbated by more incompetent umpiring, Hussain stood firm at the crease. Fortunate to survive clear bat and pad catches on 53 and 67, he and Thorpe added 167 for the third wicket, and when he reached his century he waved his bat ecstatically at his team-mates in recognition of the support they'd given him throughout the past year. His painstaking 109 gave England a vital first-innings lead of 90. Needing 161 to win, they finished the penultimate day on 91/4, but, amid great tension, Thorpe and Craig White guided them to a three-wicket victory.

One of Hussain's great successes as captain had been his sensitive handling of his opening bowlers Gough and Caddick, and they, along with Croft, the Glamorgan off-spinner, bowled England to another victory at Colombo to register their fourth consecutive series win. They were making progress, Hussain declared, but they still had some road to travel to catch up with Steve Waugh's Australia, their prime opponents that summer.

Prior to that they beat Pakistan at Lord's, only to lose to them at Old Trafford in Hussain's absence, incapacitated by a broken thumb. His misfortune with injury continued in the first Test against Australia when he sustained a broken finger. Beaten by an innings, England lost the next two games in his absence, and by the time he returned the series as a contest was over. For the seventh successive time, they had been outplayed by Australia. Their defeat in the final Test at the Oval marked the end of Atherton's distinguished Test career, and with Stewart, Gough and Caddick unavailable for the tour to India, few gave England's experimental side a ghost of a chance. According to Scyld Berry, Hussain was facing his toughest assignment yet, and if his team returned with anything better than a 3-0 loss they would have done well.

The portents indeed looked grim when they lost the first Test by ten wickets, but they displayed much character to get the better of draws at Ahmedabad and Bangalore. Once again, Hussain succeeded in motivating his men and he devised various tactical ploys to smother the Indian batsmen on flat pitches, the most outlandish of which was left-arm spinner Ashley Giles bowling into the rough outside the leg stump to Sachin Tendulkar. 'Like an alchemist, Hussain turned boys into men during England's tour of India,' reported Berry. 'Yet, by the end in Bangalore, the whole of the England team was vastly greater than the sum of their parts at the start.' [200]

After Christmas at home, they returned to India to draw 3-3 in the ODIs before moving on to New Zealand for another three-Test rubber. On a wet pitch at Christchurch, Hussain's century, one of his best, helped England to a first-innings lead of 81 and an overall victory by 98 runs.

This was the high point of the tour. The death of Ben Hollioake, a highly popular ex-team-mate, in a car crash in Australia cast a deep shadow over the players, and after looking the better side at Wellington, England lost under the floodlights at Auckland. For all the talk about endeavour and team spirit, they had gone four series without a win. They returned to form by easily disposing of Sri Lanka at home but faced greater resistance from India. They won the first Test at Lord's and they should have won the second Test at Trent Bridge, but they had to settle for a draw. India took advantage of some loose England bowling at Headingley to level the series, and Hussain seemed all too ready to settle for a draw at the Oval. According to Rahul Bhattacharya in *Wisden*, he was found to be perhaps a little short of ideas, and his stock, feverishly high after the Lord's win, had sunk to normal by the end of the series.

'And so with Hussain, the obsession with attrition as a match-winning tactic, the endless tinkering with fields and continual chat with the bowler could go too far and sometimes be too intellectual and too defensive.

'This is not to say that Hussain suddenly ceased to be an excellent captain; just that the warts were now more exposed.' [201]

The strain was beginning to get to him. Criticised for batting at number three in the ODIs by several former players, Hussain, after reaching three figures in the NatWest final against India, gesticulated angrily to the Lord's media centre in defiance of his detractors. Weeks later, at the Oval, Vaughan found him in tears because those same critics had called for his resignation as captain. Duly appointed to lead England in Australia, their mission appeared doomed from the start. Thorpe withdrew for personal reasons before departure and Hussain was attacked by Gatting for flying to Australia early to accompany his pregnant wife rather than travelling with the team.

Up against one of the best Australian sides of all time, England's task became ever more arduous as injuries decimated them. Gough,

Andrew Flintoff and Simon Jones all played little or no part in the tour, while others such as Stewart, John Crawley and Ashley Giles were forced to miss crucial games with various ailments. The injuries, besides drawing ridicule from the Australian media, took their toll on Hussain, who, according to Vaughan, became unnecessarily aggressive towards the team. Stewart, who felt the lash of Hussain's tongue during the Perth Test for not protecting tail-ender Alex Tudor against the quicks, wrote: 'Nasser felt the heat more than any of us at this time, and it was no surprise that the old familiar passion that he displayed when younger often came bubbling to the surface.' [202] Surprised by the timing of his outbursts, Stewart noted that 'the chemistry between captain and players wasn't always right in Australia, compared with other tours I've been on under Nasser's captaincy'. [203]

Hussain's mood darkened after his decision to give Australia first use of a placid surface at Brisbane. According to opener Marcus Trescothick, he took one look at the dressing room and saw something approaching fear on the faces of one or two players. The Australians responded to his generosity by racing to 339/1 and went on to win the game by 384 runs. Hussain, admitting his error, called it his worst day as captain and was forced to deny thereafter that the Australians had established a mental hold over his side.

They maintained their ascendancy at Adelaide and Perth, beating England both times by an innings. Hussain tried unavailingly to withstand the deluge at Perth with a fighting 61 before departing to a dubious decision, which brought an explosion of anger back in the dressing room. Looking utterly deflated afterwards, he admitted his side had played poorly as Botham called for his resignation.

To England's credit, they fought back at Melbourne in the fourth Test, losing by five wickets, and at Sydney they finally came good with Vaughan hitting his third century of the series before Caddick exploited a wearing pitch to bowl England to victory by 225 runs. It proved a minor consolation for Hussain at the end of a gruelling campaign but his winter of discontent wasn't yet complete.

The World Cup, due to be played in South Africa and Zimbabwe, had raised uncomfortable questions about England playing in the latter at a time when the Mugabe regime was riding roughshod over basic human rights. For weeks Hussain and his team had questioned the morality of playing in Zimbabwe, but the ICC turned a deaf ear to their concerns, insisting that with safety not an issue the match went ahead as scheduled. With the British government washing its hands of the affair, it fell to Hussain to engage in endless hours of fruitless negotiation, which proved ultimately futile when the ICC, irked by England's threatened boycott, awarded the match to Zimbabwe. The loss of four points cost England a place in the second round of the World Cup and after they played their final match Hussain announced his resignation of the one-day captaincy, admitting that he felt drained. He did, however, confirm his intention to continue to captain the Test side, expressing his ambition to win 100 caps and to lead the side more than anyone else. His words showed that he cared more about himself than the team, declared Gatting, while Botham repeated his opinion that he should quit now in order to blood more youngsters.

Hussain captained England to two easy victories against Zimbabwe in the brief Test series before stepping aside for the one-day series against Pakistan and the triangular tournament against South Africa and Zimbabwe. He cut a forlorn figure on the sidelines as a younger team responded positively to Michael Vaughan's relaxed leadership to emerge victorious, so that when England assembled at Edgbaston for the first Test against South Africa he felt his authority slipping away. He tried to regain the initiative by tossing a few grenades into the South African camp, aimed specifically at their young captain, Graeme Smith, but even these blew up in his face as Smith smashed 277 in South Africa's first innings of 594/5 declared. Unable to summon up his usual enthusiasm in the field, feeling somewhat estranged from the team and out to an indeterminate stroke for a single, in contrast with Vaughan's exquisite 145, Hussain sensed that his time was up. At the end of the match, which ended in a draw, he resigned. 'Was it brave to quit?' wrote Brearley. 'I don't think so. It would have been braver to bear with it longer, to work himself up for one last surge, to see the series through (or at least the first two or three Tests). By doing what he felt he had to do, Hussain was primarily intent on re-establishing his own equilibrium.' [204]

His batting remained unaffected by the growing strains of captaincy and he continued to score vital runs for England for another year before signing off with an undefeated century against New Zealand at Lord's. He made the swift transition to the commentary box, becoming a respected pundit for Sky Sports Cricket.

Hussain's four years in charge makes him one of England's most pivotal captains. Inheriting the captaincy at a time when her cricket had reached rock bottom at the end of the 1990s, he and Duncan Fletcher, helped by the introduction of central contracts, instilled a new sense of pride and purpose in the team. Leading by example, he inspired Caddick, Gough, Thorpe and Vaughan to greater heights and successfully blooded Trescothick, Steve Harmison and Matthew Hoggard. Yet this new-found confidence and resolution, which brought four consecutive series wins in 2000/01, failed to make any headway against Australia and, as the road became ever steeper, he found the long march increasingly arduous. It needed a change of leadership and Vaughan's more relaxed style to reach their final destination when England triumphed against a strong Australian side in 2005.

Mark Butcher

MARK BUTCHER was born in Croydon on 23 August 1972. His father, Alan Butcher, played cricket for Surrey and Glamorgan, in addition to winning one cap for England, and his younger brother Gary also represented both these counties.

Educated at Cumnor House Prep School, where he was taught football and cricket by the former Crystal Palace footballer Steve Kember, and Trinity College, Croydon, Butcher graduated through Surrey's junior sides. In 1991 he first played for Surrey in a JPL match against Glamorgan, his father numbered among the opposition, and the following year he made his championship debut.

In 1997 he won his first Test cap against Australia and formed a reliable opening partnership with Atherton, only then to experience a lean time in the West Indies.

In 1998 he scored prolifically against South Africa at home and hit a century against Australia at Brisbane. Thereafter, his form fell away in the series and in the first two Tests against New Zealand in 1999 he'd only scored 72 runs in four innings.

His surprise elevation to the England captaincy for the third Test came about because of Hussain's broken finger in the previous game at Lord's. Thorpe, his Surrey team-mate, seemed the likely stand-in, but Butcher had impressed with his leadership of Surrey that year in the absence of captain Adam Hollioake, away on World Cup duty.

Intelligent, easy-going and gregarious, it was Butcher's misfortune that his promotion occurred at a time when English cricket had sunk to such a low ebb. Humiliated in the World Cup and defeated in the previous Test against moderate opposition, the team lacked confidence and morale. Their spirits were hardly lifted by playing in front of sparse crowds at Old Trafford in miserable conditions on a sluggish pitch. Electing to bat first on winning the toss, Butcher didn't last long as England were bowled out for 199. He then struggled to motivate his team as New Zealand, with centuries from Nathan Astle and Craig McMillan, ground relentlessly on to make 496/6 declared. Even with his limited resources, Brearley thought Butcher could have done more either by varying the attack or by adjusting the field.

In England's second innings, Butcher was again out cheaply, but Atherton and Stewart consolidated and the latter remained undefeated on 83 when rain washed out most of the final day. Disillusioned with the side he'd been given, Butcher impressed at the post-match press conference when he candidly discussed England's crisis of confidence and his own loss of form. With only 86 runs in six completed innings, he was dropped for the final Test.

Although he never captained England again, he returned to the side in 2001 with success against Australia and proved an invaluable member of the side until an elbow injury put an end to his Test career in 2004. He was appointed captain of Surrey, but his four years in charge were plagued by injury, and he retired in 2009, after which he became a summariser for Sky Sports, as well as a musician.

Michael Vaughan

MICHAEL VAUGHAN was born in Eccles, Manchester, on 29 October 1974, the great, great nephew of the early 20th-century England cricketers, Ernest and Johnny Tyldesley. The family moved to Sheffield when Vaughan was nine when his father, an engineer, was offered a job there.

A fanatical sportsman, football was Vaughan's first love till his elder brother encouraged him to practise at their local cricket club, Sheffield Collegiate. Although his prodigious feats at Silverdale School won him the *Daily Telegraph* under-15 cricketer of the year in 1990, it was his grounding in the Sheffield Collegiate first team that proved critical to his development, not least facing their quick West Indian bowler Kenny Benjamin in the nets twice a week.

Having graduated through the schoolboy ranks at Yorkshire – in 1991 the county relaxed its rule about relying solely on players born within the county boundaries – he made his first eleven debut against Lancashire and Wasim Akram on a lively pitch at Old Trafford in 1993, scoring 64.

Exposed to Yorkshire's seaming wickets, it took Vaughan time to fulfil his potential, but England's new coach, Duncan Fletcher, discerned something special about his batting, and in 1999 he was picked for the tour to South Africa. His debut couldn't have been more torrid. Entering at 2-4 in the first Test at Johannesburg, he played Donald and Pollock with admirable composure to score 33.

After two years of learning his trade at the highest level, he graduated from apprentice to master in 2002, scoring 1,481 Test runs that year with a new-found flair and fluency. An accomplished captain of England under-18s and of England A, he seemed the natural successor to Hussain when the latter renounced the one-day captaincy following another disappointing World Cup campaign in 2003. 'The more I thought about it, the more I was sure I wanted the job,' he later wrote. 'I felt I was up to the task, and I was enthused by the prospect of making an impression on the game we gave to the world, maybe even leaving a rich legacy through which England would again become cricket's dominant force.' [205]

Adopting a more consensual approach than Hussain, Vaughan immediately won the backing of his young team and their exhilarating cricket carried them to victory in a three-match series against Pakistan and in a triangular tournament with Zimbabwe and South Africa.

His visionary captaincy made Hussain's combative style look rather dated, and when the latter quit after England's prosaic performance in the first Test against South Africa he was the obvious successor. His baptism proved an unenviable one since, batting first at Lord's, England were shot out for 173; they then toiled for two days in the field as Smith scored another double century in their massive 682/6 declared. Only a defiant 142 from Andrew Flintoff provided some comfort as they crashed to a ten-wicket defeat. Unhappy with his team's feckless attitude, Vaughan told them that he wouldn't tolerate anything similar again and he warned the tetchy Hussain to pull himself together if he wanted to remain part of the team.

Hussain responded positively at Trent Bridge with a determined century in England's first innings of 445, giving them a lead of 83. They batted tepidly in their second innings, but, on a deteriorating wicket, Vaughan held his nerve and debutant James Kirtley's 6-34 bowled them to victory by 70 runs.

With South Africa back in the ascendancy at Headingley with a thumping victory, everything depended on the Oval, Alec Stewart's final Test. When the visitors were 345/2 on the opening day, they seemed out of sight, only to lose their last eight wickets for 139. A brilliant double century from Trescothick, an elegant 124 from Thorpe and a scintillating 95 from Flintoff gave England a first-innings lead of 120 before the blistering pace of Harmison propelled them to a nine-wicket victory and a share of the rubber, a creditable start to Vaughan's captaincy, even though his batting had lost its fluency.

During the autumn tour to Bangladesh and Sri Lanka, he made real progress in improving levels of fitness and forging a strong team ethic. Brought closer together by their sessions in the gym, Vaughan encouraged everyone to have their say in team discussions and to share in each other's success, as well as promoting self-expression on the field.

Their camaraderie and intense work ethic bore fruit in the West Indies in the new year. A phenomenal 7-12 spell from Steve Harmison resulted in England's ten-wicket victory in the first Test at Kingston as the West Indies collapsed to 47 all out, their lowest-ever Test score.

Harmison was again the match-winner at Port of Spain and wickets for Flintoff and Hoggard, including a hat-trick, and a century from Thorpe, set up another easy victory at Bridgetown, the first time England had won a series in the Caribbean for 36 years. 'Save for his shortage of runs, Vaughan scarcely put a foot wrong,' wrote Simon Wilde of the *Sunday Times*. 'His decision to put fitness top of the agenda when he took over last year paid dividends. Nobody broke down. Tactically, he gave a ruthless, nerveless performance.' [206]

The tour saw the metamorphosis of England's four-pronged pace attack – Harmison, Hoggard, Jones and Flintoff – complete with highly attacking fields, part of the more enterprising approach that defined Vaughan's captaincy. While he was fortunate to have such a powerful arsenal, his sensitive man-management helped them to fire on all cylinders. According to Harmison, Vaughan, unlike Hussain, who seemed prickly a lot of the time, was a PR man's dream, positive, approachable and not taking himself too seriously. 'Vaughan was one of the best captains I ever played under, and one of the best liars. He'd say anything if he thought it would get the best out of you!' [207] 'He likes me to play with a smile on my face and enjoy my cricket, which is the way I've always liked to play,' wrote Flintoff. 'I don't think it any accident that I have played some of my best cricket under Michael simply because he encourages you to enjoy your cricket without fear of failure.' [208]

Yet underneath the relaxed demeanour, there lurked a steelier side manifest in the ousting of wicketkeeper Chris Read in the West Indies for Geraint Jones because of his lack of runs, and, later in 2005, of veteran Thorpe for Kevin Pietersen.

Vaughan missed the first Test of the summer against New Zealand because of a knee injury. Trescothick captained the side in his place, Andrew Strauss made a dream debut and Hussain ensured victory with an undefeated century in his final Test. He returned to lead England to two further wins against New Zealand, impressing *The Independent*'s Henry Blofeld with his growing authority. 'There is no question as to who is in charge of the side. One only has to watch for a couple of minutes to realise that Vaughan is pulling all the strings. His is an easy authority, too: he clearly knows his own mind; there is never the slightest suggestion of panic; he communicates well with the other players; he appears always to be receptive to suggestions anyone may make; and he is in constant touch with his bowlers.' [209]

Only his shortage of runs aroused adverse comment, and when Vaughan responded by scoring two centuries in the first Test against the West Indies at Lord's he bought himself precious time with the critics. With left-arm spinner Ashley Giles proving an inspired selection, England beat the West Indies 4-0 to win all seven Tests in a summer for the first time. 'Like the team, his confidence in his own leadership grew with every win,' wrote Hoggard. 'He thinks about the game a lot, he'd move fielders into positions that might have seemed strange at first, but there would always be some sound reasoning behind the move.' [210]

After such a successful year, England made for South Africa with a high level of expectation, but with Harmison, temporarily, a spent force, they never played with any consistency, and relied on several individual heroics, most notably Strauss, who averaged 72.88 in the series. He scored 126 and 94 in his side's seven-wicket victory in the first Test and was again to the fore at Durban when he and Trescothick overcame a first-innings deficit of 193 with an opening partnership of 273 in the second innings. Both men scored centuries, as did Thorpe, and at the end of the game it was South Africa who were clinging on for dear life when bad light brought proceedings to a halt prematurely.

Drained by their exertions in back-to-back Tests, England began the new year badly with a heavy loss at Cape Town. Disconcerted by his repeated failures with the bat, Vaughan shunned the additional time off to practise intensely with Duncan Fletcher. His efforts were rewarded with two half-centuries at Johannesburg, but it was his captaincy that caught the eye with his lunchtime declaration on the final day which set up England's thrilling 77-run victory. Simon Wilde wrote:

'After 18 months in the job, Michael Vaughan has progressed beyond imagining as leader. He now captains as he bats when in the best form, the rational laced with the recklessness of the irredeemable gambler. Perhaps because he knows it brings out the best, he is addicted to risk in both suits.

'Vaughan has grasped the fundamental truth about cricket captaincy: that it is in large part about gambling. It is the business of the captain to create the luck, and Vaughan did it with two declarations at the Wanderers.

'If Matthew Hoggard was the hero of that victory, Vaughan … was the architect. At the start of the final day, when Duncan Fletcher, the coach, was more concerned about securing a draw, Vaughan alone believed that a creaking England attack could yet force the win. He not only pulled it off, but galvanised the team into relocating the elusive spirit that carried them through so many victories last year.' [211]

A draw in the final Test at Centurion gave England the rubber 2-1, their first series win in South Africa for 40 years. Vaughan called it their most satisfying achievement yet, but he knew that they would need to go the extra mile against Australia. Convinced that England had been too deferential towards them in the past, he and Fletcher stressed the need to avoid being intimidated by them. They put their resolutions into practice during the two one-day tournaments prior to the Tests. In the first of these a throw from Simon Jones, destined for the wicketkeeper, accidentally hit opening batsman Matthew

Hayden in the chest. Affronted by such tactics, Hayden directed his spleen at Jones, whereupon several England fielders rushed in to support him and told Hayden to back off.

After Pietersen's showing in the ODIs against South Africa, Vaughan included him in the Test side, at the expense of Thorpe, reasoning that the former's brazen self-confidence would hold no fear against Australia. He refused captain Ricky Ponting's request to take a fielder's word for a catch and he constantly riled the Australians throughout the summer by his side's use of highly athletic substitutes to replace their bowlers while they enjoyed a rub-down massage.

England's uncompromising approach was manifest on the opening morning of the first Test when, in a highly charged atmosphere, Justin Langer and Ponting took blows to the elbow and Hayden was hit on the helmet, eliciting minimum concern from their opponents, much to Ponting's disgust. Bowling to well-prepared plans, especially going around the wicket to the left-handers, Hayden and Adam Gilchrist, England dismissed Australia for 190, and although they ultimately lost convincingly they felt they had rattled their opponents.

Afterwards Vaughan urged his men not to read the doom-laden assessments in the media and to continue to be positive. The emphasis on attack was followed to the letter. Inserted on a plumb wicket at Edgbaston, England scored 407 in 80 overs on the opening day and went on to control the match until the final hour when a gallant fightback by the Australian lower order threatened to undo everything they'd achieved. It was then that Vaughan earned his stripes by keeping his cool under immense pressure as England went on to win a gripping match by two runs.

They continued their resurgence at Old Trafford. Led by 166 from Vaughan, they were by some way the better side and only a stubborn last-wicket stand by Australia prevented England from winning again. As the Australians embraced each other on the balcony, Vaughan congratulated his men on their performance and told them to look at how enthusiastically their opponents were celebrating a draw, an indication that they were now the dominant team.

England returned to winning ways at Trent Bridge, their four-man pace attack once more bowling to precisely placed fields, and amid intense patriotic fervour they congregated at the Oval needing only a draw to regain the Ashes. That win seemed under threat at lunch on the final day when England stood only 134 runs ahead with five wickets left. It was at this point that Vaughan told Pietersen to go out and play his natural game. Having survived a torrid spell from Brett Lee before lunch, Pietersen lay waste to him afterwards to change the course of the match. When he fell for 158, he returned to the pavilion secure in the knowledge that the Ashes were back in English hands for the first time in 16 years.

Not surprisingly, the Ashes triumph proved the apogee of Vaughan's captaincy. Thereafter, it was 'Never glad confident morning again'. A serious knee injury on England's tour to Pakistan later that autumn forced him out of cricket for a year, and while he was absent the side he'd built up began to disintegrate. By the time he returned early in 2007 following the Ashes whitewash, rifts were beginning to appear in the side, not least between coach Fletcher and stand-in captain Flintoff. These rifts only deepened during the World Cup in the West Indies when Fletcher dropped Flintoff following a night of excessive drinking, and Vaughan later blamed the latter for England's poor showing in the tournament.

The World Cup marked the end of Fletcher's eight-year tenure as coach, much to Vaughan's consternation, especially since he never felt at one with his successor, Peter Moores.

Vaughan celebrated his return to Test cricket with a sublime century against the West Indies at Headingley. England beat them 3-0, but up against India later that summer they lost 1-0, their first series defeat at home in six years. Vaughan continued to bat well but his captaincy drew criticism from Mike Brearley for his unorthodox fields when the ball was moving about at Trent Bridge, the scene of their defeat. Having relinquished the one-day captaincy to Paul Collingwood, he now found his leadership subjected to greater scrutiny, especially given the latter's assured start, and his uneasy relationship with Moores.

Moores was universally regarded as an honest, thorough and enthusiastic coach who'd led Sussex to their first-ever county championship in 2003, but his automatic promotion from national academy director to national coach raised some uncomfortable questions. For, aside from his lack of international experience, the methods he used to energise Sussex weren't necessarily conducive to success at Test level, especially his rigorous training regime. Uncomfortable with the profusion of new faces, unhappy with his own form and frustrated with spinner Monty Panesar's lack of initiative, Vaughan felt the pressure like never before during England's tour to Sri Lanka in the autumn of 2007. After the second Test he grabbed the camera of the *Daily Mirror*'s Dean Wilson when he took photographs of the players enjoying a karaoke night out in Colombo. At the end of a series, which England lost 1-0, Vaughan contemplated resignation.

The clouds failed to lift on tour to New Zealand in the new year. Arriving at the end of the ODIs, Vaughan found a discontented squad disillusioned with the Calvinist ethos. After England lost the first Test, Hoggard and Harmison, at Moores's instigation, were dropped in favour of James Anderson and Stuart Broad. Their inclusion helped England win the next two Tests to take the series 2-1, but Vaughan derived little satisfaction from the result. 'I was not enjoying the system I was working in, not enjoying being captain anymore,' he wrote in his autobiography. 'Behind the glasses and under the brim of my sunhat I was just feeling miserable.' [212]

After a lean series in New Zealand, Vaughan scored a century against the same opposition at Lord's months later. It was to be his last substantial score at Test level. New Zealand were beaten 2-0 but South Africa provided stiffer opposition once they'd overcome a faltering start in the drawn first Test at Lord's.

Presented with a grassy wicket at Headingley, England made one of their most bizarre selections. Rather than picking a traditional swing bowler, Moores opted for Darren Pattinson, a Yorkshire-born Australian seamer who'd played a few games for Nottinghamshire. An unfamiliar face to Vaughan and most of the team, Pattinson bowled respectably, but without the venom of Flintoff, still injured, South Africa compiled a large first-innings lead, and with the England batsmen lacking that same self-discipline they lost by ten wickets.

Weighed down with anxiety, not least his own double failure at Headingley, Vaughan approached Edgbaston full of negative thoughts, his troubled demeanour manifesting itself in a terse clash with the BBC's Jonathan Agnew, which was totally out of character. Batting first again, he was unfortunate to be dismissed for his second duck in three innings. Vintage bowling by Flintoff and a painstaking 135 from Collingwood in the second innings helped England back into the game, but a masterly 154* from South Africa's captain Smith saw his side home by five wickets to take the rubber. It was Vaughan's third defeat in five series, and with his batting in crisis – 40 runs in five innings against South Africa – he decided to bow out. At a hastily arranged news conference the next day, he publicly announced his resignation of the England captaincy, admitting to the strain it had placed upon his family. 'I take no pleasure in seeing Michael go,' wrote Geoff Boycott. 'He has done a fine job for England. But I think the captaincy, a lack of runs and loss of confidence have all got to him in the end. It's better to go now, with dignity, than just hang on.' [213]

Vaughan was not only one of England's longest-serving captains, he was also one of its most successful, his 26 victories an all-time record. Working effectively with Fletcher, he combined an astute reading of the game with adept man-management, not least his ability to motivate Flintoff and Harmison to greater things. Playing positive, attacking cricket, England won six series in succession in 2004/05, culminating in their memorable triumph against Australia in 2005. It was Vaughan's misfortune that not only was he struck down by injury, but so were several others of the side he'd nurtured so assiduously. By the time he returned in January 2007, his authority was never quite the same, especially under new coach Moores, and once his batting gave up on him his days were numbered.

Vaughan's hope that his release from the captaincy would revive his batting proved illusory. He never played for England again, and after a dearth of runs for Yorkshire the following year he retired mid-season to become a leading cricket writer and broadcaster.

Marcus Trescothick

MARCUS TRESCOTHICK was born in Keynsham, Somerset, on 25 December 1975, the son of an accomplished opening batsman good enough to play a couple of matches for Somerset second eleven.

Introduced to the game by the age of two, Trescothick played for Keynsham under-11s, aged seven, and he was racking up centuries for Avon Schools by the age of 11 with his aggressive stroke-play. A prodigious scorer at Sir Bernard Lovell School, Oldland Common, he hit his first century for Keynsham in the Western League aged 14, and he made his debut for Somerset aged 17. Although he prospered in his first full season in 1994, he struggled for the next few years. He returned from a winter in Australia in 1998/99 a more complete player, and a superb 167 for Somerset against Glamorgan and Jacques Kallis in full spate impressed England's new coach Duncan Fletcher.

Following his one-day debut for England in the summer of 2000, Trescothick marked his Test debut against the West Indies at Old Trafford with an assured 66. He formed a successful opening partnership with Atherton, scoring his first Test century against Sri Lanka at Galle in 2001, and although he disappointed in his first two series against Australia he returned to form with 219 and 69* against South Africa at the Oval in 2003, helping England to square the rubber.

A quiet, reassuring presence in the dressing room, liked and respected by his team-mates, Trescothick captained England in a one-day international in Zimbabwe in 2001 and was vice-captain to Hussain in Australia in 2002/03. Had he scored more runs there, he, rather than Vaughan, might well have been his successor following Hussain's resignation in August 2003. 'If I am honest, I never thought he was the right person to captain England anyway,' Vaughan later wrote. 'Marcus is such a nice bloke and, like a lot of very decent people, prone to high levels of worry and stress, and I always saw him as the perfect right-hand man or vice-captain, which he was.' [214]

When a twisted knee forced Vaughan to miss the first Test against New Zealand at Lord's the next year, Trescothick deputised. Revelling in the occasion, he and debutant Andrew Strauss put on 190 for the first wicket in England's first innings, and, although incurring some criticism for persisting with spinner Ashley Giles in New Zealand's second innings rather than taking the second new ball, he looked the part.

Set 282 to win in 95 overs, England recovered from a sticky start to win by seven wickets, with Hussain bowing out with an undefeated century in his final Test.

Trescothick remained central to England's two years of uninterrupted success, culminating in their Ashes triumph of 2005. Their fortunes began to flag on the tour to Pakistan that autumn, since injuries ruled out several leading players, including Vaughan, for the first Test at Multan. Trescothick once again deputised, and for most of the game the tide flowed very much in his favour. Having bowled out Pakistan for 274 on the opening day, he batted England to a first-innings lead of 144 with a magnificent 193, but for the last part of his innings he was sorely troubled by the news that his father-in-law had suffered a severe head injury falling off a ladder. With his wife distraught and pleading for him to return home, Trescothick was caught in two minds. He eventually decided to stay, but it did nothing to quell his growing homesickness when on tour.

As for the match, Trescothick found it a positive distraction from events at home and he captained astutely during Pakistan's second innings of 341. Requiring only 198 to win on a trusty surface, England seemed comfortably placed at 64/1, but some reckless batting thereafter prompted a serious collapse and they lost by 22 runs.

Trescothick captained England in the five ODIs in Pakistan and was all set to continue in charge in the Test series against India post-Christmas when Vaughan became indisposed because of his knee, but long periods of absence from his young family were beginning to exact their price. Increasingly prone to depression, Trescothick fell into such a state that he was sent home from India to recover.

He remained on medication all summer when he played against Sri Lanka and Pakistan and was considered an automatic selection for Australia that winter. With hindsight, he should never have gone, because within days of arrival his stress-related illness resurfaced. Not only did it once again force him to return home prematurely, but he never played for England again, a tragic waste of a rare talent who could well have captained his country for a number of years. He did, however, continue to provide sterling service to Somerset both as captain and opening batsman until his retirement in 2019 after 27 years with the county.

Andrew Flintoff

ANDREW FLINTOFF was born in Preston on 6 December 1977, the son of a British Aerospace worker who played cricket for Dutton Forshaw. Educated at Ribbleton Hall High School, he performed well academically but left school prematurely. A leading light with the Lancashire age-group teams, Flintoff joined St Annes Cricket Club in Lytham at the age of 14 and immediately impressed as a precocious all-rounder of immense power. In 1995 he made his debut for Lancashire and in 1996/97 he captained the England under-19 team against Pakistan and Zimbabwe. He won his first Test cap against South Africa at Trent Bridge in 1998, but in that game, and the following one at Headingley, he achieved little.

Over the course of the next few years, he showed real promise but injury and a lack of self-discipline severely disrupted his progress. He scored his maiden Test century against New Zealand at Christchurch in February 2002, only to miss England's tour to Australia the following winter because of a hernia operation.

Returning to full fitness by the beginning of 2003, he finally came good, beginning with a spectacular 142 against South Africa at Lord's. A brilliant 95 in the final Test at the Oval helped England square the series and his buccaneering efforts with both bat and ball in 2004 won him a national following.

In 2005 he reached the peak of his powers in England's historic win against Australia, his magnetic personality and awesome all-round performance the difference between the two sides.

On tour to India in 2006, a knee injury to captain Michael Vaughan and a stress-related illness to vice-captain Marcus Trescothick created a vacancy in the captaincy. Flintoff was very keen to step up and showed the extent of his commitment by abandoning plans to return home for the birth of his second child.

With debutant Alastair Cook hitting 60 and 104*, England managed a draw in the first Test, and although they lost the second Test easily, despite two half-centuries from Flintoff, he remained bullish. Far from being waylaid by the captaincy, he found it enhanced his own game. At Mumbai in the final Test his two fifties and 3-14 in India's second innings inspired his team to a 212-run victory. Fletcher called it one of the most creditable of his time in charge and the *Sunday Times*'s Simon Wilde in *Wisden* described Flintoff's captaincy debut the most arresting since Mike Brearley's against Australia in 1977. 'In the Ashes of 2005, he already seemed the complete cricketer, but he now displayed an extra dimension: that of the caring, considerate captain, tactically astute, at ease with responsibility, yet still fiercely passionate.' [215]

He continued in office against Sri Lanka that summer, but after enforcing his opponents to follow on nearly 400 runs behind in the first Test at Lord's, he allowed them to escape defeat. While sloppy catching didn't help, his captaincy came under serious scrutiny for the first time. Not only did he under-bowl debutant spinner Monty Panesar, he flogged himself to near exhaustion in the second innings by bowling 51 overs.

England returned to winning ways at Old Trafford, only then to submit meekly to spinner Muttiah Muralitharan at Trent Bridge, giving the unfancied Sri Lankans a share of the series. By the final Test, Flintoff was struggling to inspire his men as his own form began to suffer from exhaustion and injury. A serious ankle injury forced him out of international cricket for the rest of the summer, raising doubts as to whether he was the right man to lead England in Australia in Vaughan's absence, especially since Andrew Strauss impressed with his leadership in the 3-0 win against Pakistan.

While Flintoff's captaincy had exceeded expectations in India, he had looked less assured against Sri Lanka, and if England were to stand any chance of retaining the Ashes, they needed him at his brilliant best. There were also reservations as to whether his increasingly celebrity lifestyle would set him apart from the team. 'I also had my doubts as to whether Fred's individual way of going about things would necessarily be the best example for the rest of the players to follow,' wrote Trescothick. 'Fred is very much his own man and always did his thing the way it suited him.' [216]

Fletcher fretted about Flintoff's tactical nous, man-management and self-discipline, but, while inclined to choose Strauss, he worried whether he could control a disillusioned Flintoff and his close friend Steve Harmison. It was this concern which led him to opt for the Lancastrian. 'I was not confident that we were making the right decision,' he wrote in his autobiography, 'but I also knew that if Flintoff was not captain he would be a huge hindrance to the side. This appointment would, I hoped, get the best out of Flintoff and maybe he could do the same to Harmison. However, even though I believe it took some time, Flintoff came to realise how difficult it is to motivate Harmison at times.' [217]

Although England prepared thoroughly for Australia, the tour was one of the most humiliating in its history. Deprived of several leading members of the Ashes-winning side of 2005, they were up against opponents bent on revenge and they never stood a chance from the moment the opening ball of the series from Harmison ended up at second slip. They lost badly at Brisbane but the real body-blow came in the second Test at Adelaide when they lost with a feckless batting display on the final day after dominating the majority of the game. Flintoff looked a shadow of the player who had rattled the Australians in 2005 and his captaincy seemed bereft of ideas. A man who disliked confrontation, he irked Fletcher by failing to counter Australian aggression on the field and by drinking with them late into the night after the Adelaide game. Following another shattering defeat at Perth, which saw the Ashes return to Australia, England looked a broken team. Captain and coach drifted further apart, rifts appeared among the players and Flintoff was reduced to uttering platitudes when asked to account for his side's fall from grace. They slid to further heavy defeats at Melbourne and Sydney, completing their first 5-0 whitewash against Australia since 1920/21.

Despite growing tensions with Fletcher, Flintoff captained England to victory in the Australian one-day tri-series for the first time in 20 years. With Vaughan back from injury for the World Cup in the West Indies, he reverted to being vice-captain, but following a notorious incident with a pedalo on the back of a late-night drinking session he was stripped of the vice-captaincy by Fletcher. It was an unfortunate end to a tetchy relationship. Both went into print soon afterwards to cast aspersions at the other: Fletcher accusing Flintoff of weak leadership.

Rather like Botham, Flintoff's leadership stemmed largely from his own mighty deeds, but once reduced to mere mortality his aura quickly faded as he became prone to self-doubt. No England captain could have won in Australia against such stiff opposition, but, nevertheless, he was outsmarted by his counterpart, Ponting, in what he later called the tour from hell.

His final two years as an England player were dogged by further injury and he retired from cricket in 2009. Aside from a brief reappearance in Twenty20 cricket in 2014, he has fronted large commercial campaigns for brands such as Morrisons and Jacobs, and he has carved out a profitable career for himself in the media, especially by appearing on television reality shows.

Kevin Pietersen

KEVIN PIETERSEN was born in Pietermaritzburg on 27 June 1980 into a close-knit, sports-proud family. Encouraged by his Afrikan father (his mother was English) to aim high, Pietersen learned to be highly competitive from the outset as he played cricket and rugby with his three brothers in the garden and thereafter was obsessively single-minded about improving his game.

A superb all-round sportsman at fee-paying Maritzburg College, he made his debut for Natal B aged 17, primarily as an off-spinner, and he played against Hussain's side in 1999/2000, scoring 61* batting at number nine. Dropped from KwaZulu-Natal (as it was now called) because of the quota system, he left for England in 2000 to play for Nottinghamshire. Never plagued by self-doubt, his batting pedigree soon manifested itself but his intolerance of lesser lights made him a divisive figure and he quit Nottinghamshire for Hampshire in 2004.

Newly qualified as an England player, Pietersen first played for his adopted country in an ODI against Zimbabwe in November 2004 and he overcame the raw hostility of the home crowds to score three centuries against South Africa in the one-day series there in early 2005.

Making his Test debut against Australia at Lord's later that year, he immediately took the attack to their bowlers and he capped a memorable first summer with a scintillating 158 in the final Test at the Oval, which helped England to regain the Ashes. He continued to be England's leading run scorer, but, for all his flamboyant stroke-play, the brash self-confidence, the outlandish haircuts and celebrity lifestyle didn't endear him to everyone. He also fell out with new coach Peter Moores, who replaced Fletcher in 2007, because of the former's intense training methods and overbearing style of management. His reservations were shared by Vaughan and other senior players, which helps explain the dramatic upheavals in the summer of 2008. The resignation of Vaughan from the Test captaincy following England's series defeat against South Africa at Edgbaston, coupled with the resignation of Collingwood from the captaincy of the one-day side, left the selectors in a bind. Given their preference for the new captain to take charge of both sides, they took a gamble with Pietersen, his shrewd cricket brain and dedication to excellence offset by his inexperience as a captain and his substantial ego.

Chuffed with his coronation, Pietersen gave a bullish first press conference in which he promised an attacking brand of cricket. Only once did he falter and that was when he was asked about his relationship with Moores. He admitted that they hadn't always seen eye to eye in the past but claimed that they had wiped the slate clean at a meeting the previous day.

Energetic and enthusiastic from the outset, Pietersen rejuvenated England in the field, especially fast bowler Harmison, and his own first-innings century helped them to a six-wicket victory.

They continued their mini-revival with a comprehensive 4-0 win in the ODIs against South Africa, but, thereafter, it was heavier going. After competing in the tacky Stanford Twenty20 tournament in Antigua, England lost 5-0 in the ODIs in India. The terrorist outrages in Mumbai, in which 174 people were killed, placed the tour in jeopardy as the team feared for their safety, but after a brief trip home and promises of heightened security Pietersen persuaded all the players to return for the two-Test series.

Back in India, he remained the dominant figure, winning the gratitude of the locals with his sensitivity to recent events there, but England's creditable performance in the first Test at Chennai fell away on the final day. Having declared his side's second innings on 311/9 and set India 387 to win, Pietersen's tactical inexperience was exposed, since his priority of saving boundaries allowed the Indians to take singles and twos at will. With Tendulkar scoring a brilliant 103*, India chased down their target to win by six wickets. 'Pietersen has generally made an outstanding start as England captain,' wrote Michael Atherton, 'but the last day in Chennai also illustrated how much he has to learn.' [218]

Pietersen's feeling that he hadn't received sufficient tactical input from the coach brought to the surface the simmering tension that still existed between captain and coach. Andrew Strauss wrote: 'In team meetings they went through the motions, saying the right things, but the body language between them told a different story. There was no rapport, and away from the formal settings I didn't see them speaking at all, which is an unusual situation in an international environment, with so many decisions to be made on a daily basis.' [219]

Convinced that he couldn't work with Moores and that the team wasn't progressing under his tutelage, Pietersen told Giles Clarke, the chairman of the ECB, in India that he should go. Yet despite a plethora of meetings, the issue remained unresolved by the end of the tour. With Pietersen threatening resignation, he was asked by David Collier, the chief executive of the ECB, to email the board his proposals for 2009. He duly did so, reiterating his belief that Moores should quit.

On New Year's Eve, while Pietersen was on holiday in South Africa, his email was leaked, placing the ECB in a quandary, now that the rift had become public and was not denied by either party. When Hugh Morris, the managing director of English cricket, canvassed the opinion of players, he found that while a number shared Pietersen's reservations about Moores's methods, they were reluctant to be his accomplices in a coup against a man they liked. At the same time, and for all his glowing reviews since taking command, Pietersen's pedestal was built on fragile foundations, since an influential clique in the team, led by Flintoff, disliked his form of domineering leadership. Reluctant to go back to India in the wake of the Mumbai terrorist attacks, they thought Pietersen's willingness to return was motivated primarily by his desire to secure a lucrative IPL contract, and once back they resented the way he milked the good publicity. 'There is no doubt that Kev is a good player, a really fine batsman,' wrote off-spinner Graeme Swann, 'but he was never the right man to be captain in my opinion. Some people are better leaders of men and Kev, for all his abundant talent, is not one of those natural leaders.' [220]

Consequently, the ECB, forced into a corner by a captain brazen enough to issue an ultimatum to his employers, especially when he lacked the full backing of his own players, felt they had no option but to dismiss both captain and coach. The fact that Pietersen subsequently accepted no responsibility for his downfall merely exposed his delusions of grandeur, especially when the captaincy had become less powerful compared to the age of Brearley, let alone Jardine and Archie MacLaren. 'But when it came to his own ego, Pietersen was unable to look round it,' wrote Henry Blofeld. 'He has only been able to see what is best for Pietersen and not what is best for the England side.' [221]

Pietersen returned to the ranks but his relations with the ECB never recovered. In 2012 he was suspended for sending disparaging texts to the South African dressing room undermining his captain, Strauss. Restored to favour by the new captain, Alastair Cook, he returned the compliment by helping England to a 2-1 win in India in 2012/13, but he was less successful in the 5-0 drubbing in Australia the following winter. Deemed to be a disruptive influence, he was omitted from the side by the ECB, citing a need to rebuild the team ethic, and he never played for England again. He continued to play in World Twenty20 tournaments until his retirement in 2018.

Andrew Strauss

ANDREW STRAUSS was born in Johannesburg on 2 March 1977. Raised in South Africa until the age of seven, his family moved briefly to Australia before settling in England.

Educated at Caldicott Prep School and Radley College, Strauss delighted in the countless sporting opportunities available. An accomplished fly-half on the rugby field, he played in the same Radley cricket eleven as Robin Martin-Jenkins, later of Sussex, and Ben Hutton, later his opening partner at Middlesex. Although not an outstanding schoolboy cricketer, he was a very good one, possessing an ideal temperament. While a student at Durham University, Strauss was offered a contract with Middlesex. He scored 83 on his championship debut against Hampshire in 1998 and performed respectably over the course of the next couple of seasons without looking destined for the higher peaks.

His subsequent development owed much to Australian batsman Justin Langer, who captained Middlesex in 2000. His fiercely competitive approach instilled in him a more professional ethos which immediately bore fruit on the county circuit. 'He stood out as someone with a bit extra to offer,' recalled Langer. 'Not only did he work hard and have plenty of natural ability, but he was intelligent and prepared to listen and learn. It was no surprise to me when he became England captain. He has that British Bulldog mentality and the determination to plough through the disappointments that come with a sporting career.' [222]

By 2003 Strauss's progress was such that he was chosen for England's one-day squad in Sri Lanka, and in 2004 he made a dream Test debut against New Zealand at Lord's by scoring 112 and 83.

His run feast continued throughout the next two years, including three centuries against South Africa in 2004/05 and two against Australia in 2005. When Vaughan and his deputy Flintoff were both unavailable against Pakistan the following summer, Strauss, previously captain of Middlesex, stepped into the breach and acquitted himself capably in England's 3-0 win. Disappointed to have lost the captaincy to Flintoff in Australia in 2006/07, it proved a blessing in disguise, since England crashed to a 5-0 defeat.

Strauss endured a poor series with the bat and, after a year of deteriorating form in 2007, he missed out on England's tour to Sri Lanka that autumn. He was back against New Zealand early in the new year and re-established his position with 177 in the final Test.

Two centuries in the first Test against India at the end of 2008 helped him secure the captaincy when the incumbent Pietersen was unceremoniously ditched on his return following his unwillingness to work with coach Peter Moores, who was also sacked.

With English cricket in disarray, Strauss was the ideal man to restore confidence in the dressing room with the calm authority he exuded. A consummate communicator who radiated common sense, he always appeared to find the right words for each occasion and whenever he spoke everyone listened.

Convinced that England's recent travails had stemmed from the rigid intensity of the previous regime, Strauss wanted to give the players greater discretion over the way they practised and prepared.

His philosophy was closely shared by acting coach Andy Flower, the former Zimbabwean batsman, whom he greatly admired both as a cricketer and a person, not least for his black-armband protest against the Mugabe regime in a World Cup match in Zimbabwe in 2003. Their relationship was cemented in the wake of England's humiliating innings defeat in the first Test at Kingston when they were bowled out for 51 in their second innings. Convening a team meeting in their Antigua hotel prior to the second Test, Flower calmly but firmly told them that the time for excuses was past and that from now on they had to take responsibility for their actions.

His message struck home, since England scored a stack of runs in the next three Tests and only two ultra-cautious declarations prevented them from winning the series 2-1. Yet, despite his frustration, Strauss returned from the Caribbean a proven leader, with three centuries in successive matches and the respect of the whole side, leading personalities and all. While proving to be no soft touch – Ian Bell was dropped after the first Test and told to toughen up and Pietersen was refused permission to make a brief return home to see his family – Strauss backed his men at every conceivable opportunity. 'In fact whatever situation he was confronted with, and whatever the state of his personal game,' wrote James Anderson, 'you always felt that his number-one priority was the welfare of others and that is the trait of a natural leader.' [223]

England returned to winning ways with two decisive victories over the West Indies in unseasonal weather back home, an encouraging warm-up for the Ashes. Although Australia had lost some of their aura following the recent retirement of leading players such as McGrath, Warne and Gilchrist, they arrived fresh from a series win in South Africa. Led by 150 from captain Ponting, they ran England ragged during their total of 674/6 declared in the first Test at Cardiff and only dogged batting by their last-wicket pair, Anderson and Panesar, aided by some dubious time-wasting, saved them from a crushing defeat.

Under fire for his uninspiring captaincy at Cardiff, Strauss led from the front at Lord's with his scintillating 161. Rarely playing better, he gave England the early initiative, which they never surrendered, going on to win the match by 139 runs. After getting the better of a draw at Edgbaston, they crashed horrendously at Headingley. A meticulous organiser, Strauss found his pre-match preparations severely disrupted by a truncated night's sleep because of a fire alarm in the team hotel and a last-minute injury to wicketkeeper Matt Prior. After a delayed toss he was out almost immediately as England were bowled out for 102, the prelude to a humiliating innings defeat.

Despite their pitiful performance, Strauss refused to panic, and, aside from dropping the out-of-form Ravi Bopara for the debutant Jonathan Trott, he kept faith with his players at the Oval. Australia's failure to play a specialist spinner on a turning wicket cost them dear, and with Trott hitting 109 in the second innings and paceman Stuart Broad in devastating form with the ball England romped home by 197 runs to regain the Ashes. Strauss, with two half-centuries in the match and 474 runs in the rubber, the highest on either side, was named man of the series. 'To regain the Ashes in 2009, less than eight months after taking over at a nadir, was a supreme achievement,' wrote Scyld Berry. 'Neither Vaughan, nor Brearley, nor Hutton, nor any other England captain conjured up a series victory over Australia out of quite such unpromising circumstances.' [224]

England's new-found grit and resilience was on display in South Africa that winter when they managed to share the four-match rubber. Fortunate to escape with draws at Centurion and Cape Town when on both occasions they were nine wickets down, they headed for Johannesburg for the final game one up by virtue of a resounding victory at Durban, but once there their luck ran out. Electing to bat first on a damp wicket, Strauss was out to the first ball of the match and, showing little resolution against the pace of Dale Steyn and Morne Morkel, England lost by an innings.

Jaded by a year on the road, Strauss courted controversy by missing the short tour to Bangladesh, with several of his predecessors calling it a dereliction of duty, but his absence did little to harm team spirit. He returned refreshed to lead England to two easy victories against Bangladesh at home and to a 3-1 win against Pakistan, although their overwhelming victory in the final Test at Lord's was overshadowed by a serious spot-fixing scandal involving three members of the opposition. Their fury at Pakistan's antics was compounded when the chairman of their cricket board, Ijaz Butt, claimed that England had deliberately lost the third ODI at the Oval for a large sum of money. To Strauss this was a step too far and with his team solidly behind him he proposed they boycott the fourth ODI, but having listened to Giles Clarke, the chairman of the ECB, and weighed up the ramifications of such a move, he began to have second thoughts.

Accepting that his team would now become the news story rather than the Pakistanis, he suggested that they draft a joint statement expressing their displeasure at the chairman of the PCB and then play the game, a proposal that was accepted by the majority. 'It is difficult to think of anybody else captaining England right now, so sure is Strauss's hold on the title,' wrote Atherton. 'In a difficult summer he has handled himself and his team with immense poise.

'Calmness and strength of mind have characterised his off-field performance throughout the fractious one-day series against Pakistan, as he played a central role in keeping the more militant members of his team on track in the wake of Ijaz Butt's slurs. As public and media opinion swings wildly back and forth, it is not always easy to chart such a straight course in such turbulent times, but Strauss has managed it impressively.' [225]

Determined to avoid the errors of the previous Australian tour, England planned methodically, leaving no detail untouched. Pre-tour meetings during the summer, a bonding session in Germany and a highly competitive approach to the three warm-up matches helped raise team morale on the eve of the first Test, in contrast with the disarray in the Australian camp hamstrung by selectorial indecision.

The game began badly, with Strauss's first-over dismissal and England, bowled out for 260, faced a first-innings deficit of 221. Fortunate to avoid a pair when a marginal lbw decision went his way, Strauss thereafter batted with conviction to make 110, sharing an opening partnership of 188 with Alastair Cook, who finished 235* in England's 517/1 declared.

Having seized the moral advantage at Brisbane, England enjoyed a dream start at Adelaide, where, on the flattest of wickets, they soon had Australia 2/3 with Ponting and Clarke both out for a duck. Relying on their four-man attack, as they did throughout the series, they looked to off-spinner Swann to tie one end up while the three pace bowlers pounded away at the other end. Dismissing them for 245, they replied with 620/5 declared, and when Australia staged something of a fightback Strauss turned to the occasional off spin of Pietersen, who promptly had Clarke caught at short leg in the final over.

England cleaned up the next day and, although they were soundly beaten at Perth, undone by Mitchell Johnson's devastating swing, Strauss once again held his nerve. Regarding Perth as a mere aberration by his batsmen, he fielded an unchanged side at Melbourne, other than replacing the expensive Steven Finn with Chris Tremlett. On an overcast morning he won the toss and, fielding first in conditions conducive to swing, his bowlers did him proud by bowling out Australia for 98. He and Cook then took up the cudgels by racing to 157/0 by the close, a big step along the road to a crushing victory by an innings and 157 runs, their biggest against Australia since 1956.

With another innings victory at Sydney to take the series 3-1, their first in Australia for 24 years, Strauss became only the third post-war England captain after Hutton and Brearley to win the Ashes both home and away. 'What he does have, which all the best leaders possess,' noted the *Daily Telegraph*'s Derek Pringle, 'is an understated authority though one that leaves you in no doubt as to who is in charge.' [226]

Although Strauss relinquished the one-day captaincy after England's disappointing showing in the World Cup in India, they returned to winning ways that summer. After beating Sri Lanka 1-0 in a rain-affected series, they then overwhelmed India, the top side in the world according to the ICC rankings, 4-0. In the third Test at Edgbaston, Strauss, who endured a torrid season with the bat, made 87 and put on 186 with Cook, who went on to score 294. England's victory by an innings and 242 runs meant they now replaced India at the top of the world rankings, a far cry from the bottom position they occupied in 1999. 'There really is no mystery as to why this England side are so good,' declared Steve James in the *Sunday Telegraph*. 'Possessing an outstanding group of international cricketers is a given, but it is not always enough. Leadership is key, and this team are superbly led by Andrew Strauss and Andy Flower. The players work hard, making them the fittest team in world cricket. They adhere religiously to simple plans. And they care passionately about the team ethic.' [227] According to John Woodcock, they were the best organised England team he'd known, and Shane Warne thought that they could go on and dominate world cricket for some time, but Strauss warned against complacency. His side would be judged by higher standards, not least their record on the subcontinent, which had been far from impressive over the past decade.

His words contained a prophetic touch for having reached the summit they quickly strayed from it as they lost direction and focus. Playing Pakistan in the United Arab Emirates (UAE) early in the new year, their failure to acclimatise properly backfired on them, since their failure to combat their spinners Saeed Ajmal and Abdur Rehman accounted for their 3-0 loss, their first series defeat in ten. On top of this, Strauss was once again struggling with the bat, which subjected him to greater media scrutiny. 'For the first time since he took on the job, it is being questioned whether Strauss should continue much longer,' reported *The Observer*'s Vic Marks. [228] A half-century in the second Test of a shared rubber against Sri Lanka bought him some time, but he later admitted that 'it was increasingly clear to me that the combination of batting troubles, the constant demands of captaincy and the pressing need for the England team to be pushed forward were beginning to wear me down. I wasn't enjoying my cricket any more.' [229] Determined not to be hounded out by the press, he vowed there and then that another bout of poor form would bring about his retirement.

Two centuries in the 2-0 defeat of the West Indies at home, while immensely satisfying, proved something of a false dawn. Up against Steyn, Morkel and the redoubtable South African pace attack later in the summer, Strauss struggled throughout, scoring a mere 97 runs in six innings. What's more, he became embroiled in a dressing-room spat with Pietersen.

Although never close personally, Strauss's relationship with Pietersen was a respectful one, his own South African upbringing helping him to understand Pietersen's brazen character, but that relationship began to unravel during the summer of 2012. Already embittered by a contractual dispute with the ECB, Pietersen then took umbrage against a parody Twitter account lampooning him for his arrogance, which he thought emanated from the England dressing room. Detaching himself from the rest of the team during the first part of the second Test against South Africa, his moroseness earned him a reprimand from Strauss. Even a brilliant 149 failed to lighten his mood or heal the rift with his team-mates. In his troubled state he sent a series of text messages to South African players which contained derogatory remarks about his captain, a provocative act which saw him dropped for the final Test at Lord's.

The whole imbroglio not only proved an unwelcome distraction for Strauss, who'd always placed a great emphasis on team loyalty, but it also undermined England's preparations for Lord's, and, while the players responded positively, they lost an enthralling match by 51 runs, giving South Africa the series 2-0. It was England's first home defeat under Strauss.

Dismissed for 20 and 1 in what was his 100th Test and ground down by fatigue, Strauss felt it was time to go. After mulling things over on a family holiday in Spain, he announced his retirement from all cricket in a press conference at Lord's, making clear that his lack of runs was the prime reason for his departure. Speaking with typical grace and dignity, he left to an unprecedented round of applause from the hardened journalists. 'As a person, Strauss has been remarkable for his modesty, reliability, straightforwardness,' wrote Brearley, 'he has never put a foot wrong. He made the best of his talent. He has worked hard, gone the extra mile.' [230]

Understated, courteous and reassuring, Strauss was the most English of captains, whose privileged background and noble bearing seemed like a throwback to a bygone era. Although lacking the tactical ingenuity of Brearley and the flair of Vaughan, he was their equal as a man-manager. Inheriting the captaincy during the dark days of January 2009, he, along with Flower, restored order out of chaos by creating a more relaxed, inclusive environment and winning the loyalty of the players in return, including the recalcitrant Pietersen. Yet for all his affability, Strauss was deceptively strong-willed. Committed to the highest of standards both on and off the field, nothing was left to chance in England's rise to supremacy. Thorough preparation, consistency of selection and team unity were critical to their achievement of going through nine successive series unbeaten, including two Ashes victories, the first England side to win in Australia in 24 years.

It was a measure of Strauss's standing that he kept the unequivocal support of his team when his own form fell away, and once he recognised that his decline was terminal he left on his own terms, his head held high.

After a spell in the Sky Sports commentary box, Strauss was appointed managing director of English cricket in 2015. His first act was to remove the incumbent coach Peter Moores and replace him with Trevor Bayliss, with a brief to improve England's performance in the limited overs game. He resigned in 2018 to spend more time with his ailing wife who died from cancer shortly afterwards. In 2019 he was knighted for his services to cricket.

George Mann, captain of the unbeaten MCC team to South Africa 1948-49.

Freddie Brown, an inspirational captain of England in Australia 1950-51. Next to him on the right is Len Hutton, England's first professional captain – unbeaten in six series during his three years in charge.

Peter May leading England against New Zealand, Lord's, 1958. He was unbeaten in his first five series as England captain.

Ted Dexter celebrates England's win against Australia at Melbourne, 1962-63 with Fred Trueman, David Sheppard and Colin Cowdrey. It was one of the highlights of Dexter's career.

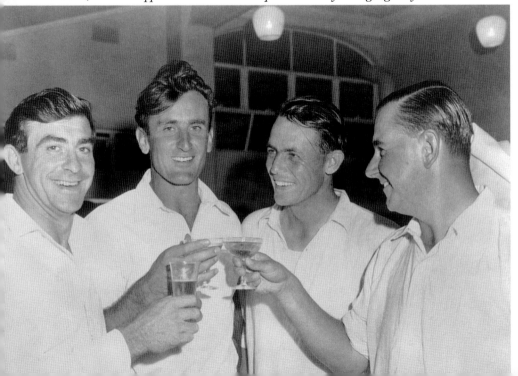

Ted Dexter with rival captain Richie Benaud at the end of the Ashes series 1962–63. The two of them became good friends.

Brian Close watches his opposite number, India's The Nawab of Pataudi, from his familiar position at short leg, Headingley, 1967.

Colin Cowdrey with rival captain Gary Sobers, Port of Spain, 1967–68. England, against all expectation, beat the West Indies 1–0.

Ray Illingworth drives Ashley Mallett for six during his match-winning innings against Australia at Headingley, 1972.

Ray Illingworth the day after his dismissal as England captain with his successor, Mike Denness, at Folkestone, 1973.

Tony Greig before his first Test as England captain: against Australia at Lord's, 1975, with debutants David Steele, Bob Woolmer and Phil Edmonds.

Tony Greig celebrates England's series win in India, 1976/77.

Ian Botham introduces his England side to The Queen, Lord's, 1980.

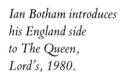

Mike Brearley celebrates England's remarkable victory against Australia at Headingley, 1981, with Ian Botham, the man of the match.

England under Brearley on the way to another win against Australia, Edgbaston, 1981.

Mike Gatting, captain of England 1986-88, the highlight of which was retaining the Ashes in Australia.

Four England captains at The Oval, 1986: Ian Botham, Graham Gooch, Mike Gatting and David Gower.

The summer of four captains: Mike Gatting and Graham Gooch with manager Micky Stewart at Lord's, 1988.

Graham Gooch, captain of England 1988-93, with his chairman of selectors Ted Dexter.

Michael Atherton, captain of England 1993-98, with his chairman of selectors Ray Illingworth.

Nasser Hussain, captain of England 1999-2003, with Mark Butcher, who captained England in one Test against New Zealand in 1999.

Nasser Hussain with his successor Michael Vaughan, who regained the Ashes in 2005 after 16 years.

Andrew Strauss, one of England's most successful captains, with his successor Alastair Cook, Lord's, 2012. Cook captained England in a record 59 Tests.

Nasser Hussain greets the current England captain, Joe Root, Old Trafford, 2019.

Alastair Cook

ALASTAIR COOK was born in Gloucester on 25 December 1984. Raised in the village of Wickham Bishops in Essex, his love of cricket alternated with his flair for singing. For five years he was a treble chorister at St Paul's Cathedral, a rigorous schedule of rehearsals and services that taught him the value of concentration and how to perform under pressure.

At the age of 13 he won a music scholarship to Bedford School and there, under the influence of coach Derek Randall, he became their most successful-ever cricketer. Drafted in to play for MCC against the school when the former was one short, Cook promptly obliged with a century.

Ever determined to improve, he never looked back, scoring a mountain of runs for Bedford and averaging a phenomenal 160.87 in his final year.

A member of the Essex Academy since he was 16, Cook made his first-team debut in 2003 and, two years later, he scored a chanceless double century against the Australians. In January 2006 he represented England A in the West Indies when called up as an emergency replacement for the senior team in India. Making his Test debut at Nagpur after two days of travel, he scored 60 and 104*. With three more centuries later that year, he quickly established himself as a prolific opener, not least in partnership with Strauss, his game founded on the basic virtues of a solid technique, formidable concentration and supreme stamina.

His qualities were never more conspicuous than in Australia in 2010/11 when he scored 766 runs at an average of 127.66, and the following summer he hit 294 against India at Edgbaston. Appointed Strauss's deputy, he led the 2010 tour to Bangladesh in his absence, scoring centuries in both Tests, and, on becoming England's one-day captain in 2011, he was the obvious man to take over the Test team when Strauss retired in 2012. Honest, decent and down-to-earth, he shunned the world of celebrity to work on his wife's family's farm. Never one for rousing rhetoric or flamboyant gestures, his captaincy was based on personal example: his commitment to fitness and practice and his sheer weight of runs.

Although Strauss's retirement was prompted mainly by his shortage of runs, his departure was overshadowed by Pietersen disparaging him in a series of texts to the South African players, an egregious act which brought about his omission from the team. Although appalled by his treatment of Strauss, Cook felt England couldn't afford to lose a player of Pietersen's ability for the forthcoming tour to India, and after several meetings between the two of them and Andy Flower he was readmitted into the fold.

With India unbeaten at home since 2004/05, England travelled there as underdogs and played according to script in the first Test at Ahmedabad when forced to follow on 330 behind. It was then that Cook rose to the occasion with an epic innings of 176. It wasn't enough to save his team from defeat, but it altered the shape of the series by showing that the Indian spinners Pragyan Ojha and Ravi Ashwin could be tamed.

He again showed true grit at Mumbai when he and Pietersen added 208 for the third wicket to give their side a first-innings lead of 86. Cook scored 122, Pietersen 186, and with their spinners Swann and Panesar out-bowling their Indian counterparts England won by ten wickets.

Triumphant again at Kolkata by seven wickets, Cook's contribution this time being 190, and, following a draw in Nagpur, England won in India for the first time in 28 years. The cricket journalist George Dobell wrote in *Wisden* that, 'Cook's air of calm, whether in adversity or triumph, his pragmatic approach to coaxing the best out of the eclectic mixture of characters under him and his desire to succeed meant the post-Strauss transition took place more smoothly than anyone could have dreamed.' [231] According to James Anderson, his decisions in the field were highly impressive. 'There was no ball following and he implemented his own ideas on when to attack and when to defend. He got the balance of that spot on, so that we went for the kill or bided our time at exactly the right points.' [232]

Cook's heroics in India had sapped his energy and on tour to New Zealand after Christmas his leadership lacked inspiration as England were fortunate to draw 0-0. Back home, they beat the same opposition 2-0, although Cook's defensive tactics in the second Test at Headingley drew adverse comment. It set the scene for the summer. England were firm favourites to beat Australia following the latter's disastrous tour to India and the sacking of their coach, but although they won 3-0 they were flattered by their margin of victory. Only at Lord's did they dominate, and while Cook was criticised for his defensive leadership, not least by Shane Warne, his team were also slated for their hard-nosed gamesmanship. 'He is a good man, he concentrates fully, and is loyal and considerate to his players,' wrote Brearley, but, concerned about his team's rather cynical approach in their quest for success, he continued: 'Is he, then, at present strong enough to stand up for what is right? And is he too defensive, too routine as a captain? Are these aspects that he needs to concentrate on? I think they are.' [233]

Given the considerable animosity between the two sides, it was England's misfortune that battle was resumed in Australia a few weeks later. While the home team rediscovered their hunger under new coach Darren Lehmann, Cook's men found they were running on empty as the relentless international schedule took its toll. Inadequately acclimatised after a couple of unsatisfactory warm-up games, they lined up at Brisbane totally unprepared for the ferocity of the attack that awaited them, chiefly in the form of fast bowler Mitchell Johnson, back in action after injury had ruled him out of the Tests in England. Bowling with awesome pace, he took nine wickets in the match to leave his opponents shocked and traumatised, none more so than Trott, who returned home with a stress-related illness.

Johnson was again their nemesis at Adelaide with 7/40 in their first innings of 172, a deficit of 398, and dismissing Cook in the first over of the second innings, beginning their slide towards another heavy defeat.

Despite an heroic century from rookie Ben Stokes, England were again outplayed at Perth to surrender the Ashes even more abjectly than Flintoff's side did seven years earlier. The match claimed two prominent victims – Swann, impeded by an injured elbow, announced his immediate retirement, and wicketkeeper Prior was dropped for the final two Tests – but a new-look side for Melbourne and Sydney yielded little improvement as they were thrashed 5-0. Even allowing for Australia's brilliance spearheaded by Johnson's 37 wickets at 13.57, England had been pitiful and Cook was deemed culpable, not only for his lack of runs but also for his uninspiring captaincy, especially in comparison with his counterpart Michael Clarke. Yet whatever his limitations, England's problems went much deeper than the captaincy. 'No man could have captained us this winter,' declared Swann. 'You could bring back Mike Brearley – he wouldn't have done any good. We were terrible.' [234]

Their defeat brought dressing-room strife when Pietersen publicly questioned the prescriptive approach of Andy Flower, one outburst too many as far as the ECB were concerned. With their new managing director of cricket Paul Downton determined to improve the team ethic, his services were abruptly dispensed with, a contentious decision exacerbated by the maladroit manner in which the ECB handled it. With no adequate explanation given for Pietersen's demise, many of his supporters, led by his cheerleader Piers Morgan, the journalist and broadcaster, directed their fury overwhelmingly at Cook, despite his voice being only one among many.

Pietersen's demise did give Cook the opportunity to enhance his authority in the dressing room, but new faces didn't automatically mean the end of old problems in the home Tests against Sri Lanka. A delayed declaration allowed Sri Lanka to escape defeat at Lord's with nine wickets down, and at Headingley, where England lost on the penultimate ball, there seemed no concerted attempt to dismiss captain Angelo Matthews as he and Rangana Herath added 149 runs for the eighth wicket. Warne called Cook's captaincy 'horrific', the worst he'd seen in 25 years, and the questions kept coming – why had the England bowlers been allowed to bowl short when a fuller length was needed and why had Cook bowled Anderson and Broad in such long spells when both were injury-prone?

Almost as serious as England's sixth defeat in their last seven games was Cook's decline in form, which had seen him go a year without a Test century. Another failure in the first Test against India and a dull draw did nothing to ease his plight, and two low scores in England's insipid defeat at Lord's brought the rising chorus of discontent to a crescendo. Atherton, Hussain and Vaughan all called for his dethronement, and even Brearley doubted whether he could survive. 'But seldom, if ever, has there been a backdrop so polarised and so fuelled by vitriol to the fate of an England captain,' wrote Vic Marks. [235] Cook, who'd already contemplated quitting during the Sri Lanka Test at Headingley, only to be dissuaded by his wife Alice, admitted it was his toughest challenge yet, but backed unflinchingly by his team and the ECB he vowed to carry on.

If Lord's proved to be the nadir of his captaincy, Southampton, six days later, began his path back to redemption. In the benign setting of the Ageas Bowl, Cook, missed on 15, battled away to score 95 and returned to a standing ovation by an overtly supportive crowd. Buoyed by his success, he followed up with 70* in the second innings and showed a deft touch in the field, especially in his use of spinner Moeen Ali, in England's 266-run victory. 'We have witnessed a remarkable rebirth by a remarkable cricketer,' wrote Andrew Strauss. 'What was clear from the reception he received at the Ageas Bowl is that he has many admirers, including his players.' [236]

His rehabilitation continued with two further overwhelming victories at Old Trafford and the Oval, his cause helped by India's complete failure to combat the swinging ball in conditions ideal for Anderson and Broad.

Not all of Cook's troubles were behind him. His approach to the one-day game looked increasingly obsolete, and after defeats by India at home and Sri Lanka away he was unceremoniously ditched before the World Cup. He was miffed by his demotion, but the additional time at home helped refresh his game when England travelled to the West Indies in the spring of 2015. He hit 76 and 59* in their win in Grenada and he scored his first Test century for two years in Barbados. His team, however, managed to lose by five wickets after an inexplicable collapse in their second innings, giving the unfancied West Indies a share of the series. 'Alastair is a top-class batsman with an excellent record,' wrote Boycott, 'but his tactical awareness and cricketing nous do not compare with the great England captains.' He berated him for the unsuccessful recall of Trott – he retired from Test cricket at the end of the series – his lack of enterprise in the drawn first Test and his failure to play two spinners there. [237]

England's failure to win in the West Indies following their inglorious showing in the World Cup cost Peter Moores his job for the second time. His replacement, the Australian Trevor Bayliss, proved a breath of fresh air. A more relaxed personality than his predecessor, he allowed a team of free spirits such as Ben Stokes, Jonny Bairstow and Moeen Ali to play to their strengths and encouraged Cook to be more adventurous. After a 1-1 draw against New Zealand, England beat Australia 3-2 with convincing wins on seaming wickets at Cardiff, Edgbaston and Trent Bridge. Although Cook's form with the bat was nothing special, his leadership had matured in the way he marshalled the field, managed his bowlers and, above all, trusted his players to play according to their lights. 'England's remarkable Ashes success is a great achievement for the team and a huge personal triumph for Alastair Cook,' wrote the BBC's Jonathan Agnew. 'He has led his team brilliantly and totally outthought his Australian counterpart Michael Clarke, who has long been considered one of the most innovative captains in world cricket.

'His field placings and bowling changes have been sharp, and at times he has been ruthless.' [238]

A taxing winter began with a 2-0 defeat to Pakistan in the UAE, but Cook's mammoth 263 gained England a creditable draw in the first Test, and although they lost the next two games, chiefly because of their lack of top-class spinners, they didn't disgrace themselves.

They fared better in South Africa, winning the four-Test series 2-1 thanks to a devastating spell of 6-17 from Stuart Broad in the third Test at Johannesburg. Even an embarrassing defeat in the final game couldn't take the gloss off their achievement. A relaxed Cook gave his batsmen the freedom to attack and he set imaginative fields, not least his placement of James Taylor at deep short leg, in which position he took two stunning catches at Johannesburg.

A convincing win against a weak Sri Lankan side at home was followed by a disappointing 2-2 draw against Pakistan. Cook, in splendid form all summer, gave a lead at the top of the order, but, once again, in the post-Strauss era, he lacked a reliable opening partner, and the rest of the upper order, aside from Joe Root and Bairstow, proved inconsistent.

That inconsistency remained on England's arduous seven-Test tour to Bangladesh and India that autumn. Before departure Cook gave a hostage to fortune by admitting in an interview with *The Cricketer* that he looked forward to returning to the ranks and, as the tour progressed, speculation about the captaincy became ever more pronounced.

Arriving back in Bangladesh after the birth of his second daughter, Cook won his 134th cap at Chittagong, becoming England's most capped player, in a match they narrowly won. They then lost the second Test at Mirpur where, on another turning wicket, Cook set unduly defensive fields. Needing 273 to win on the fourth day, he and Ben Duckett opened up with a stand of 100, but, after the tea interval, England lost all ten wickets in one session to record their first-ever Test defeat against Bangladesh.

They began creditably in India by getting the better of the draw in the first Test at Rajkot, and had Cook displayed a touch more enterprise they might well have won. Thereafter it was one long retreat as England, hampered by flawed selections, were unable to cope with captain Virat Kohli's gluttony for runs and their spinners, Ashwin and Ravindra Jadeja. Beaten by 246 runs at Visakhapatnam, their defeats grew ever heavier, with India scoring 759/7 declared in the final Test at Chennai, the highest number of runs England had ever shipped, as they lost the series 4-0. With the team looking increasingly rudderless in the field, Scyld Berry called for a change of captaincy, primarily because the Test side had ceased to grow.

A leader less defensive and formulaic than Cook was required for England to rise to the next level.

'The case against Cook as captain consists of the pros which stem from his character. So far, as his extreme determination allows, he is non-confrontational – which is ideal when dealing with umpires but not with opponents, because he tends to back off. Cook does not invade the space of a new batsman at his most vulnerable; he does not talk to him, or stand in his crease to direct his fielders, or make him wait, or bring up a close-catcher into his eye-line: ungentlemanly tactics, perhaps, but they have to be done to give a team their best chance of winning. Douglas Jardine, Len Hutton, Ray Illingworth, Mike Brearley, Andrew Strauss and Vaughan: all of England's most successful captains have been prepared to confront opponents, and team-mates.'[239]

Exhausted at the end of the trip, it was no surprise that, having mulled over his future on return, Cook resigned weeks later. It is one of the ironies of his captaincy that such a mild-mannered person should have generated such abuse, much of it on social media, but, equally, it says a lot about his character and resilience that he overcame it to lead his country for a record 59 times. During his four and a half years in charge, he saw the side he inherited from Strauss break up after the Ashes fiasco of 2013/14 and he fashioned a new one around the likes of Root, Moeen Ali, Bairstow, Stokes, Jos Buttler and Chris Woakes.

The advent of Trevor Bayliss as coach inspired Cook to captain with greater flair, best seen against Australia in 2015 and in South Africa the following winter, but his innate caution never really deserted him, not least on the 2016/17 tour of Bangladesh and India. Following eight defeats in his final year in charge, the highest number since 1993, Cook accepted that the team had stagnated under his leadership and decided it was time to go. Neither his middling record of 24 wins and 22 losses, nor his lack of enterprise, warrant him a place in the pantheon of great captains, but his essential decency aside he will be remembered as the only man to have won in both India and South Africa, and one of only three men – Grace and Brearley being the other two – to have won two Ashes rubbers at home.

Cook played for England for two more years and celebrated his 161st, and final game, against India at the Oval by scoring 147 in his final innings. He was knighted in 2019 for his services to the game and he continues to play for Essex.

Joe Root

JOE ROOT was born in Sheffield on 30 December 1990 into a family steeped in cricket. His father Matt, a former second eleven player for Nottinghamshire, represented Sheffield Collegiate, the club that nurtured Michael Vaughan, and his younger brother Billy currently plays for Glamorgan.

From a very early age Root dreamed of playing for England and spent every spare moment with a bat in his hand. Educated at King Ecgbert School, Sheffield, he was miffed as an 11-year-old to miss out on the school's annual sports personality award, the award going instead to an athlete several years older than him called Jessica Ennis, later Olympic champion in the heptathlon.

On scoring 80 for his school against Worksop College, he won a sports scholarship to the latter, where he continued to progress through dedicated practice, as he did for Sheffield Collegiate.

The youngest-ever member of the Yorkshire Academy at 13, he impressed the head coach Kevin Sharp with his commitment and technique, and having graduated through the Yorkshire system he made his debut for the first eleven in 2010. After two productive years he was picked for England's 2012/13 tour to India and made 73 on his debut at Nagpur, showing a maturity beyond his years.

He hit his maiden Test century against New Zealand in the summer of 2013 and followed up with 180 against Australia at Lord's, but the runs then began to dry up and on tour to Australia that winter he was dropped for the final Test.

The following summer he returned to form with 254 against Sri Lanka at Lord's and two centuries against India. He continued to dominate England's batting and in 2015 his future destiny as captain seemed assured when appointed Cook's deputy. A more open, outgoing personality than Cook, fully at ease with social media, his angelic looks and impish grin didn't detract from an inner core of steel.

On taking over as captain in 2017, he made a dream start by scoring 190 against South Africa in the first Test at Lord's and leading his team to a 211-run victory. His honeymoon didn't last long, however, since they lost heavily at Trent Bridge with a display of batting so reckless that Root's mentor, Michael Vaughan, accused them of showing a lack of respect for Test cricket, an attack that shocked him.

He recovered his poise at Old Trafford and was rewarded with a handsome victory, followed by another one at the Oval, their first series win against South Africa at home since 1998.

They continued with a 2-1 win against the West Indies. Root was once again awash with runs, and, after adding 248 for the third wicket with Cook in the first Test at Edgbaston, Cook lauded him as a genius. England won easily there, lost on a declaration at Headingley – his tactics mystifying Bayliss – before triumphing at Lord's. After a summer of success they looked forward to Australia with quiet optimism, but the tour was blighted even before they'd departed.

That September Stokes, England's talismanic all-rounder, became embroiled in a late-night brawl outside a Bristol nightclub, which led to his withdrawal from the tour while the case was under investigation; then once in Australia Root was forced to spend a lot of time answering questions about England's drinking culture following incidents involving Bairstow and Duckett.

Although England were spared the onslaught they faced from Mitchell Johnson four years earlier, the Australian pace attack of Mitchell Starc, Josh Hazlewood and Pat Cummins, along with the spin of Nathan Lyon, proved far superior. After losing by ten wickets at Brisbane, Root inserted Australia at Adelaide but was let down by his bowlers, enabling the home side to declare at 442/8, and although England fought back in the second innings under the lights they still lost by 120 runs.

England seized the early initiative at Perth with centuries from Bairstow and Dawid Malan, but their total of 403 was overshadowed by Australia's 662/9, leading to an innings victory. Australia's captain Steve Smith made 239 following his century at Brisbane, and his phenomenal batting contrasted favourably with Root's, who seemed distracted at the crease and failed to convert fifties into hundreds. Ponting said he looked like a little boy who needed to step up and Ian Chappell accused him of being too defensive, especially his failure to attack more with the new ball.

Defeated 4-0 in Australia, England completed a miserable winter by losing 1-0 in New Zealand, their dismissal for 58 in the first Test at Auckland a particular humiliation.

Their woes continued at Lord's in the first Test against Pakistan. Root had his worst match as captain as England played poorly to lose by nine wickets, but they recovered quickly at Headingley to win by an innings, the prelude to beating India 4-1.

In the first Test at Edgbaston, the tourists began the final day needing 84 to win with five wickets left when Root took charge. Handling his bowlers and fielders with aplomb, he not only starved Virat Kohli, India's leading batsman, of the strike, he also kept the pressure on their lower order and was rewarded with a 31-run victory.

England outplayed India at Lord's, and although they stumbled badly at Trent Bridge they won a close game at the Ageas Bowl to clinch the series. Root called the win his best as captain, a view endorsed by Vic Marks, who admired his ability to continue scoring runs and captain with calm authority.

His stock continued to rise during England's 3-0 win in Sri Lanka. In addition to a stunning century at Pallekele, he captained imaginatively and encouraged his batsmen to attack. 'I really believe this team belong to Joe now,' wrote Michael Vaughan. 'The way they go out and play, and the tactical manoeuvres, are all down to the captain. We have seen England play more positively in the subcontinent than their predecessors.' [240]

Unfortunately, they carried their aggression to excess in the West Indies early in 2019, losing unexpectedly 2-1. In the first Test at Bridgetown, Root admitted they'd erred by omitting Stuart Broad for Sam Curran, who looked ineffective in the Caribbean, and it needed the additional pace of Mark Wood to help England win a consolation victory in the third Test in St Lucia.

Following England's success in winning the World Cup, they entered the series against Australia in good heart, but at the end of a gripping encounter, which they were slightly fortunate to draw 2-2, they seemed no nearer to solving their frustrating inconsistency, a trait not helped by their flawed selection. In what was a difficult summer for Root, his captaincy came under fierce scrutiny, not only for the adverse effect it had on his batting, but also for his failure to take a positive lead in the field. In the fourth Test at Old Trafford, after England had surrendered a first-innings lead of 196, their opening bowlers fought back to reduce Australia to 44/4 at tea, but instead of going for the kill afterwards Root let his opponents off the hook by opening with his second-string attack. At the end of a match in which Australia's victory saw them retain the Ashes, the England captain felt obliged to burnish his leadership credentials, which would permit him a third tilt at winning the Ashes when England tour Australia in 2021/22. Aside from his continued hold of the dressing room, his position was cemented by an assured performance in England's win at the Oval to draw the rubber and the lack of a serious alternative to the captaincy, but his leadership remains a work in progress. His final place in history will depend to some extent on whether he can bring a greater consistency to his side, especially overseas, and whether his batting regains its former flair.

Conclusion

OUT of the 43 captains of England covered in this book, Gubby Allen was the oldest at 45 and Ian Botham the youngest at 24. In the post-war era the amateurs – unless their careers had been interrupted by the war – tended to be appointed captain of England in their mid-20s, by which time they'd gained some experience captaining their university or their county. The fact that Peter May was an exception to that rule when succeeding Len Hutton in 1955 proved no impediment, partly because of his close bonds with his predecessor and partly because of the authority he commanded as the world's finest batsman.

Because the professionals weren't deemed leadership material and were often chosen as a last resort, they tended to be much older. Illingworth and Fletcher were both 37 when first appointed captain of England, and Hutton, Close, Brearley and Gooch were 35, their added maturity an asset rather than a liability. Since the introduction of central contracts, the trend has been back towards younger captains who've risen through the England set-up but with little experience of captaining their counties.

Captaining England has proved a demanding business with an average tenure of about two years. Only May has lasted for five years (Vaughan's five-year stint included one year out because of injury), a brevity that has been in stark contrast to many of their counterparts overseas. Allan Border captained Australia between 1984 and 1994 and Ricky Ponting captained them between 2004 and 2011; Gary Sobers led the West Indies between 1965 and 1972, a figure easily exceeded by Clive Lloyd between 1974 and 1985, while his successor, Viv Richards, was in charge for six years. The Nawab of Pataudi captained India between 1962 and 1970, Mohammed Azharuddin was in charge for seven years and M.S. Dhoni for six; John Reid skippered New Zealand between 1955 and 1965 and Stephen Fleming was in charge for nine years, a figure exceeded by Graeme Smith of South Africa, who was their captain between 2003 and 2014.

Compared to England's 43 captains, Australia has had only 26, the West Indies 31 and India 30, and while some of this discrepancy can be attributed to the greater number of Tests they've played it goes deeper than this. England's mystical belief in the concept of leadership has often led to inflated expectations in the capacity of a captain to deliver success. While 13 of their captains were dismissed between 1966 and 1988, one of them twice, only three Australians – Bill Lawry, Graham Yallop and Steve Smith – have suffered the same fate throughout the whole period. When their team endured an unprecedented barren run throughout the mid-to-late 1980s, the selectors resisted the temptation to ditch their captain Allan Border. Instead, they kept faith with him and his young team, a policy triumphantly vindicated by Australia's rise to world dominance in the 1990s.

For 20 years after the Second World War the amateur captain was more or less impregnable, but the coming of the democratic 1960s coincided with English cricket's crisis of confidence. The game's growing defensiveness precipitated an alarming decline in attendances and England lost five home rubbers between 1961 and 1966. Two captains, Mike Smith and Colin Cowdrey, were dismissed against the West Indies in 1966, and from then on unsuccessful captains could expect the same fate. The cull reached its climax in the 1980s when England plunged to new depths, losing successive home series to India, New Zealand and Pakistan. In that decade they won only 20 out of 104 games they played, their 19.2 per cent success rate their worst ever, bar the 18.8 per cent in the 1940s, a decade when the country was recovering from the ravages of war. While the demands of the county game were primarily blamed for

England's woes, the amateur selection system was equally culpable. Acting without a long-term strategy, players were randomly selected and discarded on a whim, so that out of the 58 awarded a Test cap during the 1980s, 13 played no more than twice and 23 only four times. In 1988, 28 players were picked for the six Tests that summer, a figure exceeded by one the following summer, with only Gower and Jack Russell appearing in every game against Australia. This lack of consistency not only eroded the confidence of individuals unsure as to whether they fully belonged, it also undermined team spirit.

After the farcical experience of four captains in one summer in 1988 and Gower's short-lived return the following year, the captaincy entered a more stable phase with the appointment of Graham Gooch in 1989. Both he and his successor Michael Atherton remained in charge for four years, but while England adopted a more professional approach to fitness and practice their record of 26 wins out of 107 games, an average of 24.3 per cent, barely improved. Not only did they lose five Ashes series in that decade, they failed to win an overseas tour, except for two rubbers in New Zealand.

The real transformation came with the appointment of Duncan Fletcher as coach and Nasser Hussain as captain in 1999. Using the creation of central contracts to their advantage, the two of them were able to instil a more rigorous work ethic and greater consistency of selection. From 2000, when they won four rubbers in succession, England became harder to beat, and while Hussain failed twice in his quest to win the Ashes he'd planted the seeds which Vaughan successfully harvested against Australia in 2005.

Strauss surpassed Vaughan's achievement in 2011 by taking England to the top of the ICC cricket rankings, and even though he and his successors weren't able to keep them there, their record compares favourably with the team of the 1980s and 90s, especially at home.

With contemporary captains operating in close harness with the coach, they are cushioned against dismissal in a way that their predecessors would envy, unless they fall out with the coach as Kevin Pietersen did with Peter Moores. That said, they are subjected to a relentless schedule, especially if they play white-ball cricket as well as red-ball cricket, and confronted with intense public scrutiny. 'Critics of modern captains lightly ignore a contradiction,' wrote Ed Smith, the national selector. 'Modern captains have less power than ever, yet they are still held solely accountable for decisions and tactics which must have originated, by definition of the power arrangements in all top teams, in discussions between captains and coaches' [241] The increased workload, the physical and mental exhaustion and the lack of privacy helps explain why captains of the modern era – Gooch, Atherton, Hussain, Vaughan, Strauss and Cook – have lasted little beyond the four-year cycle. 'Four years in the job can be very repetitive,' declared Hussain at the time of his resignation. 'It tests you deeply, and mentally I felt I was not quite on the ball enough.' [242]

Whether captains resign voluntarily or are dismissed, few of them depart at the summit of their achievement. George Mann retired following one triumphant tour to South Africa in 1948/49, Hutton retired after his Ashes triumph in 1954/55, unbeaten in any series, and Brearley went on his own terms in 1981 after his remarkable comeback against Australia. Even highly successful captains such as Vaughan and Strauss relinquished the seals of office when personal form and the team's fortunes were on the wane.

For a country that places so much emphasis on leadership, it has to be acknowledged that England has produced relatively few great cricket captains in the period covered: Len Hutton, Brian Close – like George Mann all too briefly – Ray Illingworth, Mike Brearley, Michael Vaughan and Andrew Strauss were clearly outstanding and Freddie Brown, Peter May, Mike Smith and Nasser Hussain were very good ones, but too many of the others were locked into a defensive mentality which failed to place enough premium on winning.

Napoleon's oft-repeated comment that he would rather have a lucky general than a good one is applicable to cricket captains, since much of their reputation has rested largely on the talent available to them. Hutton's England side of the mid-1950s would rank with any in the post-war age; Illingworth's side, while lacking the same dash of brilliance, contained many a world-class player such as Boycott, Edrich, Knott, Snow and Underwood; Brearley had Willis and

Botham at their peak; Vaughan had England's best pace quartet in living memory and Strauss could call on prolific run scorers such as Cook, Trott and Pietersen and leading wicket-takers such as Anderson, Broad and Swann.

Yet while luck has helped determine the fate of many a captain, their own attributes shouldn't be underestimated. Hutton won respect for his profound knowledge of the game as well as his sheer weight of runs; Illingworth's canny leadership under duress proved critical in several close encounters, most notably at Sydney in 1971; Brearley vindicated his comeback in 1981 with those unforgettable victories against Australia at Headingley and Edgbaston; Vaughan's sunny optimism helped recover the Ashes in 2005 and Strauss unified a fractious group of players.

Although recent captains have served a four-year cycle, they have clocked up a huge number of matches in charge, with Cook holding the record with 59. With Root already three years into his captaincy and keen to lead his country in Australia in 2021/22, it will be interesting to see if he breaks Cook's record and sets a new model for the England captaincy.

Endnotes

1 *Sunday Telegraph*, 26 January 2014.
2 *Sunday Telegraph*, 2 July 2017.
3 *The Times*, 30 July 1997.
4 Mike Atherton, *Opening Up: My Autobiography*, p.63.
5 *Sunday Telegraph*, 2 July 2017.
6 *The Times*, 26 October 2012.
7 *Sunday Telegraph*, 3 August 2003.
8 *The Times*, 15 April 1986.
9 *Sunday Times*, 12 June 1988.
10 David Norrie, *Athers: The Authorised Biography of Michael Atherton*, p.146.
11 Atherton, *Opening Up: My Autobiography*, p.108.
12 *The Times*, 9 November 2016.
13 *Sunday Telegraph*, 26 January 2014.
14 Scyld Berry, *Cricket: The Game of Life*, p.361.
15 *Sunday Telegraph*, 2 July 2017.
16 J.M. Kilburn, *Cricket Decade*, p.25.
17 Alan Hill, *The Bedsers*, p.50.
18 Quoted in Denis Compton and Bill Edrich, *Cricket and All That*, p.77.
19 Donald Trelford [ed], *Len Hutton Remembered*, p.59.
20 Denis Compton, *End of an Innings*, p.28.
21 Compton and Edrich, *Cricket and All That*, p.96.
22 Jack Fingleton, *Cricket Crisis*, p.294.
23 Quoted in David Foot, *Wally Hammond: The Reasons Why*, p.151.
24 David Rayvern Allen, *Jim: The Life of E.W. Swanton*, p.192.
25 Alec Bedser, *Twin Ambitions*, p.31.
26 *Wisden Cricket Monthly*, June 1980, p.23.
27 Quoted in *E.W. Swanton, Swanton in Australia*, p.44.

28 *Wisden Cricketers' Almanack 1948*, p.56.
29 Len Hutton, *Fifty Years in Cricket*, p.58.
30 John Shawcroft, *Donald Carr: Derbyshire's Corinthian*, p.111.
31 Godfrey Evans, *The Gloves are Off*, p.56.
32 *Wisden 1949*, p.747.
33 Michael Marshall, *Gentlemen and Players*, p.154.
34 Manager's Tour Report 1948–49, MCC Archives.
35 Huw Turbervill, *The Toughest Tour*, p.20.
36 Alan Hill, *The Valiant Cricketer: The Biography of Trevor Bailey*, p.71.
37 *Wisden 1952*, p.101.
38 Neville Cardus (ed Margaret Hughes), *Cardus on the Ashes*, p.185.
39 Ian Johnson, *Cricket at the Crossroads*, p.124.
40 *Wisden 1952*, p.100.
41 Stephen Chalke, *At the Heart of English Cricket: The Life and Memories of Geoffrey Howard*, p.113.
42 *ibid*, p.114.
43 *ibid*, p.120.
44 Shawcroft, *Donald Carr: Derbyshire's Corinthian Cricketer*, p.69.
45 Chalke, *At the Heart of English Cricket*, p.86.
46 Hutton, *Fifty Years in Cricket*, p.48.
47 Trelford (ed), *Len Hutton Remembered*, p.80.
48 Colin Cowdrey, *The Incomparable Game*, p.39.
49 Hutton, *Fifty Years in Cricket*, p.90.
50 Compton, *End of an Innings*, p.125.
51 Chris Waters, *Fred Trueman: The Authorised Biography*, p.120.
52 Trelford (ed), *Len Hutton Remembered*, p.38.
53 Chalke, *At the Heart of English Cricket*, p.94.
54 Hutton, *Fifty Years in Cricket*, p.127.
55 Compton, *End of an Innings*, p.144.
56 *Wisden 1955*, p.82.
57 Alan Hill, *Peter May: The Biography*, p.106.
58 Norman Cutler, *Behind the Australian Tests – 1956*, p.226.
59 Johnson, *Cricket at the Crossroads*, p.128.
60 Andrew Murtagh, *Touched by Greatness*, p.124.
61 Bill Edrich, *Round the Wicket*, p.33.
62 Frank Tyson, *A Typhoon called Tyson*, p.189.
63 Christopher Sandford, *Tom Graveney: The Biography*, p.66.
64 Evans, *The Gloves are Off*, p.210.
65 Alan Hill, *Jim Laker: The Biography*, p.172.
66 Hill, *Peter May*, p.157.

67 *Wisden 1960*, p.810.

68 Colin Cowdrey, *MCC: Autobiography of a Cricketer,* p.125.

69 Manager's Tour Report 1959–60, MCC Archives.

70 Mike Brearley, *The Art of Captaincy*, p.40.

71 Sandford, *Graveney*, p.99.

72 *Wisden 1964*, p.801.

73 *The Times*, 19 August 1964.

74 Turbervill, *The Toughest Tour*, p.51.

75 *ibid.*

76 Trevor Bailey, *The Greatest of my Time*, p.104.

77 Colin Shindler, *Bob Barber: The Professional Amateur*, p.195.

78 *Daily Sketch*, 9 August 1966.

79 Mark Peel, *The Last Roman: A Biography of Colin Cowdrey*, p.145.

80 *Wisden 1969*, p.813.

81 Bedser, *Twin Ambitions*, p.151.

82 Quoted in Ivo Tennant, The Cowdreys, p.79.

83 Shindler, *Bob Barber*, p.157.

84 David Clark to Billy Griffith, 22 March 1964, MCC Archives.

85 Geoff Boycott, *The Autobiography*, p.80.

86 *Daily Telegraph*, 23 August 1966.

87 Quoted in Simon Wilde, *England: The Biography*, p.329.

88 Brian Close, *Close to Cricket*, p.69.

89 *The Times*, 24 August 1967.

90 Ray Illingworth, *Yorkshire and Back*, p.41.

91 *ibid*, p.44.

92 Derek Underwood, *Beating the Bat*, p.88.

93 Turbervill, *The Toughest Tour*, p.83.

94 *The Times*, 31 July 1972.

95 John Snow, *Cricket Rebel*, p.137.

96 *The Times*, 5 August 1972.

97 *Wisden 1974*, p.883.

98 Pat Pocock, *Percy*, p.80.

99 Dennis Amiss, *In Search of Runs*, p.29.

100 *The Times*, 5 August 1973.

101 Boycott, *The Autobiography*, p.179.

102 Leo McKinstry, *Boycs: The True Story*, p.135.

103 *The Times*, 5 March 1974.

104 Bob Willis, *Lasting the Pace*, p.51.

105 *Wisden 1976*, p.925.

106 Bedser, *Twin Ambitions*, p.158.

107 *The Times*, 31 August 1976.

108 Brearley, *The Art of Captaincy*, p.246.

109 Christopher Martin-Jenkins, *MCC in India 1976–77*, p.140.

110 *The Guardian*, 30 December 2012.

111 *The Times*, 14 May 1977.

112 *Sunday Times*, 2 July 1972.

113 *Daily Telegraph*, 30 June 2015.

114 *The Times*, 7 August 1978.

115 *The Guardian*, 5 January 1979.

116 Bob Taylor, *Standing Up, Standing Back*, p.134.

117 Boycott, *The Autobiography*, p.259.

118 John Lever, *The Cricketer's Cricketer*, p.66.

119 *The Times*, 4 November 2017.

120 Pat Murphy, *Botham: A Biography*, p.85.

121 Mike Brearley, *Phoenix from the Ashes*, xviii.

122 Simon Wilde, *Ian Botham*, p.184.

123 Simon Barnes, Phil Edmonds: A Singular Man, p.77.

124 Taylor, *Standing Up, Standing Back*, p.134.

125 Graham Gooch, *Captaincy*, p.7.

126 *The Independent*, 4 July 2009.

127 Benaud, *On Reflection*, p.42.

128 Ray Illingworth, *Captaincy*, p.144.

129 Barnes, *Phil Edmonds: A Singular Man*, p.79.

130 Mike Gatting, *Leading from the Front*, p.66.

131 *ibid*, p.67.

132 Stephen Chalke, *In Sun and Shadow: The Biography of Geoff Cope*, p.166.

133 Peter Roebuck, *It Sort of Clicks*, p.114.

134 *The Guardian*, 26 June 2019.

135 Gooch, *Captaincy*, p.3.

136 Boycott, *The Autobiography*, p.264.

137 Wilde, *Ian Botham*, p.160.

138 Geoff Boycott, *In the Fast Lane*, p.74.

139 Murphy, *Botham: A Biography*, p.70.

140 Robin Jackman, *Jackers: A Life in Cricket*, p.113.

141 Boycott, *In the Fast Lane*, p.204.

142 Graham Gooch, *My Cricket Diary '81*, p.113.

143 Wilde, *Ian Botham*, p.68.

144 *Wisden 1983*, p.959.

145 *The Times*, 22 May 1982.

146 *Wisden 1983*, p.77.

147 Bob Willis, *Captain's Diary*, p.88.

148 Turbervill, *The Toughest Tour*, p.135.

149 Barnes, *Phil Edmonds*, p.136.

150 Gooch, *Captaincy*, p.154.

151 Rob Steen, *David Gower: A Man out of Time*, p.183.

152 *The Times*, 9 April, 1986.

153 *Wisden 1987*, p.904.

154 *The Times*, 27 May 1989.

155 Devon Malcolm, *You Guys are History*, p.39.

156 *The Observer*, 27 August 1989.

157 Stephen Chalke, *Micky Stewart and the Changing Face of Cricket*, p.269.

158 Gooch, *Captaincy*, p.103.

159 David Gower, *The Autobiography*, p.160.

160 Ian Botham, *The Autobiography*, p.264.

161 *The Times*, 12 December 1987.

162 *ibid*, 14 January 1988.

163 *Wisden 1991*, p.968.

164 *David Gower, An Endangered Species* p219

165 Jack Russell, *Unleashed*, p.99.

166 Allan Lamb, *My Autobiography*, p.172.

167 *Wisden 1992*, p.963.

168 Russell, *Unleashed*, p.97.

169 Quoted in Gooch, *My Autobiography*, p.280.

170 *The Observer*, 9 August 1992.

171 *The Times*, 25 February 1993.

172 Gooch, *My Autobiography*, p.312.

173 *ibid*, p.341.

174 *The Observer*, 25 July 1993.

175 Atherton, *Opening Up: My Autobiography*, p.66.

176 Richard Evans, *The Ultimate Test*, p.170.

177 Alec Stewart, *Playing for Keeps: The Autobiography of Alec Stewart*, p.66.

178 David Lloyd, *The Autobiography*, p.140.

179 Malcolm, *You Guys are History*, p.104.

180 Russell, *Unleashed*, p.136.

181 Malcolm, *You Guys are History*, p.111.

182 *The Times*, 26 July 1994.

183 Norrie, *Athers: The Authorised Biography of Michael Atherton*, p.174.

184 Darren Gough, *Dazzler: The Autobiography of Darren Gough*, p.91.
185 Atherton, *Opening Up*, p.136.
186 Malcolm, *You Guys are History*, p.124.
187 *Sunday Times*, 10 March 1996.
188 Atherton, *Opening Up*, p.213.
189 Stewart, *Playing for Keeps*, p.188.
190 Russell, *Unleashed*, p.270.
191 Stewart, *Playing for Keeps*, p.222.
192 *Wisden 2000*, p.1097.
193 Gough, *Dazzler*, p.223.
194 *The Times*, 12 May 2003.
195 *Daily Telegraph*, 13 August 1997.
196 *Wisden 2001*, p.1052.
197 *The Guardian*, 6 September 2000.
198 Gough, *Dazzler*, p.280.
199 *Wisden 2002*, p.1035.
200 *Sunday Telegraph*, 30 December 2001.
201 *Wisden 2003*, p.509.
202 Stewart, *Playing for Keeps*, p.305.
203 *ibid*, p.216.
204 *The Observer*, 3 August 2003.
205 Michael Vaughan, *Calling the Shots*, p.1.
206 *Sunday Times*, 11 April 2004.
207 Steve Harmison, *Speed Demons: My Autobiography*, p.186.
208 Andrew Flintoff, *Being Freddie: My Story so Far*, p.143.
209 *The Independent*, 14 June 2004.
210 Matthew Hoggard, Hoggy: *Welcome to my World*, p.143.
211 *Sunday Times*, 30 January 2005.
212 Michael Vaughan, *Time to Declare: My Autobiography*, p.355.
213 *Daily Telegraph*, 3 August 2008.
214 Vaughan, *Time to Declare*, p.123.
215 *Wisden 2007*, p.1053.
216 Marcus Trescothick, *Coming Back to Me: The Autobiography*, p.284.
217 Duncan Fletcher, *Behind the Shades*, p.319.
218 *The Times*, 18 December 2008.
219 Andrew Strauss, *Driving Ambition: My Autobiography*, p.189.
220 Graeme Swann, *The Breaks are Off: My Autobiography*, p.181.
221 *Daily Express*, 8 January 2009.
222 Quoted in *The Observer*, 9 January 2011.
223 James Anderson, *Jimmy: My Story So Far*, p.297.

224 *Sunday Telegraph*, 30 August 2012.
225 *The Times*, 24 September 2010.
226 *Daily Telegraph*, 30 December 2010.
227 *Sunday Telegraph*, 14 August 2011.
228 *The Observer*, 1 April 2012.
229 Strauss, *Driving Ambition*, p.305.
230 *The Guardian*, 1 September 2012.
231 *Wisden 2013*, p.378.
232 Anderson, *Jimmy: My Story So Far*, p.302.
233 *The Times*, 13 September 2013.
234 *Daily Express online*, 29 January 2014.
235 *The Guardian online*, 20 July 2014.
236 *Sunday Times*, 3 August 2014.
237 *Daily Telegraph*, 5 May 2015.
238 *BBC Sport online*, 8 August 2015.
239 *Sunday Telegraph*, 4 December 2016.
240 *Daily Telegraph*, 20 November 2018.
241 Brearley, *The Art of Captaincy*, xv.
242 *The Independent*, 29 July 2003.

Bibliography

Allen, David Rayvern, *Jim: The Life of E.W. Swanton* (London: Aurum, 2004).

Amiss, Dennis, *In Search of Runs* (London: Stanley Paul, 1976).

Anderson, Jimmy, *My Story so Far* (London: Simon and Schuster, 2013).

Atherton, Mike, *Opening Up: My Autobiography* (London: Hodder and Stoughton, 2003).

Bailey, Trevor, *The Greatest of My Time* (London: Eyre and Spottiswoode, 1968).

Barnes, Simon, *Phil Edmonds: A Singular Man* (London: The Kingswood Press, 1986).

Bedser, Alec, *Twin Ambitions* (London: Stanley Paul, 1986).

Benaud, Richie, *On Reflection* (London: Collins Willow, 1984).

Berry, Scyld, *Cricket: The Game of Life* (London: Simon and Schuster, 2015).

Botham, Ian, *The Autobiography* (London: Ebury Press, 2007).

Botham, Ian, *The Incredible Tests* (London: Pelham Books, 1981).

Boycott, Geoffrey, *Put to the Test* (London, Arthur Barker, 1981).

Boycott, Geoffrey, *Boycott: The Autobiography* (London: Macmillan, 1987).

Brearley, Mike, *Phoenix from the Ashes* (London: Hodder and Stoughton, 1982).

Brearley, Mike, *The Art of Captaincy* (London: Hodder and Stoughton, 1985).

Brearley, Mike and Doust, Dudley, *The Ashes Retained* (London: Hodder and Stoughton, 1979).

Brearley, Mike and Doust, Dudley, *The Return of the Ashes* (London: Pelham, 1978).

Cardus, Neville, (ed Margaret Hughes) *Cardus on the Ashes* (London: Souvenir Press, 1989).

Chalke, Stephen, *At the Heart of English Cricket: The Life and Memories of Geoffrey Howard* (Bath: Fairfield Books, 2001).

Chalke, Stephen, *In Sunshine and Shadow: The Biography of Geoff Cope* (Bath: Fairfield Books, 2017).

Chalke, Stephen, *Micky Stewart and the Changing Face of Cricket* (Bath: Fairfield Books, 2011).

Close, Brian, *Close to Cricket* (London: Stanley Paul, 1968).

Close, Brian, *I Don't Bruise Easily* (London: MacDonald and James, 1978).

Compton, Denis, *End of an Innings* (London: Oldbourne, 1958).

Compton, Denis and Edrich, Bill, *Cricket and All That* (London: Pelham Books, 1978).

Cowdrey, Colin, *MCC: The Autobiography of a Cricketer* (London: Hodder and Stoughton, 1976).

Cowdrey, Colin, *The Incomparable Game* (London: Hodder and Stoughton, 1970).

Cutler, Norman, *Behind the Australian Tests – 1956* (London: Putnam, 1956).

Denness, Mike, *I Declare* (London: Arthur Barker, 1977).

Dexter, Ted, *Ted Dexter Declares* (London: Stanley Paul, 1966).

D'Oliveira, Basil, *Time to Declare* (London: J.M. Dent, 1980).

Edrich, Bill, *Round the Wicket* (London: Frederick Muller Ltd, 1959).

Edrich, John, *Runs in the Family* (London: Stanley Paul and Co, 1969).

Emburey, John, *An Autobiography* (Haywards Heath: Partridge Press, 1987).

Evans, Godfrey, *The Gloves are Off* (London: Hodder and Stoughton, 1960).

Evans, Richard, *The Ultimate Test* (London: Partridge Press, 1990).

Fingleton, Jack, *Cricket Crisis* (London: Cassell, 1947).

Fletcher, Duncan, *Behind the Shades* (London: Simon and Schuster, 2007).

Fletcher, Keith, *Ashes to Ashes* (London: Headline, 2005).

Flintoff, Andrew, *Being Freddie: My Story so Far* (London: Hodder and Stoughton, 2005).

Foot, David, *Wally Hammond: The Reasons Why* (London: Robson Books, 1996).

Fowler, Graeme, *Fox on the Run* (London: Viking, 1988).

Fulton, David, *The Captains' Tales* (London: Transworld Publishers, 2011).

Gatting, Mike, *Leading from the Front* (London: Queen Anne Press/ Fontana, 1988).

Gibson, Alan, *The Cricket Captains of England* (London: Cassell, 1979).

Gooch, Graham, *My Autobiography* (London: Collins Willow, 1995).

Gooch, Graham, *My Cricket Diary '81* (London: Stanley Paul, 1982).

Gooch, Graham, *On Captaincy* (London: Stanley Paul, 1992).

Gough, Darren, *Dazzler: The Autobiography of Darren Gough* (London: Penguin, 2002).

Gower, David, *An Endangered Species* (London: Simon and Schuster, 2013).

Gower, David, *The Autobiography* (London: Collins Willow, 1992).

Harmison, Steve, *Speed Demons: My Autobiography* (London: Trinity Mirror Sport Media, 2017).

Hill, Alan, *Brian Close: Cricket's Lionheart* (London: Methuen, 2002).

Hill, Alan, *Jim Laker: The Biography* (London: Andre Deutsch, 1998).

Hill, Alan, *Peter May: The Biography* (London: Andre Deutsch, 1996).

Hill, Alan, *The Bedsers: Twinning Triumphs* (Edinburgh: Mainstream, 2001).

Hill, Alan, *The Valiant Cricketer: The Biography of Trevor Bailey* (Worthing: Pitch Publishing, 2012).

Hoggard, Matthew, *Hoggy: Welcome to my World* (London: Harpersport, 2009).

Howat, Gerald, *Len Hutton: The Biography* (London: Mandarin, 1988).

Howat, Gerald, *Walter Hammond* (London: Allen and Unwin, 1984).

Howe, Martin, *Norman Yardley: Yorkshire's Gentleman Cricketer* (Cardiff: Association of Cricket Statisticians and Historians, 2015).

Hussain, Nasser, *Playing with Fire* (London: Penguin, 2004).

Hutton, Len, *Fifty Years in Cricket* (London: Stanley Paul and Co, 1984).

Illingworth, Ray, *Captaincy* (London: Pelham Books, 1980).

Illingworth, Ray, *Yorkshire and Back* (London: Queen Anne Press, 1980).

Jackman, Robin, *Jackers: A Life in Cricket* (Worthing: Pitch Publishing, 2012).

James, Steve, *The Plan: How Fletcher and Flower Transformed English Cricket* (London: Transworld, 2012).

Johnson, Ian, *Cricket at the Crossroads* (London: Cassell, 1957).

Kilburn, J.M., *Cricket Decade: England v Australia 1946 to 1956* (London: The Windmill Press, 1959).

Knott, Alan, *It's Knott Cricket* (London: Macmillan, 1985).

Lamb, Allan, *My Autobiography* (London: Collins Willow, 1986).

Lee, Alan, *Lord Ted: The Dexter Enigma* (London: Gollancz/Witherby, 1995).

Lever, John, *A Cricketer's Cricketer* (London: Unwin Hyman, 1989).

Lewis, Tony, *Playing Days* (London: Stanley Paul, 1985).

Lloyd, David, *The Autobiography* (London: Collins Willow, 2000).

McKinstry, Leo, *Boycs: The True Story* (London: Collins Willow, 2000).

Malcolm, Devon, *You Guys are History* (London: Harper Collins, 1998).

Marshall, Michael, *Gentlemen and Players* (London: Grafton Books, 1987).

Martin-Jenkins, Christopher, *MCC in India 1976/77* (London: MacDonald and James, 1977).

Martin-Jenkins, Christopher, *World Cricketers: A Biographical Dictionary* (Oxford: Oxford University Press, 1996).

Miller Douglas, *Charles Palmer: More than a Gentleman* (Bath: Fairfield Books, 2001).

Miller, Douglas, *M.J.K. Smith: No Ordinary Man* (Cardiff: Association of Cricket Statisticians and Historians, 2013).

Murphy, Pat, *Botham: A Biography* (London: J.M. Dent and Sons, 1988).

Murtagh, Andrew, *Touched by Greatness: The True Story of Tom Graveney, England's Much-Loved Cricketer* (Worthing: Pitch Publishing, 2014).

Norrie, David, *Athers: The Authorised Biography of Michael Atherton* (London: Headline, 1996).

Peel, Mark, *Ambassadors of Goodwill: MCC Tours 1946/47–1970/71* (Worthing: Pitch Publishing, 2018).

Peel, Mark, *The Last Roman: A Biography of Colin Cowdrey* (London: Andre Deutsch, 1999).

Pocock, Pat, *Percy* (London: Clifford Frost Publications, 1987).

Roebuck, Peter, *It Sort of Clicks*, (London: Willow, 1986).

Russell, Jack, *Unleashed* (London: Collins Willow, 1997).

Sandford, Christopher, *Tom Graveney* (London: H.F. and G. Witherby, 1992).

Shawcroft, John, *Donald Carr: Derbyshire's Corinthian* (Cardiff: Association of Cricket Statisticians and Historians, 2014).

Sheppard, David, *Parson's Pitch* (London: Hodder and Stoughton, 1964).

Shindler, Colin, *Bob Barber: The Professional Amateur* (Nantwich: Max Books, 2015).

Snow, John, *Cricket Rebel* (London: Hamlyn, 1976).

Steen, Rob, *David Gower: A Man out of Time* (London: Victor Gollancz, 1995).

Stevenson, Mike, *Illy: A Biography of Ray Illingworth* (Tunbridge Wells: Midas Books, 1978).

Stewart, Alec, *Playing for Keeps: The Autobiography of Alec Stewart* (London: BBC, 2004).

Strauss, Andrew, *Driving Ambition: My Autobiography* (London: Hodder and Stoughton, 2013).

Swann, Graeme, *The Breaks are Off: My Autobiography* (London: Simon and Schuster, 2011).

Swanton, E.W., *Gubby Allen: Man of Cricket* (London: Hutchinson/ Stanley Paul, 1985).

Swanton, E.W., *Sort of a Cricket Person* (London: Collins, 1972).

Swanton, E.W., *Swanton in Australia* (London: Collins, 1975).

Taylor, Bob, *Standing Up, Standing Back* (London: Collins Willow, 1985).

Tennant, Ivo, *Graham Gooch: The Biography* (London: H.F. and G. Witherby, 1992).

Tennant, Ivo, *The Cowdreys: Portrait of a Family* (London: Simon and Schuster, 1990).

Tossell, David, *Tony Greig: A Reappraisal of English Cricket's Most Controversial Captain* (Worthing: Pitch Publishing, 2011).

Trelford, Donald (ed), *Len Hutton Remembered* (London: H.F. and G. Witherby Ltd, 1992).

Trescothick, Marcus, *Coming Back to Me: The Autobiography* (London: Harpersport, 2008).

Turbervill, Huw, *The Toughest Tour: The Ashes Away Series 1946 to 2007* (London: Aurum Press Ltd, 2010).

Tyson, Frank, *A Typhoon Called Tyson* (London: William Heinemann Ltd, 1961).

Underwood, Derek, *Beating the Bat* (London: Stanley Paul, 1975).

Vaughan, Michael, *Calling the Shots: The Captain's Story* (London: Hodder and Stoughton, 2005).

Vaughan, Michael, *Time to Declare: My Autobiography* (London: Hodder and Stoughton, 2009).

Waters, Chris, *Fred Trueman: The Authorised Biography* (London: Aurum, 2011).

Wilde, Simon, *England: The Biography: The Story of English Cricket* (London: Simon and Schuster, 2018).

Wilde, Simon, *Ian Botham: The Power and the Glory* (London: Simon and Schuster, 2012).

Wilde, Simon, *On Pietersen* (London: Simon and Schuster, 2014).

Willis, Bob, *Lasting the Pace* (London: Collins, 1985).

Willis, Bob, *The Captain's Diary* (London: Willow, 1983).